KU-036-376

To my parents, Bill and Marian Hurkman, who taught me how to see.

—Alexis Van Hurkman

To the memory of Maurice Katrib—his spoken and edited word lives on.

In memorium: Ralph Fairweather, a valued colleague, cherished friend, and respected member of the Final Cut Pro community.

—DigitalFilm Tree

Apple Pro Training Series

Advanced Color Correction and Effects in Final Cut Pro 5

Alexis Van Hurkman / DigitalFilm Tree

PLEASE CHECK DISC ON ISSUE AND DISCHARGE

WS 2226986 X

3 2007

Apple Certified

Apple Pro Training Series: Advanced Color Correction and Effects in Final Cut Pro 5
Alexis Van Hurkman and DigitalFilm Tree
Copyright © 2006 by DigitalFilm Tree and Peachpit Press

Published by Peachpit Press. For information on Peachpit Press books, contact:

Peachpit Press
1249 Eighth Street
Berkeley, CA 94710
(510) 524-2178
(800) 283-9444
Fax: (510) 524-2221
http://www.peachpit.com
To report errors, please send a note to errata@peachpit.com
Peachpit Press is a division of Pearson Education

Apple Series Editor: Serena Herr
Editor: Bob Lindstrom
Managing Editor: Nancy Peterson
Production Coordinator: Laurie Stewart, Happenstance Type-O-Rama
Technical Editor: DigitalFilm Tree
Technical Reviewer: Brendan Boykin
Copy Editors: Darren Meiss, Liz Welch
Contributing Authors, First Edition: Andrew Balis, Steve Martin, Michael Wohl
Compositor: Robin Kibby, Happenstance Type-O-Rama
Indexer: Jack Lewis
Cover Art Direction: Charlene Charles-Will
Cover Illustration: Alicia Buelow
Cover Production: George Mattingly / GMD

Notice of Rights
All rights reserved. No part of this book may be reproduced or transmitted in any form by any means, electronic, mechanical, photocopying, recording, or otherwise, without the prior written permission of the publisher. For information on getting permission for reprints and excerpts, contact permissions@peachpit.com.

Skiing and surfing footage provided by Teton Gravity Research; all rights reserved.
Footage from Santa-Anita Racetrack © 2005 provided by Meads Durket San-Diego, with editing by Terminal, and post-production by Below The Radar.
The Chocolate Curse © 2003 Brett Shapiro, www.thechocolatecurse.com. All rights reserved.
The Pick Up © 2003 Courtesy of At The Big Picture Company, Anthony Assini, and John Leichter. All rights reserved.
Excerpt from the short film Gold Fever © 2003 Courtesy of Brazos Pictures Film, with special permission from Stephen Purvis, www.brazospix.com. All rights reserved.
Aquatic Footage © 2003 Howard Hall Production, Courtesy of Howard and Michelle Hall, www.howardhall.com. All rights reserved.
Scenes from Slapdash provided by Garden Gnome Entertainment; written, directed, and edited by Colin Hebert.
The footage supplied with this book can only be used in association with the lessons included. Any other use, including but not limited to incorporating footage in another project, duplicating or distributing requires explicit permission from the copyright holders listed above.

Notice of Liability
The information in this book is distributed on an "As Is" basis, without warranty. While every precaution has been taken in the preparation of the book, neither the authors nor Peachpit Press shall have any liability to any person or entity with respect to any loss or damage caused or alleged to be caused directly or indirectly by the instructions contained in this book or by the computer software and hardware products described in it.

Trademarks
Many of the designations used by manufacturers and sellers to distinguish their products are claimed as trademarks. Where those designations appear in this book, and Peachpit Press was aware of the trademark claim, the designations appear as requested by the owner of the trademark. All other product names and services identified throughout the book are used in an editorial fashion only and for the benefit of such companies with no intention of infringement of the trademark. No such use, or the use of any trade name, is intended to convey endorsement or other affiliation with this book.

ISBN 0-321-33548-1
9 8 7 6 5 4 3 2 1
Printed and bound in the United States of America

UNIVERSITY OF CHICHESTER

778.
59
ADV

Contents at a Glance

Table of Contents

Titling with LiveType

Getting Started

Welcome to the official advanced training course covering Color Correction and Effects in Final Cut Pro. You should already know Final Cut Pro as a comprehensive editorial environment. However, Final Cut Pro is also a feature-rich compositing and effects environment. Using the features covered in this book, you can create eye-catching motion graphics and perform sophisticated compositing and keying tasks right in the Timeline, alongside the rest of your edited program. Final Cut Pro also has a professional set of color-correction tools, which combine with the editorial tools to create a high-quality finishing environment capable of broadcast quality output.

The course material in this book is presented in three sections. The first section focuses on effects, starting with techniques for creating motion graphics such as animated titles, multi-layered compositions, filtering, and speed effects; then continuing through more typical compositing tasks like keying.

The second section focuses exclusively on color correction in Final Cut Pro, showing you how you can correct and enhance the images in your edited programs, and taking you through the process of finishing a program by balancing all the shots with one another to create the final look of your project.

The third section, contained on the accompanying DVD, covers working with LiveType, and explores how to set up a LiveType environment, share media with Final Cut Pro, create motion menus for DVDs, and produce animated type.

Although each section focuses on a particular aspect of effects work, it's important to understand that the effects and color-correction tools in Final Cut Pro work together, and techniques learned in the first section will carry into the subsequent sections. Additionally, many compositing and motion effects tools from the first section can be used with color correction filters to create even more sophisticated adjustments.

This book assumes that you're already familiar with Final Cut Pro as an editing tool, although you'll learn editing techniques that make the creation of specific effects more efficient.

The Methodology

The emphasis of this book is hands-on training. Each exercise was designed to help you start working with Final Cut Pro at a professional level as quickly as possible. The book assumes a basic level of familiarity with the Final Cut Pro interface and with the fundamentals of postproduction, but it assumes no previous knowledge of the Final Cut Pro color-correction and effects toolset. (If you are relatively new to Final Cut Pro, it might be helpful for you to read *Apple Pro Training Series: Final Cut Pro 5.)* The lessons are designed to be completed in order, as subsequent lessons build upon skills learned previously.

Course Structure

This book was designed to help you master motion graphics, compositing, and color-correction techniques as they're performed in Final Cut Pro. Each lesson expands on basic concepts, giving you the tools to customize your project workflows and configure the program for your own purposes.

▶   Lessons 1–9: Advanced Effects
    The first section focuses on the Final Cut Pro motion graphics and effects toolset. Real-world exercises let you explore motion effects, composite modes, filters, animation, nesting, variable speed, titling, and keying, while developing working habits useful for a wide variety of different tasks.

▶   Lessons 10–15: Color Correction
    The second section guides you through Final Cut Pro's color correction environment, with a strong focus on the fundamental process of color correction. You'll learn how to objectively evaluate images using the video scopes, and how to precisely control contrast and color using the Final Cut Pro color-correction filters.

    You'll learn how to identify and correct common problems, but you'll also learn about the creative uses of color correction—how to use the same tools to create a variety of "looks" that go beyond simple corrective measures.

    You'll then widen your focus as you work on scenes from actual movies, learning how to balance clips within a sequence to match one another to complete a project's look.

    Finally, you'll learn how to isolate narrow portions of an image for specific adjustments using secondary correction.

► Lessons 16–18: Titling with LiveType

The third section includes three lessons on DVD discussing the use of the LiveType application included with Final Cut Pro. You'll discover ways to import and export video and media between LiveType and Final Cut Pro while developing animated type effects. You'll also learn how to use LiveType as a tool for structuring DVD menus.

System Requirements

Before beginning to use this book, you should have a working knowledge of your computer and its operating system, as well as a basic level of proficiency with Final Cut Pro.

Basic system requirements for Final Cut Pro 5 include:

► Mac OS X 10.3.9 or later

► G4 (500 MHz or faster) or G5

► 512 MB of RAM or more

► AGP Quartz Extreme or PCI Express graphics card

► DVD drive

► Separate hard drive for media is recommended

► To use DVCPRO HD footage, 1 GHz minimum processor speed and 1 GB of RAM are required.

Consult the Final Cut Pro technical specifications page (www.apple.com/finalcutstudio/finalcutpro/specs.html) for more details on specific system requirements and qualified third-party devices such as cameras, capture cards, and other peripherals.

Copying the Lesson Files

All the necessary files you need to complete the lessons are found on the DVD-ROM disc that comes with this book.

Installing the Lesson Files

1   Insert the *APTS Advanced FCP* DVD into your DVD drive.

2   For best results, drag the entire Adv FCP Color Book Files folder from DVD to the top level of your computer's hard drive or an attached media drive.

There is a total of approximately 1.5 GB of data on this disc.

NOTE ▶ When you keep all the lesson files and media files from the disc together in one single Adv FCP Color Book Files folder on your hard drive, just as you find them on the DVD, you will ensure that the tutorial project files for each lesson will open with their media files correctly linked, and ready for you to begin the lesson.

3   To begin each lesson, launch the application for that lesson and then open the project file or files listed at the beginning of each lesson.

Reconnecting Broken Media Links

For any number of reasons, you may need to separate the lesson files from the media files when you install and use them. For instance, you may choose to keep the project files in a user home directory and the media files on a dedicated media drive. In this case, when you open a project file, a window will appear asking you to reconnect the project files to their source media files.

Reconnecting files is a simple process. Just follow these steps:

1   When you first open a lesson's project file, a Final Cut Pro dialog will appear listing one or more files that are offline. Click the Reconnect button.

A Final Cut Pro Reconnect Files window appears.

2   Click Search.

Final Cut Pro will search any attached hard disks looking for the missing files. When it finds the first file, a Mac OS X Reconnect dialog will appear.

3   Select the highlighted file and click Choose.

In the Final Cut Pro Reconnect Files dialog, all of the offline files will be moved to the lower Files Located pane.

4   Click Connect.

5   Be sure to save the newly reconnected project file, or you will have to perform the reconnect operation every time you open it.

About the Apple Pro Training Series

Advanced Color Correction and Effects in Final Cut Pro 5 is part of the official training series for Apple Pro applications, developed by experts in the field and certified by Apple Computer. The series is the official course curriculum used by Apple Authorized Training Centers worldwide, and offers complete training in all Apple Pro products. The lessons are designed to let you learn at your own pace. Although each lesson provides step-by-step instructions for creating specific projects, there's room for exploration and experimentation. Each lesson concludes with review questions and answers summarizing what you've learned, which can be used to help you prepare for the Apple Pro Certification Exam.

For a complete list of Apple Pro Training Series books, see the course catalog at the end of this book, or visit www.peachpit.com/applebooklet.

Apple Pro Certification Program

The Apple Pro Training and Certification Program is designed to keep you at the forefront of Apple's digital media technology while giving you a competitive edge in today's ever-changing job market. Whether you're an editor, graphic designer, sound designer, special effects artist, or teacher, these training tools are meant to help you expand your skills.

Upon completing the course material in this book, you can become a certified Apple Pro by taking the certification exam at an Apple Authorized Training Center. Successful certification as an Apple Pro gives you official recognition of your knowledge of Apple's professional applications while allowing you to market yourself to employers and clients as a skilled, pro-level user of Apple products.

For those who prefer to learn in an instructor-led setting, Apple offers training courses at Apple Authorized Training Centers worldwide. These courses, which use the Apple Pro Training Series books as their curriculum, are taught by Apple Certified Trainers and balance concepts and lectures with hands-on labs and exercises. Apple Authorized Training Centers have been carefully selected and have met Apple's highest standards in all areas, including facilities, instructors, course delivery, and infrastructure. The goal of the program is to offer Apple customers, from beginners to the most seasoned professionals, the highest quality training experience.

For more information or to find an Authorized Training Center near you, go to www.apple.com/software/pro/training.

Resources

This book is not intended as a comprehensive reference manual, nor does it replace the documentation that comes with the application. For comprehensive information about program features, refer to these resources:

▶   The Reference Guide. Accessed through the Final Cut Pro Help menu, the Reference Guide contains a complete description of all features.

▶   Apple's Web site: www.apple.com.

▶   Stay current: As Final Cut Pro 5 is updated, Peachpit may choose to update lessons or post additional exercises as necessary on this book's companion Web page. Please check www.peachpit.com/apts.fcpcolor for revised lessons.

Advanced Effects

1

Lesson Files	Lessons > Lesson_01 > 01_Project_Start
Media	Media > Lesson_01-02_Media
Time	This lesson takes approximately 90 minutes to complete.
Goals	Use motion parameters to transform clips
	Create motion effects using the onscreen controls in the Canvas
	Reset attributes
	Copy and paste attributes from one clip to another
	Arrange multiple clips into a single composition
	Use the Crop and Distort tools
	Work with multilayered Photoshop files

Motion Effects

Motion effects in Final Cut Pro are used to geometrically transform images in your sequences. Using motion parameters such as Scale, Rotation, Center, and Crop, you can create anything from a simple split screen to a multilayered motion graphics sequence integrating video and imported graphics images. By mastering the manipulation of these parameters, you can create exciting visuals, as well as solve simple, everyday editing problems.

In this lesson, you will learn the fundamentals of motion properties and then create a finished composition—an opening sequence for a program about surfing culture. You also will learn how to quickly reshape, distort, reposition, crop, and superimpose video clips; save time by reusing motion settings; and refine your effects for professional results.

Launching a Project

To begin, you'll open a project file and change the window layout to one best suited for the kinds of motion graphics work you'll be doing.

1   Open Lessons > Lesson_01 > **01_Project_Start.**

2   Double-click the **Surf Intro** sequence to open it into the Timeline, if it's not already open.

3   Choose Window > Arrange > Two-Up.

By default, the Final Cut Pro standard window layout maximizes the area available for the Timeline by shrinking the Viewer and Canvas and making room for the Browser. Although this is an excellent layout for editing, you may find that the two-up window layout is more useful for working on effects because it increases the size of the Viewer and Canvas while reducing the Timeline's width. Motion graphics and compositing tasks involve more activity in the Viewer and Canvas as you adjust parameters and onscreen controls than in the Timeline, so this redistribution of screen real estate makes sense.

If your computer's display is big enough, it might be to your advantage to increase the height of the Timeline so you can view more superimposed clips.

4   Move the playhead to the border between the Timeline and the Viewer or Canvas. When it turns into the resize arrow, drag up the border to simultaneously resize all four windows in the interface.

You'll find that different compositing tasks emphasize different parts of the interface, alternately requiring more room in the Canvas, then in the Timeline, then in the Viewer. The Final Cut Pro window resizing controls allow you to quickly make room where you need it, while keeping your workspace organized.

5   To make even more room in the Timeline for your clips, drag down the divider between the video and audio tracks.

Using RT Extreme Settings

With a few exceptions, most of the effects you'll be using in this book will play in real time on current Macintosh systems. You should be aware, however, that there are also a few options available to optimize real-time playback performance on your computer. These settings are found in the Real-Time Effects (RT) pop-up menu at the top-left of the Timeline.

Clicking the RT pop-up menu reveals the following options:

These settings should maximize the real-time performance of most Macintosh computers; the following settings are especially important:

▶ Unlimited RT frees Final Cut Pro to attempt the processing and playback of effects combinations that exceed the guaranteed capabilities of your computer. In other words, if you're piling on more effects than your Mac can reasonably handle, it'll try anyway. Sections of your sequence that trigger this behavior are identified by an orange render bar at the top of the Timeline ruler. Unlimited RT playback may result in dropped frames as your Mac attempts to keep up with the processing demands being placed upon it. Safe RT restricts Final Cut Pro to displaying only those

effects that can be played in real time at the current frame rate of your project. Sections of your Timeline that exceed your computer's capabilities are
not displayed, and are identified by a red render bar at the top of the
Timeline ruler.

▶ The Dynamic settings in the Playback Video Quality and Playback
Frame Rate sections allow Final Cut Pro to dynamically reduce and
increase the resolution and/or frame rate of the Canvas to continue
real-time playback of effects. For consistency, if you want to fix the
quality at which your images play back on screen, you can choose one
of the resolutions or frame rates that appear below in the RT pop-up
menu. Lower resolutions and frame rates exchange image quality for
increased real-time playback capabilities when you're working with
effects-intensive projects.

In the current project, the Browser contains a project file that shows Unlimited
RT in action.

1 Double-click the **Unlimited RT Demo** sequence to open it into the
Timeline.

Depending on your computer's capabilities, the three sections of the
sequence containing effects should have orange render bars.

2 Play the sequence, and watch the results in the Canvas.

As the sequence plays, you should observe that playback is smooth in the
sections of the sequence with no effects, and you see varying numbers of
dropped frames in each orange bar–marked Unlimited RT section. This
is an exceptionally useful mode in which to work because you can get
real-time previews of your compositions even when you pile on the effects.

This defers the need to render a sequence except when you need to see the final, full-resolution result.

NOTE ▶ The results of this exercise will vary depending on your Mac's speed, number of processors, and graphics card.

3 When you're finished, Control-click the Unlimited RT Demo tab in the Timeline and choose Close from the shortcut menu.

Monitoring Canvas Playback Quality

One last note before you get started: the image quality of effects in the Canvas will vary depending on the effects you've applied and your computer's ability to keep up with the processing demands of Final Cut Pro.

Note that clips in the Timeline that are identified with green, yellow, dark yellow, or orange render bars are displaying *approximations* of their final appearance. This is useful for quickly seeing the results of your work, but when your project is complete you should always render these sections to verify the appearance of the final effect.

Effects in these color-identified sections of the Timeline are always rendered prior to being printed to video or edited to tape unless you override this behavior with the Record to Tape > Use Playback Settings option in the RT pop-up menu. Video that is exported to QuickTime or Using Compressor is always rendered at full quality.

Understanding Motion Parameter Basics

Now you'll take a quick tour of the ways you can transform clips. These techniques will be used extensively in later exercises.

1 Double-click **Surf_Background** to open it into the Viewer, and click the Motion tab.

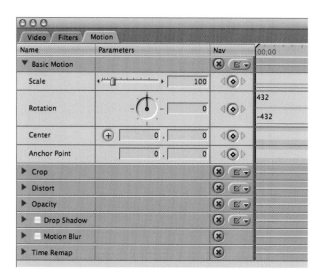

The Motion tab contains motion parameters that are associated with every video clip. The controls in this tab are separated into groups, which you can open or close using disclosure triangles to the right of each group name. By default, the Basic Motion parameters are exposed, revealing the Scale, Rotation, Center, and Anchor Point controls.

TIP ▶ The parameters in the Basic Motion group can be altered graphically using the Selection tool when the Canvas is in Image+Wireframe mode.

2   Drag the Scale slider to the left, until it's set at around 60.

As you make this adjustment, you can see the clip shrink in the Canvas.

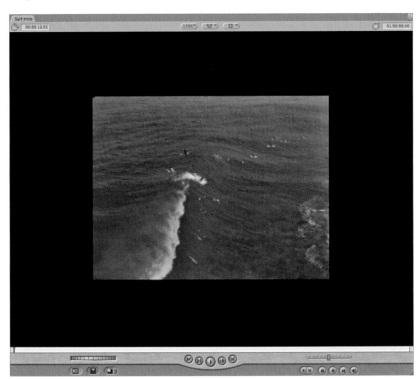

The Scale parameter is a simple percentage, which can be adjusted from 0 (which makes the image non-existent) to 1000, which is probably larger than you'll ever need (unless you're going for the texture of insanely magnified pixels).

TIP Whenever possible, try to avoid scaling video clips larger than 100 percent, since this will likely result in a significant softening of the image. If you must, limit the enlargement to 115 percent at the maximum, which is the general threshold at which enlargements tend to become noticeable. As always, the result is highly dependent on the quality of the footage, the amount of compression that's applied to it, and the type of shot.

3   Move the pointer to the Canvas. From the View pop-up menu, choose
Image+Wireframe.

This makes a wireframe appear over the clip in the Canvas. If you don't
see the wireframe, make sure that the clip is selected in the Timeline.

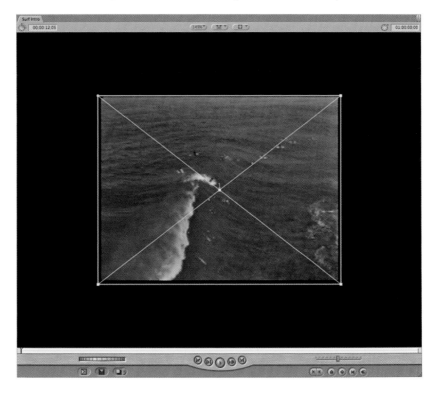

Wireframes serve two purposes. First, they let you know which clips have been selected. Second, they provide you with onscreen controls to graphically adjust most of the motion parameters (displayed in the Motion tab of the Viewer) in the Canvas.

4   In the Canvas, move the pointer directly over one of the corner points of the wireframe.

5   When the pointer turns into a crosshair, drag the corner point towards the center of the clip's image in the Canvas, thereby shrinking the clip.

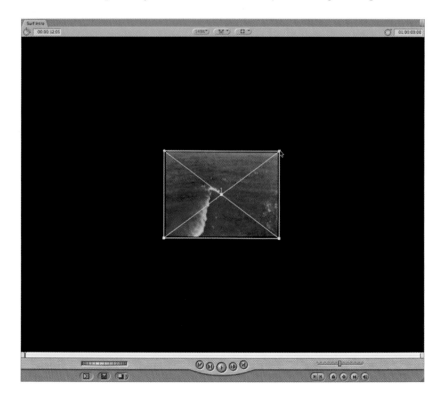

As you drag the clip's corner, notice how the Scale parameter updates in the Motion tab of the Viewer. By default, resizing is done proportionally, around the center of the clip.

6   Shift-click one of the wireframe corners, and drag it up and to the left.

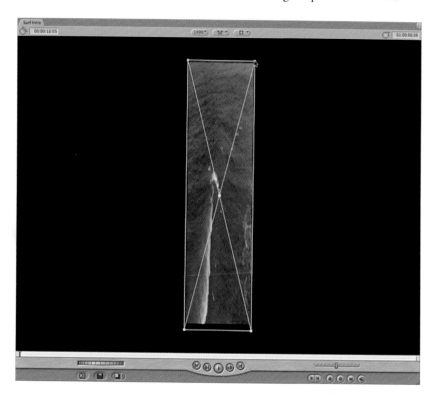

By pressing the Shift key while you resize an image in the Canvas, you can resize it freely, squeezing or stretching it out of its original proportions by simultaneously adjusting the Aspect Ratio parameter (currently hidden in the Distort parameter group in the Motion tab of the Viewer).

TIP ▶ You can modify many of the onscreen Canvas controls by using keyboard shortcuts.

7   Command-click one of the wireframe corners, and drag it around the Canvas.

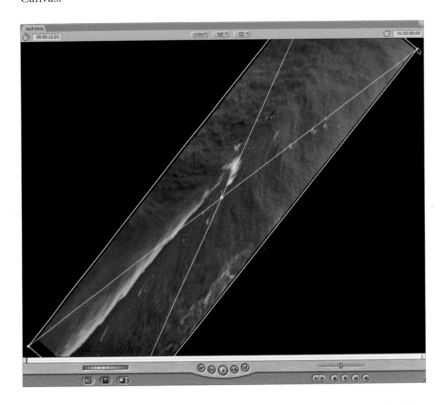

By pressing the Command key while you resize an image, you can simultaneously resize and rotate the image in the Viewer. You should notice that the Rotation parameter also updates while you make this adjustment.

As you can see, there are two methods you can use to adjust many motion parameters for a clip—using the controls in the Motion tab of the Viewer, or more graphically by setting the Canvas view to Image+Wireframe and adjusting the controls that appear over the clip. Additional onscreen controls are available, which you will explore later in this lesson.

Resetting Attributes

Before you continue, it's time to reset the practice adjustments you've made. Aside from manually returning a clip to its default settings, there are two ways you can restore a clip's attributes.

1 Click the Reset button, located in the Motion tab of the Viewer to the right of the Basic Motion section header.

This resets all the controls in the Basic Motion section—in this case, resetting the Scale and Rotation parameters. Unfortunately, it doesn't restore the Aspect Ratio parameter located in the Distort parameter group. Fortunately, another method for resetting a clip's parameters is more comprehensive.

2 Control-click the **Surf_Background** clip in the Timeline, and choose Remove Attributes from the shortcut menu.

3   In the Remove Attributes dialog that appears, select the parameter groups
    you want to restore to their default settings and click OK. By default, the
    Distort setting is already selected.

The image is now returned to its default size and position, ready for you to
create your first composition.

The Remove Attributes dialog displays checkboxes for every parameter
group, filter, and speed setting that can be applied to a group. If you want
to immediately set a clip to its default state, this is the way to do it.

TIP ▶ You can also use the Remove Attributes dialog to remove attributes from multiple clips at once. For instance, one clip may have a filter
and another clip an altered motion setting. Simply select all clips with
effects before Control-clicking and choosing Remove Attributes from the
shortcut menu. Then select the attributes you want to remove.

Creating a Multilayered Show Open

In this exercise, you'll build on the previously described techniques to create
an intro for a video program on surfing, imaginatively titled *Surf*. As is typical
for many show opens, a wealth of unused B-roll was made available from the
shoot, providing you with the opportunity to create a multilayered composition of surfing shots. A designer has also thoughtfully provided a multilayered
Photoshop file that you will use as the actual title and logo for the show.

The final composition will consist of a background clip, four foreground clips, and four graphics layers on top of that. In the process of marrying all of these elements together, you'll explore many basic compositing techniques used to create motion graphics for video.

Previewing the Final Composition

Before you get started, take a look at the final product to orient yourself.

1   Double-click the **Surf Intro - Finished** sequence to open it into the Timeline.

2   Press the spacebar to play the sequence.

NOTE ▶ If your computer's real-time playback is dropping too many frames to keep up with all the effects in this sequence, make the Timeline or Canvas the active window, and choose Sequence > Render All > Both (Option-R) to render the sequence prior to playing it.

As you work on the exercises in this lesson, feel free to refer to the finished version of the project to help guide your adjustments by clicking back and forth between the Surf Intro and Surf Intro - Finished tabs in the Timeline or Canvas.

Editing Superimposed Video Layers

The first thing you need to do is edit in the clips you want to use in this composition. Because you'll be superimposing clips throughout the lessons in this book, a small refresher is probably in order to ensure that you can perform this step as quickly as possible.

1   Click the Surf Intro tab.

There's a single item in the Timeline: the **Surf_Background** clip that happens to be the placeholder clip from your imaginary original program. You need to superimpose the clips you're going to be arranging in the middle of this composition.

2   In the Browser, open the Clips bin.

There are two ways to edit superimposed clips into a sequence.

3   Press Home to move the playhead to the beginning of the sequence, press I to set an In point, then drag the **Surf_Shot_02** clip into the Canvas, and drop it onto the Superimpose Edit Overlay.

A new video track is created above track V1, and the clip is edited into it. You can also superimpose the clips by using keyboard shortcuts only, which you'll do next.

NOTE ▶ To use the F9 through F12 keyboard shortcuts to make edits in this next step, you need to disable these keyboard shortcuts in the Dashboard & Exposé panel of the System Preferences window.

4   With the Timeline active, press Home to move the playhead back to the beginning of the sequence, and press I to set an In point in the Timeline. Press Command-4 to make the Browser active, use the arrow keys to select the **Surf_Shot_01** clip, and press the Return key to open that clip into the Viewer. Press F12 to edit the selected clip into the sequence with a Superimpose edit.

Notice that **Surf_Shot_01** has been superimposed over the track indicated by the source/destination controls, which is still track V1. The first clip you edited in, **Surf_Shot_02**, has been moved up to a new video track to make room. This demonstrates that superimposed clips are always edited into a sequence above the destination track. If there are clips already in the track above, they're all moved up one track to make room.

The second method of superimposing clips in the Timeline is a more hands-on technique (for those of you who prefer to keep your hands on the mouse).

5   Drag the **Surf_Shot_03** clip to the beginning of the Timeline, and drop it into the gray area above track V3.

A new video track is created, and the clip is edited in above the other clips. One advantage to dragging a clip into place is that it spares you the step of having to change the source/destination track pairing when you want to add a clip to the very top of a growing stack of clips.

NOTE ▶ In this latest method, the clip will snap, if it's turned on, so you can use the beginning of the clip in the Timeline or the playhead for precise alignment. Like most of the GUI direct manipulation functions, this very intuitive method is faster if you're using a graphic tablet as your interface.

6 Drag the **Surf_Shot_04** clip to the top of the superimposed stack of clips. These are all of the video clips you'll be using for this opening sequence.

Cropping Images

Cropping, as the name implies, allows you to cut off part of the top, bottom, and sides of an image. You might do this to hide unwanted edges of an image, to eliminate all but just the portion of a clip you want for your composition, or to open up room for other images.

If you look closely at the edges of the image in the Canvas in the following illustration, you'll notice a thin black border.

Borders such as these along one or more edges of the frame are a common occurrence in video from a variety of sources. Many camcorders commonly record these black borders along one side of the frame. Some video capture cards introduce similar borders. In other cases, the equipment used to telecine film to video may introduce such borders.

In this exercise, you'll trim these unwanted borders from clips that are resized and superimposed into the overall composition. You'll also be cropping into some of the images to make room for other elements. Along the way, you'll be turning on features in the Canvas that make it easier for you to perform these and other compositing tasks.

1   Move the playhead to the beginning of the sequence, and from the View pop-up menu, choose Show Overlays. If you don't see the Title Safe overlays, choose Show Title Save from the View pop-up menu.

The Title Safe overlays appear in the Canvas.

As you create compositing layouts for broadcast video programs, it's typical to refer to the Title and Action Safe boundaries of the picture. Most home televisions display a video image by overscanning it. In other words, approximately 20 percent of the outer parts of the image is "cut off" behind the bezel of the television, to provide a "full-screen" image. (The actual percentage of overscan varies between televisions.)

To give guidance to the motion graphics designer, the outer overlay indicates the Action Safe area, which is the area you can reliably expect will be cut off by most televisions (consisting of the outer 10 percent). The inner overlay indicates the Title Safe area (which excludes the outer 20 percent of the picture) that should be visible on virtually every television.

In this image, you can see a common aspect found in many captured clips: a thin black border. Some video clips have this along only one side, and others have more (such as footage that originated on film and was telecined to video). Compared to the outer Action Safe overlay, you can assume that this part of the picture will be outside the area that anyone will see on television. On the other hand, if you're going to be resizing the image to fit within a composition (as in this example), you can't let these borders show.

2   In the Timeline, double-click **Surf_Shot_04** to open it into the Viewer. Click the Motion tab, and then click the disclosure triangle next to the Crop parameter group.

3   Drag the Left slider to the right until you've cropped the image all the way to the Action Safe overlay.

Notice that as you crop the top image, the area that's being cropped is indicated by a separate *crop* wireframe, and the images that appear underneath start to peek through.

The sliders are really useful when you need to make precise adjustments. However, there's a tool you can use to crop images directly in the Canvas that's a little more interactive.

4   Click the Crop tool.

5 In the Canvas, move the pointer to the right edge of the image. When the pointer turns into the crop cursor, drag the edge to the left, all the way to the Action Safe overlay, to crop it.

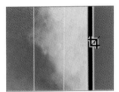

This would be useful if you just wanted to exclude the unwanted border around the image prior to shrinking it, but you actually want to crop in to isolate the surfer within the frame.

6 From the Zoom menu at the top of the Canvas, choose Fit All.

The image in the Canvas shrinks to display more gray border around the image. This makes it easier to manipulate the outer edges of wireframes located at the edge of the frame. You could also do this by reducing the magnification of the image, but Fit All is an automatic operation.

TIP If your monitor is really big, you might be able to set the viewing size to 100 percent and leave plenty of room around the edges for wireframe manipulation.

7   In the Canvas, scrub through **Surf_Shot_04** to get a sense of where the surfer goes in the frame.

In this clip, the surfer moves from his position at the right of the frame to a point just about halfway through the frame, before he "cuts back".

8   Use the Crop tool on the right edge of **Surf_Shot_04** to drag the crop wireframe to touch the surfer at the beginning of this motion, and drag the crop wireframe at the left edge of the clip to touch the surfer at the end of his motion. Also, crop just a little of the top and bottom of the image to get rid of the black border.

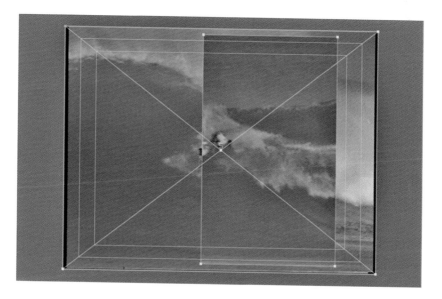

Next, you'll crop each superimposed clip to isolate the greatest area of motion. With so many clips in the Canvas, however, operating on the wireframe of a layer underneath can be difficult, so you should solo each video track containing the clip you want to work on.

9 Option-click the Track Visibility control for track V4.

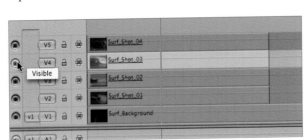

This control turns off the visibility of every other video track, leaving the clips in the track you Option-clicked the only ones that are visible. Option-clicking the same Track Visibility control a second time makes all of the tracks visible once again.

10 Click the clip in the Canvas.

Notice that selecting the clip in the Canvas also highlights it in the Timeline. The opposite also works. Selecting a clip in the Timeline also highlights that clip in the Canvas. This is a good way to select clips that may appear underneath other clips in a multilayered composition, as well as to select multiple clips for simultaneous operations.

So far, you've been individually cropping each side of an image. You can also crop two adjacent sides at once using the corner crop handles.

11 Move the Crop tool to the upper-right corner of the selected clip in the Canvas, and drag down and left to crop the top and right sides at the same time.

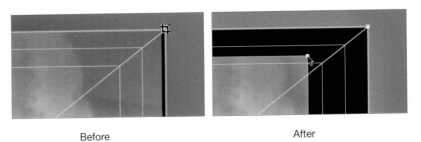

Before   After

12 Using the corner crop handles, crop all four sides of **Surf_Shot_03** to isolate and center the surfer within a smaller region.

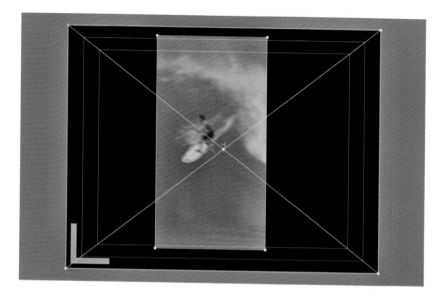

Since the **Surf_Background** clip is also hidden, you can clearly see the background of the sequence, which defaults to black. Sometimes, to more clearly see what you're doing, it helps to choose a different background, strictly for display purposes.

13 In the View pop-up menu in the Canvas, choose Checkerboard 1.

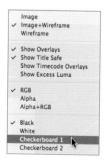

14 Option-click the Track Visibility button of track V3 to isolate it in the Timeline, click the isolated clip in the Canvas to display the wireframe, and crop the four sides to similarly isolate the surfer's movement within a smaller frame. (This time, crop the top and bottom a little closer.)

As you make this adjustment, you can see the clip image against a checkered background.

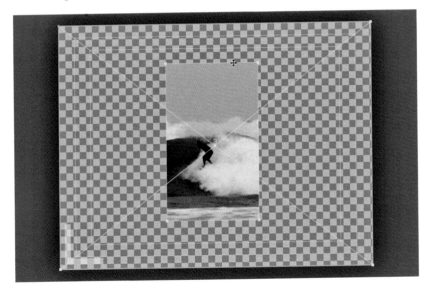

As with the resizing operations you performed, there are also keyboard shortcuts you can use to alter the behavior of the Trim tool.

15 Option-click the Track Visibility button of track V2 to isolate it in the Timeline. Click the isolated clip in the Canvas to display its wireframe, then press Command while you drag the left side of the image to crop both sides evenly.

> **NOTE** ▶ You can also press Shift-Command while dragging an edge with the Crop tool to crop all four sides proportionally to the clip's aspect ratio.

16 Press Command and drag down the top edge of the clip, to crop the top and bottom of the clip by the same amount.

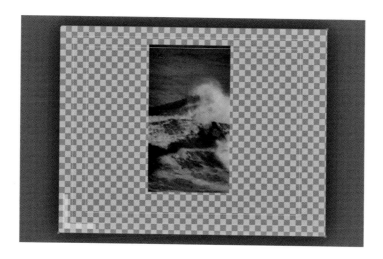

Resizing and Repositioning Clips

Now that you've cropped each of the superimposed clips, it's time to arrange them horizontally in the Canvas. In the process, you'll control the selection of clips using onscreen controls in the Canvas and items in the Timeline.

1 Press Home to return the playhead to the beginning of the sequence, and Option-click the Track Visibility button of track V2 to turn on the visibility of all clips.

As you can see, the topmost clip is **Surf_Shot_04**. Clip ordering in the Canvas depends on the track order in the Timeline—clips in higher-numbered video tracks appear in front of clips in lower-numbered video tracks.

2 Double-click **Surf_Shot_04** to open it into the Viewer, and click the Motion tab, if necessary, to view the clip's motion parameters.

It's not necessary to open a clip into the Viewer to transform it in the Canvas, but looking at its settings in the Motion tab while you make adjustments lets you see the numeric value of the changes you're making.

3 Press the A key to switch to the default Selection tool, and drag one of the four resize handles (the outer corners, not the inner crop handles) towards the center of the clip until the Scale parameter in the Motion tab of the Viewer is around 56. It's not necessary to be exact.

4 Double-click **Surf_Shot_03** to open it into the Viewer, and drag one of its resize handles towards the center of the clip until the Scale parameter in the Motion tab of the Viewer is around 70. It's not necessary to be exact.

TIP When you open a clip into the Viewer, whichever tab was open for the previous clip remains open, but it is updated to reflect the settings of the newly-opened clip.

At this point, the clips underneath the top two clips in the Timeline are getting obscured. It's time to move the top two clips into position.

5 Open **Surf_Shot_04** clip the Viewer, then Shift-drag the clip to the left until the first value in the Center parameter is about 147.

> **NOTE ▶** You may have to release the mouse button periodically to let the center parameter in the Motion tab update to its current position.

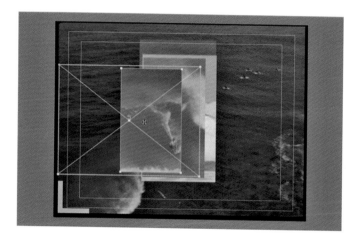

6 Select **Surf_Shot_03** in either the Timeline or Canvas, and Shift-drag it to the right to roughly match this position:

Double-click **Surf_Shot_03** to open its settings in the Viewer. If you look at the Motion tab, you'll see that the Center parameter setting is at about 85.

At this point, the onscreen controls of the two front clips are obscuring those of the clips below them. Fortunately, you can still select any clip in the Canvas by selecting it in the Timeline.

7   Move and resize the remaining two clips until your composition in the Canvas resembles this:

TIP ▶ Refer to the **Surf Intro - Finished** sequence to see how your version compares at this point to the finished project.

Positioning Clips Precisely in the Canvas

From time to time, you'll find yourself wanting to nudge a clip's position in the Canvas one pixel at a time. Other compositing applications typically use the arrow keys for this function. In Final Cut Pro, the arrow keys are used to navigate and position clips temporally in the Timeline. However, selecting a clip and then pressing Option with an arrow key lets you nudge a clip spatially in the Canvas.

1 Select **Surf_Shot_03** in the Canvas.

2 With the Canvas active, press Option-Down Arrow nine times to more closely align the top and bottom of this clip with the superimposed clip appearing all the way to the left. This will only work with the Canvas selected.

Distorting Images

The settings in the Distort parameter group of the Motion tab are useful for many purposes. By adjusting the Aspect Ratio slider, you can mix 4:3 and 16:9 material in the same sequence. By using the corner parameters or the Distort tool in the Tool palette, you can warp an image by its corner handles to create artificial perspective, to make an image fit into a design, or to fit the clip into a composite (such as making a graphic look like a sign on a wall by matching the perspective of the wall).

In this exercise, you'll use the Distort tool to add some angles to your design.

1 In the Tool palette, click the Crop icon and hold down the mouse button. When the related tools appear, select the Distort tool and release the mouse button.

TIP You can also press the D key once, or the C key twice to change to the Distort tool.

2   Select **Surf_Shot_04**, then drag each of the four corner handles (not the inner crop handles) to warp the image so that it looks like this:

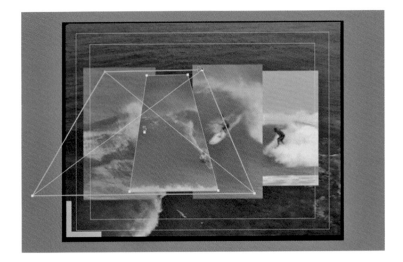

Using the Distort tool, you can independently drag each corner handle to create a wide range of effects.

3   Select **Surf_Shot_03**, and Shift-drag the upper-left corner to the left using the Distort tool.

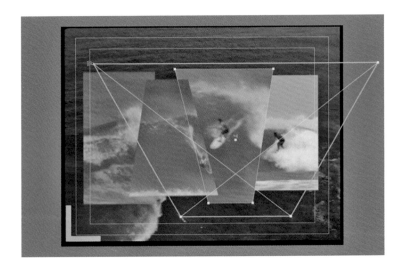

The top corners move outward simultaneously as the bottom corners move inward, simulating a perspective shift, as if the clip were tilting.

4   Use the Distort tool to warp **Surf_Shot_02** and **Surf_Shot_01** to look like this:

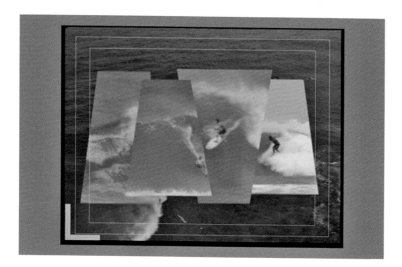

Changing the Clip Timing

At this point, the layout is starting to take shape, but it's a little static. An easy way to add some life to the composition is to stagger the introduction of each of the clips so they appear one at a time. You can then take advantage of their pre-edited durations to have them fade out, one at a time, making room for the title graphic to be added later.

1   Select all of the superimposed clips above the **Surf_Background** clip in the Timeline by dragging a bounding box over them.

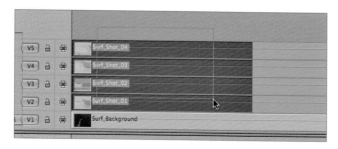

2   Type *+1.* (+1 and a period) so that a tooltip titled *Move* appears at the top of the Timeline. Press Return.

The period is a placeholder for two zeros, so you've specified that the selected clips should move 1 second forward.

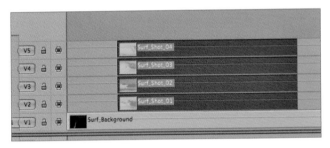

3   Command-click **Surf_Shot_01** to deselect it while leaving the clips above selected. Then type *+15* and press Return to move the selected clips forward 15 frames in the Timeline.

4   Keep moving the clips forward in staggered fashion, deselecting the bottom clip by Command-clicking it, and shifting the remaining selected clips forward by 15 frames until the sequence looks like this:

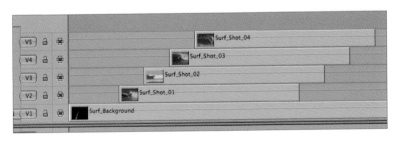

5   Control-click the end point of each clip, and choose Add Transition 'Cross Dissolve' from the shortcut menu.

After you've added a dissolve to the end of each clip, your sequence should resemble this:

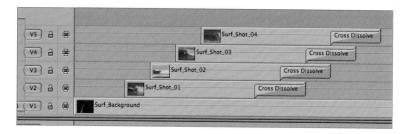

6   Play the sequence from the beginning. Each clip should appear 15 frames later than previous one, dissolving away in the same staggered order.

Adding Graphics from a Layered Photoshop File

Now, it's time to add the title graphics. In this project, the title graphics have been created as a layered Adobe Photoshop file. Final Cut Pro can import files from any version of Photoshop. However, Final Cut Pro supports only those features available in Photoshop 3. Opacity settings, composite modes (only those available in Photoshop 3), layer order, and layer names are imported; but newer features appearing in versions of Photoshop later than 4.0, such as layer effects and editable text, are not supported.

Layered Photoshop files are imported like any other media file, but the way they appear inside your project is quite different.

1   Choose File > Import > Files, and select **Surf_Title.psd** from the
     Lesson_01-02_Media folder.

NOTE ▶ If you have trouble finding the **Surf_Title.psd** file, it's also available inside the Clips bin in the Browser.

As you can see, instead of being imported as a clip, the layered Photoshop
file has been imported as a sequence.

2   Open the **Surf_Title.psd** sequence.

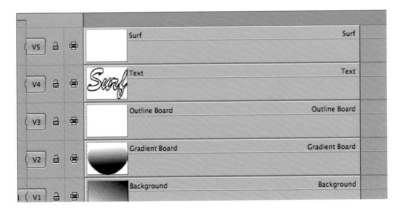

In the Timeline of the **Surf_Title.psd** sequence, each layer of the Photoshop file has been translated into a graphic on an individual video
track.

3   From the Zoom pop-up menu at the top of the Canvas, choose Fit All.

You can see that the graphic itself is quite large. It's fairly typical for motion graphics artists to provide artwork at a larger size than it will eventually be used. That way, you don't have to enlarge any clips beyond 100 percent and risk softening the image if it is later decided to enlarge the graphics.

4   Turn off the Track Visibility control for track V1, which contains the background clip.

You can tell from the checkerboard background that the top four layers have a built-in *alpha channel*. An alpha channel is a fourth image channel—in addition to the red, green, and blue channels—that defines regions of transparency in an image. All compositing is done either by creating alpha channels for clips within Final Cut Pro using the Crop tool, using the Travel Matte transfer modes and certain filters; or by importing clips with built-in alpha channels and then compositing them over other clips.

5   From the View pop-up menu, choose Alpha.

This sets the Canvas to display the alpha channel as a grayscale image.

White areas of the alpha channel are 100 percent solid; black areas are 100 percent transparent. Gray areas of an alpha channel (if there are any) represent the semi-translucent values in-between, with light-gray areas being more translucent than dark-gray areas.

6   From the View pop-up menu, choose RGB to display the image.

Adding the Logo to the Composition

In your composition, you need only the top four images, so you'll copy and paste these into the sequence you've been working on.

1   Drag a bounding box around the clips in tracks V2 through V5, then press Command-C to copy them.

2   At the top of the Timeline, click the Surf Intro tab.

If you simply pasted these clips into your Timeline, the default behavior would be to paste them into the same tracks from which they originated, starting at the position of the playhead. Unfortunately, this would overwrite the existing clips in your sequence. You can override this behavior by using the Auto Select controls in the Timeline header.

The Auto Select controls let you determine which tracks in the Timeline are affected by operations such as edits and copying and pasting.

3   Control-click the gray area above the top video track in the Timeline and choose Add Track from the shortcut menu.

4   Option-click the Auto Select control for track V6.

This has the same effect as soloing a track's Track Visibility control. Option-clicking an Auto Select control turns on that control, and turns off all the other Auto Select controls. Option-clicking a soloed Auto Select control turns all the other Auto Select controls back on.

5   Move the playhead to 01:00:03:00, and press Command-V to paste the copied clips to track V6 (and above).

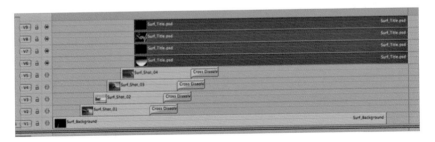

All of the superimposed graphics you copied are pasted into your composition sequence, with the bottommost graphic layer appearing in the Auto Select–enabled track, with all the other superimposed graphics clips appearing above it, automatically making new video tracks.

In the Canvas, the graphics now appear superimposed over all of the other clips you've just placed.

Rotating the Surfboard

Next, you'll want to rotate the surfboard so that it's laying on its side.

1   Press Shift-Command-A to deselect all the clips in the Timeline, and then select the clip in track V6, so that you're selecting only the surfboard graphic (not the text).

2   Press A to switch to the Selection tool, then move the pointer to the inner corner of the upper-right wireframe handle.

3 When the pointer becomes the rotate cursor, drag in a circular motion to rotate the clips in the Canvas.

You can freely rotate any clip about its anchor point, but there's a keyboard shortcut that's really handy when you want to rotate a clip in 45-degree increments.

4 Press the Shift key. With the Rotate cursor, drag the inner corner of a wireframe handle. Notice how the graphic snaps vertically, diagonally, and horizontally. Drag the surfboard logo's gradient layer so that it's horizontal.

5 On track V7, select the surfboard outline and press the Shift key while dragging its rotation onscreen control to match the orientation of the surfboard logo gradient layer you rotated in step 4.

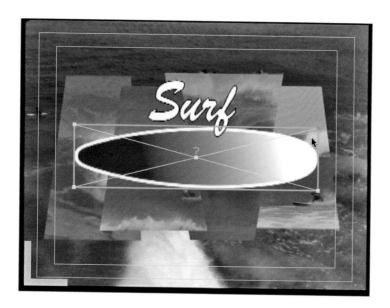

Creating Transparency

Now that the surfboard is correctly oriented, you need to make the center semi-transparent to let some of the surfing action show through. Although opacity has no onscreen controls in the Canvas, there are still two ways of making opacity adjustments.

1   On track V6, double-click the clip to open it into the Viewer. Click the Motion tab, and click the disclosure triangle next to Opacity.

    This is the Opacity slider, which lets you make uniform opacity changes to an entire clip. If the clip already has an alpha channel, the Opacity slider affects only the visible areas. Opacity is a percentage from 0 (transparent) to 100 (solid).

2   Drag the Opacity slider to the left until the value field reads 30.

As you drag the slider, you can see the middle of the surfboard become increasingly transparent.

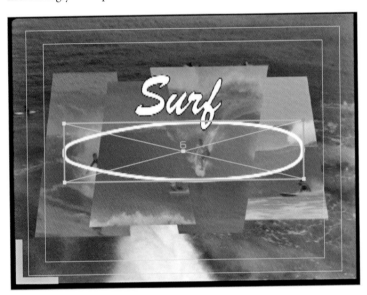

3   Click the Clip Overlays control.

The Clip Overlays control toggles the visibility of the Opacity and Level clip overlays that appear respectively over video and audio clips in the Timeline. The Opacity overlay provides another means of controlling clip opacity.

If you look at the Opacity overlay for the clip in track V6, you can see that its opacity is lower than the other clips, because you've already made an opacity adjustment to that clip.

4   Move the pointer directly over the Opacity overlay for the clip in track V6. When the pointer turns into the resize arrow, drag up until the tooltip that appears shows a value between 45 and 50.

When you release the mouse button, the Canvas updates to show the new opacity setting. Unlike the Opacity slider in the Motion tab, the Opacity overlays do not allow interactive adjustments to the image in the Canvas. The overlays are generally more useful for keyframing dynamic opacity changes, which you'll learn in a later lesson, or when you simply need to make a quick opacity change and you don't want to open the clip in the Viewer.

Copying Attributes

The last task to complete the title is to move and resize the text component of the title graphic, and add drop shadows to the four superimposed video clips. For both of these exercises, you'll be applying the same settings to multiple clips. To make this process faster, you'll use the Paste Attributes command.

Adjusting the Text Layers

Now that you've moved the surfboard, you need to transform the text of the title graphic to fit the new layout.

1   Select the clip in track V9, and drag it into the Canvas so that it fits at the center of the surfboard graphic.

2 Resize it so that it's approximately as large as this:

When you move the top clip, you can see that the black outline was actually created with a second graphic layer underneath, which is now offset. You could copy and paste the values from the top clip's Motion tab to the corresponding parameters in the bottom clip, or you could drag the bottom clip in the Canvas to approximate the size and position of the top clip. But there's an easier way.

3 Select the clip in track V9, and press Command-C to copy it.

4 Control-click the clip in track V8, and choose Paste Attributes from the shortcut menu.

5   In the Paste Attributes dialog, select Basic Motion, then click OK.

The clip in track V8 is transformed to match the scale and position of the clip you copied. As you can see, Paste Attributes is the opposite of the Remove Attributes command you learned earlier. It allows you to paste the attributes from any copied clip into the Motion parameter settings of another.

Adding Drop Shadows

Now you'll finish off the composition by adding drop shadows to the superimposed video clips and adding transitions to the In points of all the graphics layers in tracks V6 through V9.

1   Move the playhead to the beginning of **Surf_Shot_04**.

2   Double-click **Surf_Shot_04** to open it into the Viewer. Click the Motion tab, and click the disclosure triangle next to the Drop Shadow parameter group.

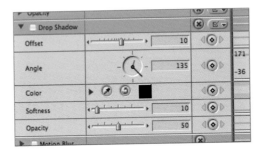

Unlike most of the parameter groups (with the exception of Motion Blur), the Drop Shadow group can be turned on and off as a whole, because all the parameters within this group adjust the same effect.

3   In the parameter group header, turn on the Drop Shadow checkbox.

A drop shadow immediately appears underneath the selected clip. Drop shadows give the illusion of depth to objects within a composition.

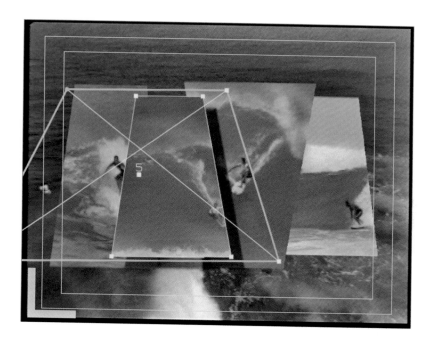

4 To lighten the drop shadow a bit, drag the Softness slider so that the value field reads 50, and the Opacity slider so that it reads 30.

Now that you've customized the settings of one drop shadow, you don't have to go through all of these steps for the drop shadows in the remaining three clips. You can use Paste Attributes just once.

5 Make sure that **Surf_Shot_04** is selected in the Timeline, and press Command-C to copy it.

6 Select **Surf_Shot_03**, **Surf_Shot_02**, and **Surf_Shot_01**. Control-click them, and choose Paste Attributes from the shortcut menu.

7   Turn on Drop Shadow in the Paste Attributes dialog, and click OK. (Don't select any other parameters.)

The drop shadow parameters are automatically copied to every selected clip in the Timeline.

8   In the Browser, click the Effects tab. Open the Video Transitions > Iris bin, and drag the Oval Iris transition to the beginning of every clip on tracks V6 through V9.

9   Press Home to move the playhead to the beginning of the sequence. Then play the sequence to see how you've done.

Lesson Review

1. Where are each clip's motion parameters located?

2. What motion parameters can you manipulate with the Selection tool using the onscreen controls in the Canvas?

3. What two motion parameters can you manipulate in the Canvas using separate tools?

4. How can you copy the motion effects settings from one clip to another?

5. How do you create a drop shadow for a clip?

6. How do you import a multilayered Photoshop file, and how does it appear within Final Cut Pro?

Answers

1. In the Motion tab, whenever that clip is open in the Viewer.

2. Scale, Rotation, and Center.

3. Crop and Distort each have separate tools.

4. Copy the clip with the settings you want to copy, then use the Paste Attributes command on the clip you want to paste these settings into.

5. In the Motion tab, turn on the Drop Shadow parameter group, and adjust the Offset, Angle, Color, Softness, and Opacity settings to create the desired shadow effect.

6. Photoshop files are imported using the File > Import > Files command. They appear within Final Cut Pro as sequences, with each layer of the Photoshop file superimposed on its own video track.

2

Using Filters

Filters are an easy way to turn an ordinary clip into an instant graphic design element with a minimum of work. There are a variety of filters that serve more utilitarian functions as well, but this lesson focuses on the use of filters for motion graphics.

Applying and Manipulating Filters

The filters in Final Cut Pro are grouped into categories—Blur, Color Correction, Distort, Key, and so on. Filters are capable of creating a wide variety of effects. The filters found in the Perspective category alter a clip's geometry, similar to the Motion parameters. The filters in the Distort category warp and deform clips in various ways. Some categories of filters—Keying and Color Correction, in particular—are covered in their own lessons later in this book.

You can browse the filters by clicking the Effects tab of the Browser and opening the Video Filters bin.

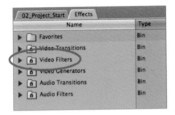

In the next several exercises, you'll use some of the more design-oriented filters to enhance the composition you assembled in Lesson 1, and in the process you'll learn the foundations of filter management that you'll use in later lessons.

Getting Started

In this first series of exercises, you'll apply filters to clips in a sequence and manipulate parameters to customize their effect.

1   Open Lesson_02 > 02_Project_Start.

2   Choose Window > Arrange > Two Up.

3   From the View pop-up menu at the top of the Canvas, choose Black.

4   Open the Filtered Surf Intro sequence.

Combining Filters to Create a Stylized Background

First, you'll apply a set of filters to the **Surf_Background** image in track V1 to make it a little more abstract.

1   Scrub through the Timeline, and notice how the surfer in the background moves from left to right, while the surfers in the foreground clips move from right to left.

To unify the design a little, you should reverse the orientation of this shot.

2   Option-click the Track Visibility control for track V1 to solo it.

With the background soloed, it will be easier to see the changes you're about to make.

3   In the Browser, click the Effects tab to reveal the effects bins, then drag the Video Filters > Perspective > Flop filter onto the **Surf_Background** clip in the Timeline.

The image is reversed in the Canvas. The Flop filter is an example of filters that transform a clip's geometry.

TIP The Flop filter is one of the most frequently used filters in Final Cut Pro. It's frequently used by editors who are trying to match the continuity of insert shots that were filmed with the wrong orientation.

Now that the motion is correctly oriented, a few more filters will make this shot a little more interesting. This time, you'll add a filter using the Effects menu.

4   In the Timeline, select the **Surf_Background** clip, then choose Effects > Video Filters > Stylize > Find Edges.

NOTE ▶ When applying a filter from the Effects menu to a clip in the Timeline, be sure to first select the clip you want to filter. If no specific clips are selected, every clip with Auto Select enabled and every track at the current playhead position will have the filter applied to it.

The Find Edges filter is now applied to the clip.

You can also access every filter and filter category in the Effects tab of the Browser from the Effects > Video Filters submenu. This is useful if you're using a window layout that moves the Effects tab to an inconvenient location for drag-and-drop operations.

The effect you've just applied is a little extreme, so you'll open up the filter to adjust it.

5 Double-click the **Surf_Background** clip to open it into the Viewer, then click the Filters tab.

The Filters tab displays the parameters for each of the filters you've applied to a clip. It's also the place where you can delete or rearrange the ordering of a clip's filters.

So far, you've added two filters to this clip, and they both appear in the Filters tab, stacked in the order in which you applied them.

6   Drag the Amount slider to a value of 45.

Many filters have an Amount parameter, which mixes a percentage of the original, unfiltered image back into the filtered version. In this case, the more abstract outline created by the Find Edges filter is superimposed with the original image, within the filter itself. The end result is a mixture of both, in which the outline is highlighting the original image.

Controlling Filter Combinations

Next, you'll see how the order in which filters appear in the Filters tab affects the resulting image.

1   From the View pop-up menu in the Canvas, choose Black.

2   With the **Surf_Background** clip open in the Viewer, and the Filters tab open, click the Effects tab and drag the Video Filters > Matte > Widescreen filter to the Filters tab.

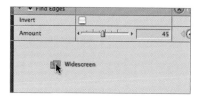

This is the third way you can add a filter to a clip, by dragging it directly to the Filters tab of a clip loaded into the Timeline.

TIP ▶   There is a fourth method of adding a filter to a clip—dragging the filter onto the Canvas. It will be applied to whichever clip is at the play-head position.

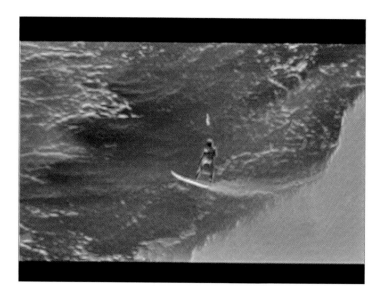

Adding this filter results in cropping the top and bottom of the clip. This simulates a widescreen video that has been letterboxed to fit the 4:3 aspect ratio of standard definition video. There are many aspect ratios available from the Type pop-up menu in this filter.

TIP ▶ By default, this filter is set to 1.66:1, which, curiously, splits the difference between the aspect ratios of Widescreen-presentation 35mm (1.65:1) and Super-16 (1.67:1).

3   Drag the Video Filters > Image Control > Sepia filter onto the Filters tab to add it to the **Surf_Background** clip.

This filter selectively tints an image with the color of your choosing. By default, the tint is, well, Sepia. You're not trying to make this look like an old western movie, however, so you should choose a different color.

4   In the Filters tab, click the Sepia filter's Tint Color control.

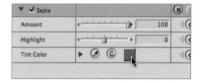

The standard color picker appears.

Clicking anywhere on the color wheel lets you choose a hue (the color itself) at a particular level of saturation (intense or pale). The vertical slider to the right lets you choose the luminance level, or how bright or dark the color should be. There are other color controls you can use for this process, selectable at the top of the Colors window, but this is the default color picker.

TIP ▶ Click the magnifying glass, and the cursor will be replaced with a large magnifying glass, with which you can click anywhere on the screen to choose a color from any window in any application.

5   Pick a blue color. The color you choose appears in the swatch above the color wheel and vertical slider. When you're done, click OK.

Immediately, you'll notice that the entire image is colored blue.

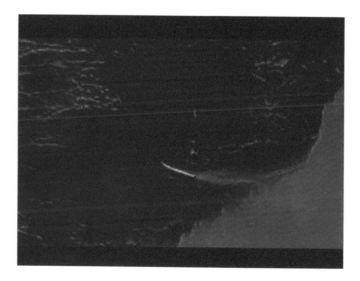

You should also notice that the letterboxed border at the top and bottom of the clip are tinted blue. This was not the desired effect, but it illustrates the importance of applying filters in the proper order.

When Final Cut Pro renders the filters applied to a clip, it does so starting at the top of the filter list and moves down, rendering the first filter, then sending the resulting output to the second filter and rendering, then sending the resulting output to the third filter and rendering, and so on.

This means that each filter affects the total image output by the filter before it. In this case, you applied the Widescreen filter before the Sepia filter, so the Sepia filter added color to everything, the top and bottom borders included. Fortunately, there's an easy fix.

6   In the Filters tab, click the title bar of the Sepia filter, and drag it up to a position above the Widescreen filter. (As you drag, a position indicator bar shows you where the filter will be placed when you release the mouse button.)

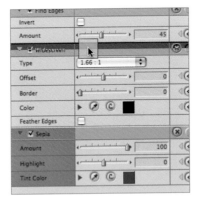

This produces the desired result.

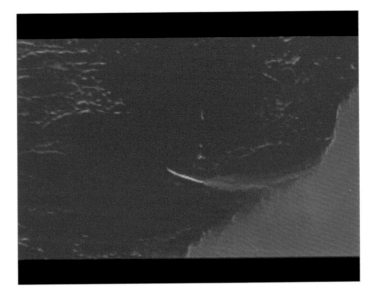

7   Drag the Amount slider of the Sepia filter to the left to a value of 50 to
reduce the amount of tinting.

> **TIP** ▶ Don't worry if you can't seem to drag the Amount slider exactly
> to 50. The default resolution of the slider is a little rough. To obtain more
> precise control over a slider's movement, press the Command key while
> dragging.

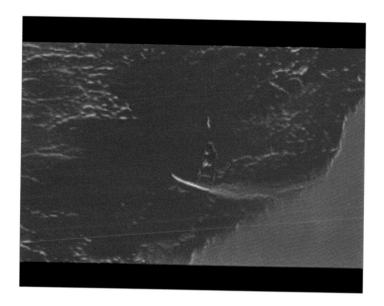

Adjusting a Filter's Start and End Points

Filters have timing controls. You can set individual Start and End points for
each filter, which limits the duration of that filter's effects. In the next exercise,
you'll adjust the Sepia filter's Start and End points so that the clip is tinted
only when the superimposed video clips appear.

1   Make sure that the **Surf_Background** clip is still open in the Viewer, and
Option-click the Track Visibility control on track V1 to turn on all the
other tracks again.

2   Move the playhead in the Timeline to the In point of **Surf_Shot_01**.

If you look in the Filters tab of the Viewer to the right of the parameters, you'll see the keyframe graph area, separated by a dividing line. The keyframe graph is similar to the Timeline, although it's a Timeline used for creating and editing keyframes to create animated effects (which you'll learn much more about in Lesson 5).

You should notice that the playhead's position in the keyframe graph area is offset from the left side of the graph by the same amount the playhead in the Timeline is offset from the beginning of the clip. The playhead in the Timeline and Canvas is mirrored by the playhead in the keyframe graph area. This lets you quickly line up key points in the keyframe graph with edit points, clips, or markers in the Timeline.

In the keyframe graph, notice the pairs of small black lines in the gray bars that extend out of the headers for each filter. These are the Start and End points of each filter. Between them is a light-gray section that shows which section of the clip is affected by that filter.

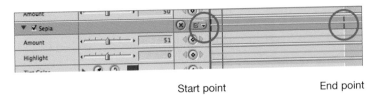

Start point   End point

By default, each filter's Start and End points correspond to the total duration of the clip to which they're applied.

3 Move the pointer to the small black lines, into the keyframe graph area, until it becomes the resize arrow.

4 Drag the Sepia filter's Start point until it lines up with the current position of the playhead.

5 In the Timeline, move the playhead to the Out point of the **Surf_Shot_04** clip.

6 Drag the End point of the Sepia filter to the current position of the playhead.

At this point, the Start and End points of the Sepia filter correspond to the total duration over which all four superimposed surf shots play.

7 Play through the sequence.

You should see that the Sepia filter has no effect until it turns on at the beginning of **Surf_Shot_01**. At the end of **Surf_Shot_04**, it turns off again.

> **TIP** ▶ You can also set Start and End points for filters as you apply them by using the Range Select tool to select a section of a clip in the Timeline, and then dragging a filter onto the selected portion of the clip.

Slipping Filter Start and End Points

In the event that both the Start and End points of a filter's effect need to be moved, you can simultaneously slip a filter's Start and End points together in the keyframe graph of the Viewer.

1   Move the pointer to an area between the Start and End points you adjusted in the previous exercise.

2   When the pointer turns into the Slip tool, you can click this area and drag to simultaneously move the Start and End points.

3   When you're finished, press Command-Z to undo this change.

Adding Filters to Multiple Clips

Oftentimes, you'll find yourself wanting to copy a filter from one clip in a sequence to another. Likewise, you might want to apply one filter to an entire group of clips. Final Cut Pro provides you with several ways to accomplish these tasks.

To begin, you'll add a filter to the topmost superimposed clip, and adjust its settings.

1   In the Timeline, select the **Surf_Shot_04** clip, then choose Effects > Video Filters > Channel > Channel Blur.

    The image is slightly softened.

2 Open the **Surf_Shot_04** clip into the Viewer, and click the Filters tab to view the Channel Blur filter's parameters.

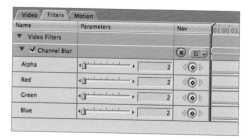

Channel Blur is a very useful filter. Unlike the other blur filters, which generally blur the entire image, the Channel Blur filter lets you selectively blur each individual channel of an image, with sliders for the Alpha, Red, Green, and Blue color channels. By blurring individual color channels to different degrees, you can create highly stylized results.

3 Drag the Alpha, Green, and Blue sliders all the way to the left, so their value fields read 0.

4 Drag the Red slider to the right until its value field reads 20.

The resulting image has a diffuse red haze over it, but it retains color and detail from the still-sharp green and blue channels. Next, you want to apply this filter to the other superimposed clips in this sequence. There are numerous ways to do this, but you'll probably find that you use two key techniques over and over again.

Dragging Filters onto Multiple Clips

In the Viewer, you already have open the Filters tab with the Channel filter you want to copy, so the fastest thing to do is to drag this filter onto all of the clips in the Timeline you want to filter.

1   Drag to select **Surf_Shot_01**, **Surf_Shot_02**, and **Surf_Shot_03**.

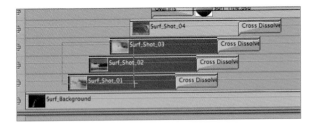

2   Drag the Channel Blur filter from the Filters tab onto any one of the selected clips in the Timeline.

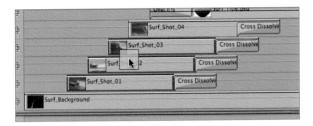

Play through the clips, and you'll see that the filter you dragged is now applied to each of the selected clips, with all of the settings intact.

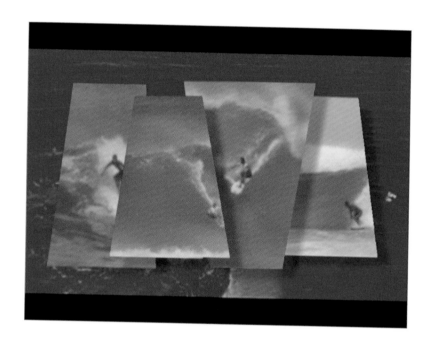

3 In preparation for the next exercise, press Command-Z to undo the change you just made.

Using Paste Attributes

As you saw in Lesson 1, the Paste Attributes command lets you copy settings from one clip and paste them into others. The Paste Attributes command also lets you paste all of the filters from a copied clip onto one or more selected clips. This is a good technique to use if you don't want to open a clip into the Viewer, or if you want to copy all the filters from one clip to others.

1 In the Timeline, select **Surf_Shot_04** and press Command-C to copy it.

2 Drag to select **Surf_Shot_01**, **Surf_Shot_02**, and **Surf_Shot_03**.

3 Press Option-V to use the Paste Attributes command.

You could also Control-click any of the selected clips and choose Paste Attributes from the shortcut menu.

4   In the Paste Attributes dialog, select the Filters box, then click OK.

The filter is applied to all of the selected clips.

Creating Favorite Filters

As you work on more and more projects, you'll discover interesting ways to use filters to create unique effects. If you have a particular filter with specific settings you really like, use often, or need to reuse frequently for a specific client or project, you can save it as a favorite.

Favorite filters appear in the Favorites bin, which appears in the Browser at the top of the Effects tab.

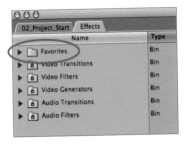

TIP ▶ The contents of the Favorites bin also appear in the Effects > Favorites submenu.

The Favorites bin is a place for you to store effects you use often or have customized for future use. There are a number of ways you can store and manage favorite effects.

First, you'll save a single filter with custom settings as a favorite filter.

1   Open the **Filtered Surf Intro** sequence, if it's not open already.

2   Open the **Surf_Shot_04** clip into the Viewer, and click the Filters tab.

3   With the Viewer active, choose Effects > Make Favorite Effect (or press Option-F). The filter, with all of its settings, is saved into the Favorites bin.

4   In the Browser, click the Effects tab, and click the disclosure triangle next to the Favorites bin to open it.

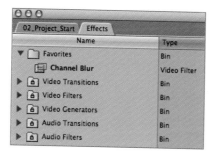

You can see the filter you've just saved inside the bin. By default, favorite filters are saved with the name of the original filter. To keep the contents of the Effects tab organized, and to save yourself some confusion later on, rename favorite filters to reflect their distinguishing features.

5   In the Favorites bin, click the Channel Blur filter once, pause briefly, then click it a second time, so that its name is highlighted.

6   Type a new name (for example, *Channel Blur Red*) and press Return.

Creating Filter Packs

You can also save groups of filters to the Favorites bin, a so-called filter pack (simply a group of filters in a sub-bin within the Filter's tab). For example, if you've created an aged-film effect using a Desaturate filter combined with a strobe effect, you can save both filters as a filter pack, which includes the settings you've made and the order in which they're applied. After you've saved a filter pack, you can apply the entire group of filters by dragging the filter pack bin onto one or more clips in the Timeline.

In this exercise, you'll save the filters applied to **Surf_Background** as a group so you can reuse them, in the same order, on other clips.

1   In the Timeline, select **Surf_Background**.

2   Choose Effects > Make Favorite Effect (Option-F).

A bin named Filtered Surf Intro (Filters) appears in the Favorites bin.

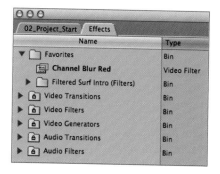

NOTE ► Do not double-click to open the filter bin into its own window—this will alphabetize the filters and change the order in which the filters are listed, rather then preserving the order in which they were originally applied.

3 Rename the Filtered Surf Intro (Filters) bin to *Background Treatment*, or some other descriptive name.

To apply this filter pack to another clip, drag it from the Effects tab of the Browser onto one or more selected clips in the Timeline.

NOTE ► Filter packs are easiest to apply by dragging from the Effects tab of the Browser. When using the Effects menu, you can only select one favorite filter at a time from the filter pack, so you need to click into the menu several times to apply multiple filters.

Organizing the Favorites Bin

When you rely on a lot of custom favorites, you may want to spend some time organizing the contents of your Favorites bin so that you can locate what you need, quickly and easily. For example, if there are four different clients you work with regularly on recurring shows, and each has specific filters used for each show, you could create a hierarchy of sub-bins, one for each client.

In this exercise, you'll create some new Favorites bins and explore ways to organize them.

1   In the Effects tab of the Browser, Option-double-click the Favorites bin icon to open the bin as another tab in the Browser.

2   Control-click the unused gray area inside the Favorites bin and choose New Bin from the shortcut menu.

3   Rename the new bin as desired.

Once you've created a hierarchy of bins in the Favorites bin, you can organize the contents however you like. In particular, since there are so many other types of effects that you can store in the Favorites bin (transitions and motion effects, for example), you may want to create sub-bins for each.

NOTE ▶ Although you can store favorite filters, transitions, and motion effects in the same bin, the only type of favorite settings you can apply to a clip as a group are filters. When the effects in a given bin are different types (filter, transition, or motion), you must apply them individually.

Moving and Preserving Favorites

As you build up a collection of favorites, you will need to take special steps to preserve them, in case you need to reinstall the software on your computer or move your setup to a new computer.

When you save a filter, motion, or transition to the Favorites bin, that information is stored by Final Cut Pro in its preferences file. If you reinstall your system, move to a new system, or delete the preferences file as a part of regular system maintenance or troubleshooting, you unfortunately will lose all your favorites!

However, you can use a special method to transfer your favorites into a new preferences file, in case you need to delete your original preferences file for any reason. You can also use this method to back up your favorites beyond the preferences file, and to move them to any new workstation.

1 Create a new sequence.

2 Add one slug generator clip for each effect or group of effects you want to save. (When you use slugs instead of actual video clips, you won't be presented with an "offline media" warning when moving this project to a computer without the same media.)

The Slug generator is available in the Generator pop-up menu near the bottom-right corner of the Viewer's Video tab.

When you select the Slug generator, the Viewer is filled with black, and you can edit this black slug clip as you would any other clip in the Viewer.

TIP You can also create slug by dragging from the Viewer whenever it's empty.

3   Drag all the effects you want to save to the different slug clips in the Timeline. To save any favorite transitions, just apply them to any edit point between the slug clips in the Timeline.

4   Customize the name of each slug clip by selecting it and pressing Command-9 to display the Item Properties dialog. Each slug can have its own name. Any custom transition names will be carried over automatically.

5   Save this project and name it *Favorites*.

6   At this point, you can move the project file to a different computer or safely delete the preferences files (after quitting Final Cut Pro).

7   To restore the effects, open your Favorites project. If you've changed computers or deleted your preferences, you will notice that the Favorites bin is empty. Then, one by one, restore your Favorite effects by selecting a clip in the Timeline, and choosing Make Favorite Motion or Make Favorite Effect. For any filter packs, go back to the Favorites bin and name the newly-created bin of effects by the customized name of the slug in the Timeline. For any favorite transitions, just recreate the favorite by dragging each transition from the Timeline to the Favorites bin.

Lesson Review

1. How can you can add a filter to a clip?

2. Where do a filter's parameters appear?

3. Does the order in which filters are applied to a clip in the Filters tab matter?

4. What are two ways to apply a filter to multiple clips at once?

5. What do filter Start and End points affect?

6. What happens when you use the Make Favorite Effect command on a clip with multiple filters?

Answers

1. Drag a filter from the Effects tab onto a clip in the Timeline. Select a clip in the Timeline, and choose a filter from the Effects > Video Filters sub-menu. Drag a filter from the Effects tab to a clip in the Viewer. Drag a filter from the Effects tab to the Canvas to apply it to a selected clip at the position of the playhead.

2. In the Filters tab of a clip open in the Viewer.

3. Yes.

4. In the Timeline, select all of the clips you want to filter, then drag a filter onto one of the selected clips, and it will be added to all of them. You can also select a group of clips, and use the Paste Attributes command.

5. The duration and timing of a filter's effect on the clip to which it's applied.

6. A filter pack is created in the Favorites bin of the Effects tab.

3

Lesson Files   Lessons > Lesson_03 > 03_Project_Start

Media   Media > Lesson_03_Media

Time   This lesson takes approximately 60 minutes to complete.

Goals   Apply various composite modes to clips

Choose between the similar Add and Screen functions

Create a "silk stocking" effect to soften and diffuse an image

Project a video image onto a textured background element

Modify opacity to lighten or darken a composite mode effect

Combine composite modes with nesting effects

Lesson 3
Composite Modes

By now, you know how to add clips to multiple layers in the Final Cut Pro Timeline to create complex images and special effects. This lesson will introduce you to ways of combining, or *compositing,* images onscreen in order to create a wide variety of effects.

Understanding Composite Modes

In order to have more than one image occupy the same onscreen space and time, you must mix the two images together, or composite them. Final Cut Pro offers more than 10 composite modes. Each composite mode works by applying different mathematical equations to the pixels in the clips. You don't necessarily need to understand how the math works to use the different modes, but you do need to familiarize yourself with the look that each mode produces in order to know which one will best suit your needs.

1   Open the **03_Project_Start** file in the Lesson_03 folder.

2   In the Clips bin, double-click the **CompModes** clip.

3   Play the clip in the Viewer.

This clip contains examples of various composite modes applied to the Sunset clip superimposed over a simple white-to-black vertical gradient.

The gradient background is useful to help you understand how composite modes work. Some modes tend to make the overall image lighter; some tend to make it darker; others yield a combination of light and dark effects.

Applying a Composite Mode

To apply a composite mode, you must have two clips in your Timeline that overlap in space and time.

1   Double-click to open the **Basic** sequence in the Browser and play it back.

You can view each clip by toggling the Track Visibility controls on and off.

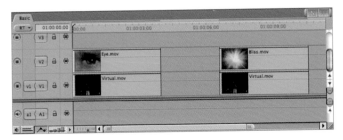

The **Basic** sequence contains two pairs of clips. You will apply a different composite mode to each one.

2   Select **Eye.mov** and choose Modify > Composite Mode > Add.

This mode adds the mathematical color value of each pixel to the clip beneath it. Areas that are black (0) remain unchanged (0 added to anything has no effect), whereas areas that are light in both images become brighter.

If your system will not playback a Composite Mode in real time, change your RT setting to Unlimited RT, and render or press Option-P for "near-real-time".

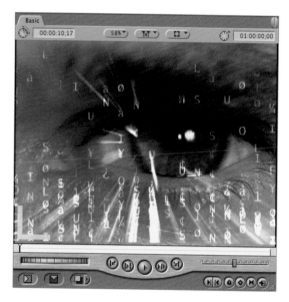

Add

Composite modes must be applied to the clip on the upper track. Applying a composite mode to a clip on track V1 will have no visible effect.

3   Position the playhead over the **Bliss.mov** clip.

4   Control-click **Bliss.mov** and choose Composite Mode > Subtract.

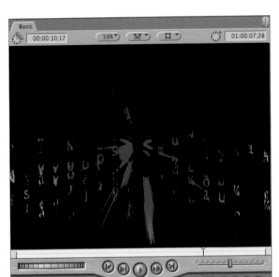

Subtract

Although the Subtract mode also performs a simple arithmetic operation on each pixel, the result may not be what you expect. Subtracting white from a color has the effect of inverting that color. Subtracting black always results in black.

Even if you can't follow the math that creates the various effects, you can learn by trial and error as you experiment with the various modes.

Experimenting with Modes That Lighten
Add, Screen, and Lighten are all similar modes that have an overall lightening effect when applied to a clip.

1   Open the **Lightening** sequence.

This sequence contains four sets of clips. The first three are identical, except that each has a different mode applied.

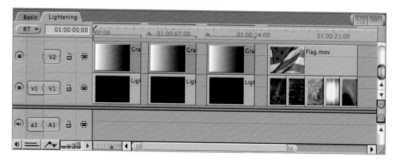

2   Render if necessary and play back the sequence to see the different effects.

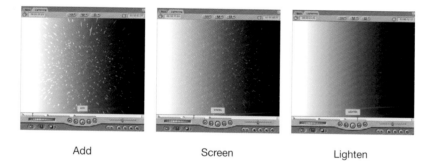

| Add | Screen | Lighten |

The Screen effect differs from the Add effect in that a ceiling is set at pure white, so no pixel will ever "bloom" and create the burning effect that the Add mode can create. The Lighten mode affects only pixels that are darker than 50% gray.

NOTE ▶ The Add mode can create clips that exceed broadcast-safe white levels.

3   Select **Flag.mov** and experiment with the Add, Screen, and Lighten modes to see the different results on each of the clips on V1.

You can easily see the difference in white levels between Add and Screen by viewing the sequence using the Waveform Monitor in the video scopes and switching the composite mode for the V2 clip between Add and Screen.

Using Screen Mode to Create a Diffusion Effect

The Screen effect can be used to create a glowing diffusion effect to soften and brighten an image without losing any detail or sharpness. This is similar to what happens when you put a ProMist filter or a silk stocking on your camera lens.

1   Create a new sequence and name it *Silk Stocking*.

2   Edit **Lake** into the sequence on V1.

3   Duplicate **Lake** by Shift-Option-dragging the clip onto the V2 track, or use a Superimpose edit to edit another copy onto V2, above the V1 clip.

4   Select the clip on V1 and choose Effects > Video Filters > Blur > Gaussian Blur.

5 Double-click the clip to open it into the Viewer.

6 Click the Filters tab. The Blur controls should be visible.

7 Set the Blur Amount to *10*.

The Canvas won't appear to change because the clip on V2 is completely obscuring the clip on V1 you are altering.

8 Select the clip on V2 and set the composite mode to Screen.

Before   After

You can expand this simple technique to create a wealth of unique and interesting effects. For example, instead of blurring the lower clip, try one of the Stylize filters at a low setting such as Diffuse or Find Edges. You can also experiment with different composite modes on the upper clip.

Using Screen Mode to Create a Lens Flare or Explosion Effect

Any time you want to add a bright light source such as a lens flare or an explosion to a clip without altering the overall look of the clip, Screen mode does the trick. It treats any black pixels as transparent, so even if your source clip has no predefined alpha channel (transparency), you can composite the clip successfully.

1   Using the sequence you just created, drag the **Ion Bubble** clip into the sequence on a track above the **Lake** shots.

2   Set the composite mode for **Ion Bubble** to Screen.

3   Set the Canvas to Image+Wireframe.

4   Drag the **Ion Bubble** clip to the upper-left corner so that it looks like an explosion is occurring in the trees.

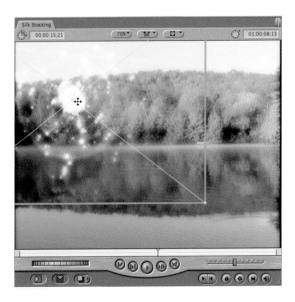

5   Render, if necessary, and play back the sequence.

Experimenting with Modes that Darken

Two of the Final Cut Pro composite modes typically darken the resulting composite: Multiply and Darken.

1   Open the **Darkening** sequence.

This sequence contains three sets of clips. The first two are set to Multiply and Darken, respectively.

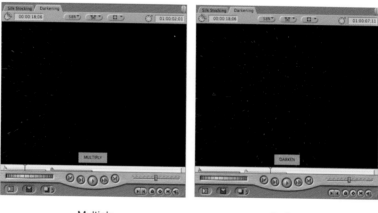

Multiply   Darken

The difference between Multiply and Darken is similar to the difference between Screen and Lighten. Multiply treats white pixels as transparent and black pixels as opaque. The Darken mode affects only pixels brighter than 50% gray.

Multiply is one of the most commonly used composite modes. The pixel values in the two images are literally multiplied, but don't try to do the math yourself. The result merges the two images without adding brightness. This has the effect of combining the textures of the images into a single organic whole.

2   Select the **Flag.mov** clip on V2 and set the composite mode to Multiply.

3   Step through the clip to observe how the clip interacts with the different clips beneath it.

4   Set **Flag.mov** to Darken.

5   Observe the difference.

Using Multiply to Create a Textured Effect

The Multiply effect can be used to apply a texture from one clip to another.

1   Open the **Texture Text** sequence.

This sequence contains a text generator.

2   Drag **Stage** from the Clips bin in the Browser to the sequence and drop it on track V2 directly above the text clip.

3   Set the composite mode on **Stage** to Multiply.

The order of the clips affects how the composite mode is applied.

4   Reverse the order of the clips in the Timeline so **Text** is above **Stage**.

5 Set the composite mode for **Stage** to Normal.

6 Set the composite mode for **Text** to Multiply.

This gives the impression that the word *Show* is being projected onto a textured white background.

7   Delete the **Text** clip.

8   Drag the **Sunset** clip from the Browser into the sequence and place it on the track above the **Stage** clip.

9   Set the composite mode for **Sunset** to Multiply.

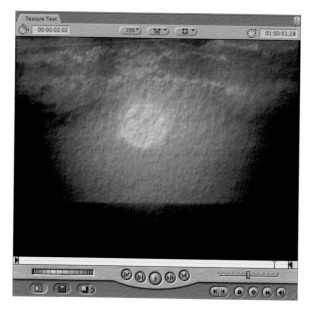

The **Sunset** clip looks like it is being projected onto the textured stage background. This trick is particularly effective when projected onto a static background image. Choose any texture file, such as a brick wall, canvas bag, or metal grate.

Using the Overlay Composite Mode

Overlay is a special composite mode that combines the effects of Screen and Multiply. Pixels darker than 50% gray are multiplied and clips lighter than 50% gray are screened. Overlay mode can be used when either a Multiply or Screen effect is too dramatic on its own.

1   Open the **Overlay** sequence.

2   Set the composite mode for the **Gradient** to Multiply.

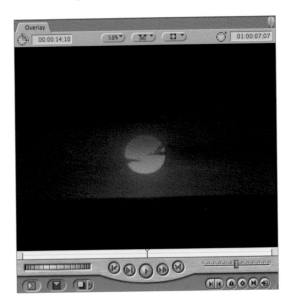

This composite effect is much too dark.

3   Set the composite mode for the **Gradient** to Screen.

Now the whiter areas of **Gradient** wash out much of the sunset.

4   Set the composite mode to Overlay.

Now the dark areas successfully sharpen the sky, and the lighter areas sharpen the ocean.

5   Toggle the track visibility of the **Gradient** on V2 to see the difference.

Using Subtract and Difference Modes

The Subtract and Difference composite modes work similarly to the Invert filter (which we'll address next) in that they have the effect of changing pixel colors to values on the opposite side of the color wheel, depending on the clips that are being composited. There is no obvious application for Subtract and Difference modes when creating effects that suggest a real-world environment, but they can be used to create a variety of interesting specialized effects. Using black-and-white clips makes it easier to see how these modes work.

1   Open the **Subtract & Difference** sequence.

This sequence contains two pairs of clips. The first pair is monochromatic, and the second is full color.

2   Set the composite mode of **Binary Scan Vertical.mov** to Subtract.

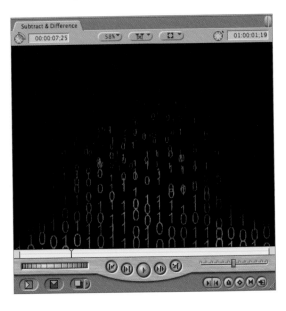

This subtracts the pixel values of the two clips. Just like the opposite of adding, this tends to darken the image. If a pixel's combined value equals 0 or less, it is represented as black.

3   Set the composite mode of **Binary Scan Vertical.mov** to Difference.

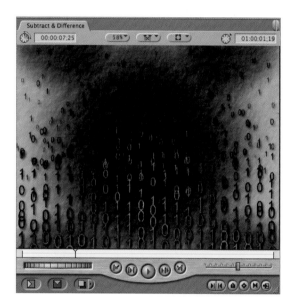

Difference creates a much more complex combination of the two images. Whereas Subtract stops at absolute zero (black) with its math, Difference will invert the image if the value goes below zero. In general, Difference results in a much more interesting and complex composite than Subtract.

Making Composite Effects More Versatile with the Invert Filter

You can use the Invert filter to modify one of the composited clips to reverse the effect of the composite mode. This trick can be employed with any composite mode setting, but it is most effective with the Subtract and Difference modes.

1 Select **Binary Scan Vertical.mov** and choose Effects > Video Filters > Channel > Invert.

2 Change the composite mode of **Binary Scan Vertical.mov** back to Subtract.

The Invert filter gives you two additional ways to use the effect.

Using Subtract and Difference with Color Clips

1 Select the **Pulse Rate.mov** clip and set the composite mode to Subtract.

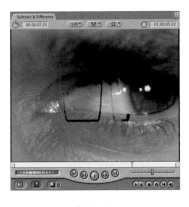 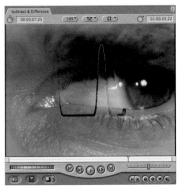

Subtract   Difference

When subtracting one color from another, you may have unexpected results.

2   Select **Pulse Rate.mov** and set the composite mode to Difference.

3   Render, if necessary, and play back.

The Difference filter creates a rainbow on the pulse line as it moves across the variously colored pixels in the face and eye.

Modifying the Opacity of Composited Clips

You can further vary a composite mode's effect by altering a clip's opacity. Because changing the transparency of a clip can mute its colors or otherwise change its appearance, changing a clip's opacity can have dramatic effects on how the composite mode works.

1   Turn on Clip Overlays by clicking the button in the lower-left corner of the Timeline.

2   Adjust the opacity of **Pulse Rate.mov** to about 25%.

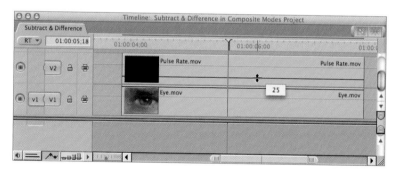

Reducing the opacity causes the colored highlights to disappear and the composited clip to become more integrated with the background clip. Whenever you experiment with composite modes, remember to adjust the clip's opacity to vary the effect.

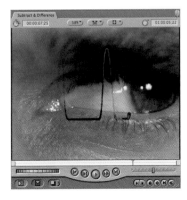 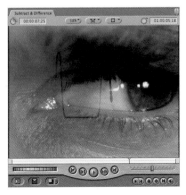

100% opacity   25% opacity

Using Hard Light and Soft Light Modes

The Hard Light and Soft Light composite modes are designed to create the effect that the clip is being projected onto the background image either as a hard, high-contrast light source or as a soft, diffused light source that yields softer shadows.

1   Double-click the **Hard and Soft Light** sequence to open it in the Browser.

2   Set the composite mode on **Flag.mov** to Hard Light.

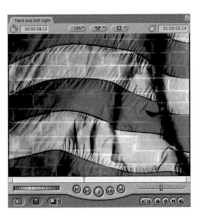

Hard Light

3 Render, if necessary and play back the sequence.

The four background clips illustrate how the effect looks when applied on various images. Notice how the shadows and folds of the flag are accentuated.

4 Set the composite mode of **Flag.mov** to Soft Light.

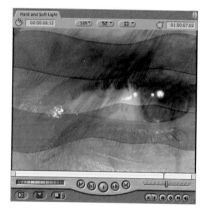

Soft Light

In this mode, the white stripes become almost entirely transparent. The texture of the flag is softened, and the background becomes more prominent.

Using Complex Composite Mode Effects

Once you get the hang of the different composite modes, you'll identify the ones you like best in different situations. In some cases, you can combine effects for even greater flexibility.

Combining Modes on Multiple Layers

Every clip in a sequence has a composite mode that determines how it is mixed with the clips beneath it in the Timeline.

1 Open the **Complex** sequence. This sequence contains the **Sunset Over Sea.mov** clip. In this exercise, you will make the clip look like it was shot on film, and that the film reel ran out during the filming.

2 Set an Out point at the end of the clip in the Timeline.

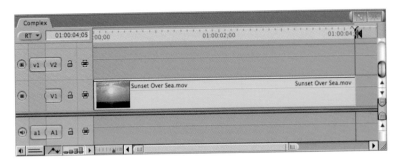

3 Drag the **Tail Burn 2** clip from the Clips bin in the Browser window onto track V2. Align the clip to end with the **Sunset Over Sea.mov.**

The clip should appear on track V2 and end on the same frame as the sunset clip.

4 Set the composite mode of **Tail Burn 2** to Screen.

5 Edit the **Film Scratch** clip from the Clips bin in the Browser to track V3 of the Timeline. It should line up with the beginning and end of the sunset clip.

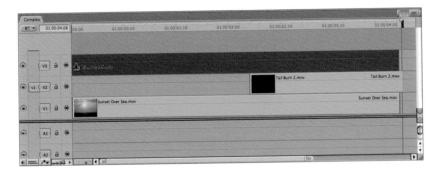

6 Set the composite mode of **Film Scratch.mov** to Subtract.

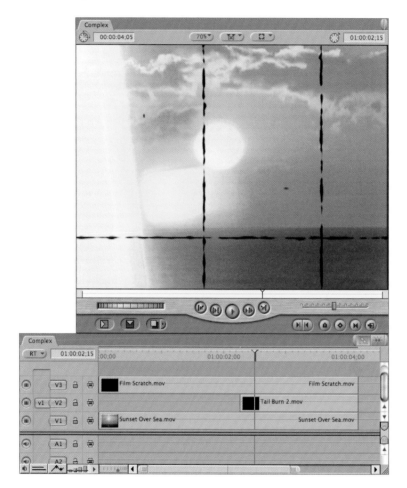

7   Render, if necessary and play back your sequence.

Now the sunset clip appears to have been taken from the very end of a scratched-up roll of film.

Using Nesting to Control and Combine Composite Modes

Sometimes, simply compositing one clip on top of another won't create your desired effect. You may want to control how one combined shot is composited with a third clip. You can do this with a *nested* sequence.

1   Create a new sequence by pressing Command-N. Name it *The Eye*.

2   In the Viewer window, access the Generators pop-up menu and load a text generator.

3   Click the Controls tab and type *EYE* into the text field. Use the default font (Lucida Grande) and set the Size to 200. Make the Style bold and the Font Color pink.

4   Edit the text clip into the sequence.

5   Return to the Generators pop-up menu and choose Render > Gradient to load a gradient into the Viewer. Leave all the controls at their default settings.

6   Edit Gradient to the track above the Text clip in the sequence.

7   Set the composite mode of Gradient to Multiply.

This applies **Gradient** to the color of the text, leaving the remainder of the clip black.

8   Drag the two clips from tracks V1 and V2 onto V2 and V3.

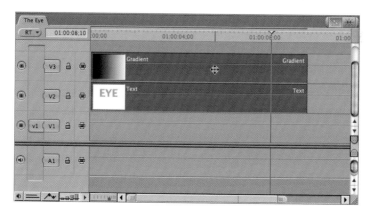

This makes room to use another clip as a background.

9 Drag **Eye** from the Clips bin in the Browser onto track V1 directly beneath the two clips.

Because of the way composite modes work, the gradient on track V3 is darkening the right side of the **Eye** clip as well as the text on V2. To eliminate this undesired effect, you must nest the clips on tracks V2 and V3.

10 Select the **Text** and **Gradient** clips.

11 Choose Sequence > Nest Items.

The Nest Items dialog box appears.

12 Name the new sequence *Gradient Text* and click OK.

The new sequence has a black background that obscures the **Eye** clip entirely.

13 Select **Gradient Text** and set the composite mode to Screen.

Now the gradated text is screened on top of the video clip. You could also try other modes such as Difference or Subtract to create alternate effects.

Lesson Review

1. Does the stacking order of superimposed clips affect the result of a composite mode effect?

2. What are good uses for the Screen composite mode?

3. How can you invert a composite mode's effect?

4. When compositing clips, what control can you use for adjusting the transparency of a superimposed clip?

5. How can you control how composite modes work with three or more superimposed clips?

Answers

1. Sometimes.

2. The Screen composite mode is good for superimposing lighting effects, such as lens flares or diffuse glowing effects.

3. Apply an Invert filter to one of the superimposed clips.

4. Reduce the composited clip's Opacity.

5. Nest the superimposed clips within a sequence in the Timeline, then apply a composite mode to the nested sequence.

4

Lesson 4
Travel Mattes

Travel mattes offer another way to composite two images together, and are commonly used to create a video-in-text effect, which is a video image matted inside the shape of text. You'll use travel mattes to create a video-in-text effect, as well as explore some other scenarios when a travel matte is the perfect choice, such as creating a gradient filter effect and revealing portions of video images.

What Are Travel Mattes?

First, let's distinguish the differences between standard mattes (and masks) versus travel mattes. A standard matte is a filter used to cut out, or crop, an image by using defined points or shapes, leaving part of the frame transparent. Conventional matte treatments include 4- and 8-point garbage mattes to crop out miscellaneous parts of an image before blue- or green-screen keying.

Travel mattes work a little differently in that they are more like compositing than matting. A travel matte is not a filter like a standard matte. A travel matte is a composite mode used to combine elements of two different images. Using a travel matte, one video image is matted by another.

Assume for a moment that you want to cut out an image in the shape of a word. This can be done by creating a travel matte that combines a video clip and a text clip. When the video is matted by the text, it appears as video-in-text.

Video clip   Text clip   Video-in-text

There are two types of travel mattes: alpha and luma. Both are used to combine two images, yet they use different information to create the matte, as you will see during this lesson.

Using Alpha Travel Mattes

An alpha travel matte uses the transparency (alpha channel) from one clip to matte another clip.

Creating an Alpha Travel Matte

Let's give it a try.

1   Open Lesson_04 > **04_Project_Start**.

2   If the **Travel Mattes1** sequence is not in front in the Timeline, click its Timeline tab to bring it to the front.

3   Move the Timeline playhead to the first clip in the Timeline, **circuit board**. This is one of the two clips you will use in this exercise.

4   Move the playhead to the next clip in the Timeline, a text generator.

   This clip will be used to matte the first clip, as you will see next.

5   Drag **circuit board** over the text clip, as shown, and drop it on V2.

6   Highlight the video clip on V2 and choose Modify > Composite Mode > Travel Matte - Alpha. Instantly, you should see a video-in-text effect.

   TIP ▶ You can also Control-click a clip directly in the Timeline and choose Composite Mode > Travel Matte - Alpha from the shortcut menu.

7   Render, if necessary the composite and play back the composite

This is one way to use a travel matte, to composite two clips. The top clip (also called the source clip) is a video image that is stamped into the shape of text. It is placed on a higher video track. The bottom clip (or the matte clip) is a text generator that contains an alpha channel. Any clip that has an alpha channel can be used to matte a source clip with an alpha travel matte. The matte clip is placed on a video track just below the source clip.

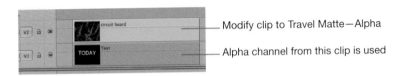

can be used to matte a source clip with an alpha travel matte. The matte clip is placed on a video track just below the source clip.

Choosing to Blur

When using travel mattes to create a video-in-text effect, you have the choice of whether or not you want to see the video clearly in the text. In other words, do you want to discern the content of the scene clearly, or is the video in the text simply a way to add texture to the text? In this exercise, you will blur the video clip to alter the result of the travel matte, creating a more subtle effect that shifts the emphasis from the video image to the text.

1   In the Timeline, double-click the **circuit board** clip to load it into the Viewer, and then click the Filters tab.

2   Choose Effects > Video Filters > Blur > Gaussian Blur to apply a Gaussian Blur filter.

3   Change the Radius of the blur to about 30.

As you adjust the slider (increase the blur), watch the result in the Canvas.

The higher the blur, the less defined the image, eventually giving way to just a blur of light and color by the time the Radius is 30.

4 Render the composite, if necessary and play it back.

The video in the text plays back as subtle shifts in light, color, and movement.

> **TIP** ▶ When you want to create this type of textured text, choose a source clip with high-contrast areas, camera or subject movement, or varying color.

Adding a Background

When applying a travel matte, the source clip is matted into the shape of the matte clip, creating transparency in the resulting composite. At first, it may appear as though you have created video-in-text against a black background. If the composite is left as is, then this would be a black background, but there are many more possibilities.

1 In the Canvas, click the View pop-up menu to choose Checkerboard 1.

Notice that the only portion of the image that is opaque (solid) is the shape of the text. The rest of the frame is transparent.

Because the travel matte has left a fairly large part of the frame transparent, any clip may be placed below the travel matte composite in the Timeline to create a background.

2   Switch the Canvas background back to Black.

3   Move the travel matte composite up one video track in the Timeline.

TIP ▶ To quickly move a clip or group of clips up in the Timeline, highlight both clips and press Option–Up Arrow.

4   Open the Clips bin in the Browser and locate the clip **sparkling water**. Edit it to V1 in the Timeline, under the composite.

You now have added a background to the video-in-text effect.

5   Optionally, add a Sepia filter to the **circuit board** clip on V3 so that the text's hues are closer to the colors of the background. Choose Effects > Video Filters > Image Control > Sepia.

As you have seen, the video used in the travel matte can be altered with filters, such as Gaussian Blur and Sepia, to create an entirely new look.

Fine-Tuning Travel Mattes

There are numerous ways to modify a travel matte composite, but the result will depend on which clip is altered. In the next exercises, you will make adjustments to the source clip, the matte clip, and the two clips together.

Adjust Source and Matte Clips Independently

Use the following steps to alter the results by making individual adjustments to each clip.

1   Open the **Travel Mattes2** sequence by clicking its tab in Timeline. (If it is not open, open it from the Browser.)

2   Move the playhead over the composite in the Timeline.

The clip **sunset on beach** is on V2. A text clip of the word *SUNSET* is on V1. The composite shows the video of the beach seen through the text. (A travel matte composite mode has been applied to the top clip.)

NOTE ▶ This text clip is created with a wide, heavy font so that you can see the matted image more clearly.

3   In the Canvas, switch to Image+Wireframe.

4   In the Timeline, select the video clip on V2 to activate its wireframe in the Canvas.

5 Shift-drag the active wireframe in the Canvas down until you can see the sun in the text. Shift-dragging constrains the movement to only one direction, such as up and down or left and right.

Moving the source clip reveals different parts of the video seen in the text.

6 Shift-drag a corner point of the Canvas wireframe inward a bit to make the image smaller. Release the mouse button before the image is smaller than the text. Shift-dragging scales the image out of proportion, making it possible to fit more of the video frame inside the text.

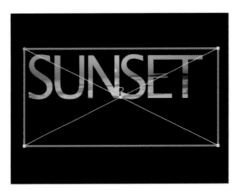

7 Select the text clip in the Timeline to activate its wireframe.

8 In the Canvas, click and drag the text clip. Notice that the video remains still while the text moves, revealing different areas of the video image.

This would be undesirable if you wanted to move the text to a new location and still see the same area of the video in the text.

9 Press Command-Z to undo the text move in the Canvas.

10 Select *both* clips in the Timeline. In the Canvas, you should see both wireframes active.

11 In the Canvas, click and drag either wireframe and move it around the screen.

The two clips reposition together. Depending on your goal, you can adjust the video seen in the text by independently moving the source clip's wireframe, or you can move the two wireframes together to reposition the text and video as one unit, keeping the video that is visible through the text the same.

Modify the Composite as a Whole

When you nest two clips together, you are able to treat them as one clip, and affect the entire composite as a single item when applying effects, animating a motion path, changing the scale, or other motion effect. When you create a motion path for the nest that contains the clips, as you will do next, all the clips move together in unison on the screen, because the animation is applied to the nest, instead of applied to one clip or the other.

Now you will animate the travel matte composite you have built so that it travels from one side of the screen to the other.

1   In the Timeline, highlight both clips of the travel matte composite.

2   Choose Sequence > Nest Items (Option-C).

3   In the Nest Items dialog box, change the name to *Nested Composite* and click OK.

4   Once the clips are nested, select the nest in the Timeline to activate its wireframe in the Canvas.

5   Click and drag the wireframe to the left until it is almost fully outside the frame.

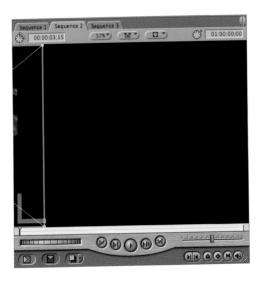

6   In the Canvas, choose Zoom > Fit All.

This resizes the Canvas view so that you can see the wireframe outside of the frame.

7   Continue to drag the clip to the left until it is fully out of the frame.

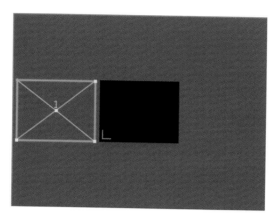

8   Press Home to move the playhead to the head of the sequence (and the nest).

9   Set a keyframe at this point in the Canvas.

TIP▸ Control-click the Add Keyframe button and choose Center to set a keyframe only for the Center point and not for all the motion settings.

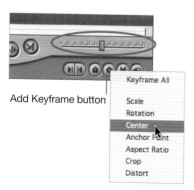

Add Keyframe button

10   Move the playhead near the end of the nest in the Timeline.

11   In the Canvas, drag the wireframe to the right until it exits the frame.

You should now see a motion path from one side of the screen to the other.

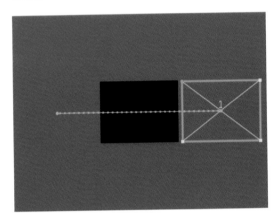

12   Render the animation, if necessary, and play it back.

In this exercise, you used nesting to treat the travel matte composite as one item, which made it easier to animate the two clips together.

Using a Gradient Source Clip

Any video or graphic can be used as the source clip in a travel matte, and using a gradient yields many interesting effects.

1   Open the **Travel Mattes2** sequence if it is not already open in the Timeline.

2   From the Generator pop-up menu in the Viewer, choose Render > Custom Gradient.

3   Edit this gradient into the Timeline on V2, into a blank space on the Timeline, to the right of the previous composition. Set it to a duration of 4 seconds.

4   Double-click the gradient from the Timeline to reopen it into the Viewer to modify it.

5   In the Viewer, click the Controls tab.

6   Set the Gradient Direction angle to 180 degrees, the Gradient Width to about 30, and set the Start coordinates to about 0, −100, to move the line of the gradient up the screen a bit. (There are two Start parameters; use the one nearer the top.)

Optionally, you can add a Gaussian Blur filter (set to 20) to soften the edge of the gradient clip.

7   Create a new text clip. Use a somewhat wide font and large point size, such as 100-point Impact. Change the text to *Fading Away*.

8   Edit this text clip to V1 in the Timeline, directly beneath the gradient.

9   Select the gradient clip in the Timeline and change its composite mode to Travel Matte-Alpha.

Depending on where the line of the gradient is, at this point you might see an image similar to this illustration, a full black frame, or text that is all white.

10 In the Timeline, select the gradient clip to activate its wireframe in the Canvas.

11 Click the gradient wireframe in the Canvas and slide it up or down in small increments to reveal the line of the gradient. Release the mouse button when the line of the gradient is visible in the letters of the text.

There are many ways to use this effect by playing with the gradient and its position. You can make the text look as though it was fading away, with just the top of the text barely visible, for example. Or you can change the colors of the gradient to create other looks. If you animate the center point of the gradient clip itself, you can start with the text as one color, and transition over time into another hue.

TIP The Highlight gradient can also be used to create the effect shown in this figure:

Using Luma Travel Mattes

So far you've looked only at alpha travel mattes, but there is another type of travel matte available in Final Cut Pro: the luma travel matte. Luma travel mattes also produce an image matted by a clip placed below it, but they use luminance (brightness) levels of the clip image instead of an alpha channel to determine whether a pixel remains solid (opaque) or becomes transparent.

Here's how it works: Wherever there is pure black in the matte clip, the matte is fully opaque and none of the source image on top (the foreground image) shows through. On the other hand, wherever there is pure white in the matte clip, the matte clip is fully transparent, and all the pixels in the foreground are preserved in the final composite. The really interesting stuff happens where there are shades of gray, which results in semi-transparency in the final composited image.

Let's dive into a few real-world scenarios where a luma travel matte is ideal for creating an effect.

Blending Two Images in a Luma Matte

In the previous exercise, you used a gradient generator as a source clip. Now, you will use a gradient as a matte clip. As a default gradient ranges from black to white, it combines the two extremes used by a luma travel matte. Next, spend a moment seeing how grayscale information relates to matting an image.

1   In the Browser, locate the clip **sunset on beach**, and edit it to a blank area of the **Travel Mattes2** Timeline on V1.

2   In the Browser, locate the clip **kelp forest and fish**, and edit it to the Timeline on V3, above **sunset on beach**, leaving track V2 empty at this point.

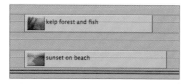

The images of these two clips will be blended together in the next steps.

3   From the Generator > Render pop-up menu in the Viewer, load a custom gradient into the Viewer.

4   Edit the gradient onto V2, between the two clips already on V1 and V3.

5   Trim down all three clips to the same length.

6 In the Timeline, Control-click the clip on V3 and choose Composite Mode > Travel Matte-Luma from the shortcut menu.

In the Canvas, notice that the result is a split screen of sorts. In the center of the screen, the two images blend together.

7 Compare the image in the Viewer and the Canvas to get a better idea of how the gradient on V2 is being used to blend together the clips on V1 and V3, based on the luminance (brightness) values of each pixel.

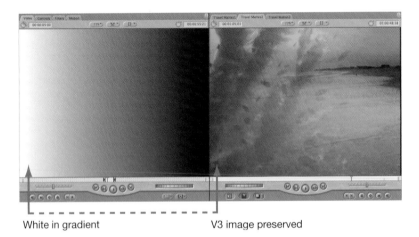

White in gradient   V3 image preserved

Wherever the gradient is white, the image on V3 is preserved in the composite. Wherever there is black in the gradient, V3 is transparent and only V1 is visible. Wherever the gradient is gray, there is semi-transparency.

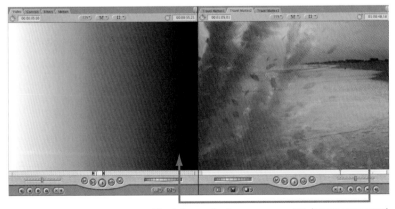

Black in gradient   V1 image preserved

8 In the Canvas, choose View > Image to turn off the wireframe.

9 Double-click the gradient in the Timeline to open it back into the Viewer.

10 In the Viewer, click the Controls tab of the gradient.

11 To make the gradation line a bit smaller, change Gradient Width to *75*.

This adds a bit more contrast between the two images, as the left and right edges of the frame become less transparent. It also pushes the gradient line to the left too much, which you will correct next.

12 To reposition the gradient line, click the crosshair button next to Start. The button darkens when activated.

13 Move the cursor to the Canvas. The cursor appears as a crosshair.

14 Click and hold in the middle of the Canvas. (Do not release the mouse button.)

15 Drag left and right to see the line of the gradient change. It will continuously update as you move the cursor.

16 Release the mouse button when the line is somewhat centered in the screen and you see an equal mix of the two images.

17 Set Gradient Direction to 135 to make a diagonal transition between the clips.

18 Because this last action also impacts the line of the gradient, use the Start crosshair to fine-tune the positioning of the gradient line to create a more equal mix of the two images.

19 Render, if necessary, and play back the composite.

This type of effect can also be well used in a narrative situation, as a way to show simultaneous action in two different scenes. It is also more film-like than a straight split screen.

Creating a Grad Filter Effect

Another handy way to use a gradient as the matte clip is to emulate a *grad* lens filter. *Grad* is short for *gradient*. A grad lens filter graduates from clear to a color tint or a neutral density. Cinematographers often use grad filters to alter part of the frame without affecting the whole frame. Although a common use of these filters is to darken or intensify the color of a sky, grad filters can be used in a variety of situations.

In this exercise, you will use a gradient generator and a travel matte to intensify the color of the sky as if a grad filter had been used on the video camera.

1   In the Browser, locate clip **L5-castlepeak-1** and edit it into a blank spot in the **Travel Mattes2** Timeline on V1.

2   Shift-Option-click the clip to duplicate it, and then drag it upward. Place the copy on V3, leaving V2 empty. (Pressing Option duplicates the clip; pressing Shift constrains the movement of the clip to one direction— up/down or left/right.)

Now, you'll blend together parts of these two clip's images to create the grad filter effect.

3   Select the clip on V3 and apply a brightness/contrast filter by choosing Effects > Video Filters > Image Control > Brightness and Contrast (Bézier).

4   Open the V3 instance of **L5-castlepeak-1** into the Viewer, and on the Filters tab, adjust the Brightness to approximately –25.

5   Edit a new custom gradient onto track V2, between the two video clips already in the Timeline, on V1 and V3. (Again, to access the custom gradients, click the Generator pop-up menu in the Viewer and choose Render > Custom Gradient.)

6   Open the gradient back into the Viewer and click the Controls tab.

7   On the Controls tab in the Viewer, set the Gradient Direction angle to *180* to make it horizontal.

8   Set Gradient Width to about *50* to start. You will come back to these controls to fine-tune them later.

9   Control-click the video clip on V3 and choose Composite Mode > Travel Matte-Luma from the contextual menu.

After the travel matte is applied to the clip on V3, the gradient will serve to reveal the top of the clip on V3 (the darkened clip), and reveal the bottom part of the original, untouched clip from V1. In the Canvas, you should now see that the top of the image is dark, and the bottom of the image is normal.

10 In the Viewer, click the Video tab.

Notice the position of the gradient line and where that relates to the composite seen in the Canvas. The line separating the two images will still need to be fine-tuned because right now it falls in the greenery of the scene and should only be affecting the sky.

Clip on V3

Clip on V1

Next, you'll adjust the gradient so the lighter clip on V1 reveals the ground portion of the frame, and the darker clip on V3 reveals the sky portion of the frame. Additionally, setting the gradient line near the horizon line can help to disguise it and create a more realistic result.

11 Click the Controls tab of the Viewer to make adjustments to the gradient.

12 Click the crosshair for Start to activate it.

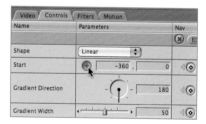

13 Move the cursor to the Canvas and click with the crosshair about two-thirds of the way up the screen.

This is a general starting point. You will need to fine-tune this positioning a bit after the next step.

14 Change the Gradient Width to about *30*.

You should now see an image similar to this:

15 Continue to fine-tune the gradient Width, Start, or Direction as needed so that the line of the gradient is somewhat hidden along the horizon.

Creating a Stylized Grad Filter Effect

Now you will continue to tweak the grad filter effect to produce a look that is bolder and somewhat surreal.

1 Add a Gaussian Blur filter to the gradient and set the Radius to *40*.

This will help to soften the line of the gradient as you intensify the look of the clip on V3 in the next steps.

2 On the Controls tab of the gradient, set the Gradient Direction angle to about *170* degrees.

3 Click the Start crosshair on the Controls tab in the Viewer and set it to the upper-left corner of the Canvas, as shown in this figure:

4   Adjust the Gradient Width as desired.

5   Open the clip on V3 into the Viewer and click the Filters tab.

6   Set Brightness to about *–50* in the Brightness/Contrast filter.

Experiment with other variations by adding additional effects filters to the clip on V3 and/or modifying different elements of the gradient, this time without concern for hiding the line of the gradient.

Lesson Review

1.   How many video clips are required to composite a travel matte over a background clip?
2.   What does the middle clip do in a travel matte composite?
3.   How does an alpha travel matte work?
4.   How does a luma travel matte work?
5.   Which generator can be used to quickly create travel matte composites?

Answers

1. Three: a top, middle, and bottom clip.

2. The middle clip defines the matte, which determines which parts of the top image are solid and which parts are transparent.

3. A clip with a grayscale image is used as an alpha channel to define areas of transparency for the clip in the track above.

4. The luminance (brightness) from a clip (which can be either color or grayscale) is used to define areas of transparency for the clip in the track above.

5. Gradient, Custom Gradient, or Highlight generators.

5

Lesson Files Lessons > Lesson_05 > 05_Project_Start

Media Media > Lesson_05_Media

Time This lesson takes approximately 120 minutes to complete.

Goals Use the Final Cut Pro coordinate system

Create motion effects with keyframe animation

Create and modify motion paths

Use Bézier handles to customize effects

Copy motion effects to other images using motion favorites

Create a template to reuse a composition and replace the images

Animating Effects

In previous lessons, you've created *static* effects that remain unchanged for the duration of the clip to which they're applied. In this lesson, you'll create effects that change over time—*motion effects*.

Motion effects are important elements that add polish to any program. They are used to create anything from an animated split screen to a pan-and-scan movement on a still photograph. When you animate multiple parameters at once, you can create even more eye-catching animations such as images flying across the screen.

Creating Motion Effects

Final Cut Pro lets you create a wide variety of motion effects using *keyframe animation*. Keyframes are the basic building blocks of motion effects. They let you stamp a particular setting on a clip's motion or filter parameter at a specific time. When you add two or more keyframes to a single parameter, each with different values, the parameter is animated.

The settings are automatically calculated in each frame occurring between two keyframes, in order to create a smooth transformation from the state of the parameter in the first keyframe to the state of the parameter in the next keyframe. For example, if you add two keyframes to the keyframe graph of the Scale parameter—the first with a value of 50, and the second with a value of 100—that image will grow in size from 50 to 100 percent as the playhead moves from the first to the second keyframe.

Keyframes can be used to animate all of the motion parameters you have explored in previous lessons, as well as the parameters of any filter that you add to a clip. In the exercises in this lesson, you'll learn many techniques for adding and manipulating keyframed animation to motion and filter parameters.

Getting Started

1   Open Lesson_05 > **05_Project_Start**.

2   Choose Window > Arrange > Two Up.

Choosing the Render Quality of Motion Settings

Final Cut Pro is capable of real-time playback when editing, when performing many compositing tasks such as making simple superimpositions, when creating motion effects, and when using RT filters. However, as you delve into the creation of intensive multilayered motion graphics, you'll eventually hit the limits of your computer's real-time playback capabilities.

As a result, you may find it necessary to render the output from time to time to see your composition at the highest quality. You should be aware that the Motion Filtering Quality pop-up menu (available in the Video Processing of the sequence settings) lets you set the quality of rendered results.

There are three options: Fastest renders a low-quality result, but produces the quickest render times, and is useful when you simply need a speedy preview. Normal results in high-quality images. Best predictably renders the best quality, but with slower render times.

> **NOTE ▶** In Final Cut Pro 4.5 and earlier, the fastest quality was the only level of quality for the rendering of all image transformations. Final Cut Pro 5 introduced significantly higher quality rendering options, which default to Normal.

If you're using a slower computer, you can lower the Motion Filtering Quality to speed up the rendering of exercises in this lesson. If you're using a faster machine, go ahead and use better settings.

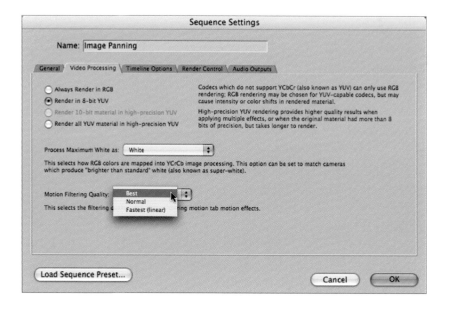

These settings have no effect on real-time previews. The quality of real-time previews is controlled by the settings in the RT pop-up menu in the Timeline.

Learning the Final Cut Pro Coordinate System

Before you begin animating motion parameters for each clip, you should understand the Final Cut Pro coordinate system.

The center of each clip, and the center of the Canvas, is located at coordinates 0,0. The first value is the X coordinate (the horizontal position), and the second value is the Y coordinate (the vertical position). Changing the Y coordinate to a negative value moves the corresponding clip's image up, whereas changing the Y coordinate to a positive value moves the clip down. Similarly, changing the X coordinate to a negative value moves the parameter left, whereas positive values move the parameter right.

The following illustration shows the coordinate system used by many of the motion parameters in Final Cut Pro.

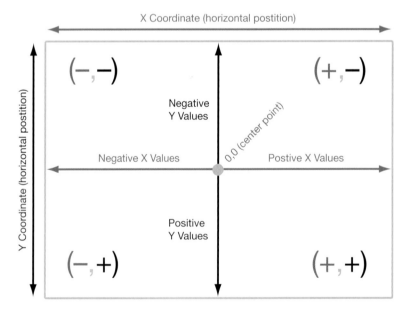

The next exercise will help you become familiar with the coordinate system.

1 Option-double-click the Exercise 01 bin to open it into its own tab, then open the **Exercise 01 - Coordinates** sequence.

A series of Final Cut Pro–generated graphics divide the Canvas into the four quadrants. A circle sits in the middle, at the default position of all clips edited into the Timeline.

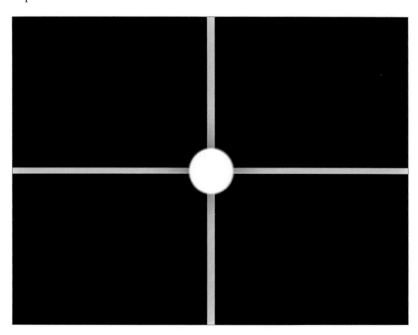

2 Open the **Circle** clip in the Timeline into the Viewer, and click the Motion tab.

As you can see, the Center parameter is set to 0,0—which is the default center position of the Canvas, no matter what size it is.

3   From the View pop-up menu at the top of the Canvas, choose Image+
Wireframe.

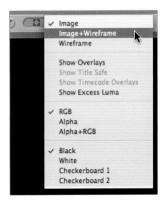

4   In the Canvas, drag the circle down and to the right, so that it sits somewhere within the lower-right quadrant.

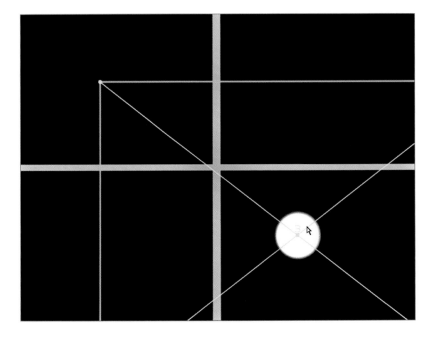

When you release the mouse button, the Center parameter in the Motion tab updates to show the clip's new position in the Canvas.

Your results will most certainly vary, but what you should notice is that both the first and second coordinates (X and Y) are positive values.

5 Drag the circle into each of the three remaining quadrants and release the mouse button, checking the Center parameter each time.

With practice, you can numerically make changes to parameters that use coordinates, without dragging clips around in the Canvas. This is especially useful when you need to very precisely line up different clips, or when you have to make specific changes to a sequence's layout. You'll be doing this several times in the next exercise.

Creating an Animated Multilayer Sequence

In the following exercises, you'll be animating motion and filter parameters to create a multi-paned montage of automobile drivers. You'll also control the orientation of scale transformations using each clip's Anchor Point parameter.

1 In the 05_Project_Start tab, Option-double-click the Exercise 02 bin to open it into its own tab.

2   Open the **Multilayer Animation - Finished** sequence, and play it to see the final result you'll be working to create.

You can refer to this finished project as you work on the exercises.

Arranging the Final Composition

When creating an animated sequence that assembles itself over time, a good strategy is to first lay out all of the video layers and elements in the animation's final state. This makes the animation more straightforward to keyframe later. This also gives you an opportunity to arrange your video layers to make them easier to animate.

1   Open the **Multilayer Animation** sequence into the Timeline.

The clips for this sequence have already been edited into a superimposed stack of four layers. The order in which the clips have been stacked is significant—the layers appearing higher in the stack will be revealing the video layers underneath as their scale is animated.

First, you need to resize the layers to fit them into their final arrangement.

2 From the View pop-up menu at the top of the Canvas, choose Image+Wireframe to display each selected video clip's onscreen controls.

3 In the Canvas, click the image to select it and display its wireframe, then drag one of the corners towards the center to scale it down.

By default, the image is scaled around its center. In the finished version of the sequence, this image is located at the upper-left corner of the screen, so it is preferable to have the image scale relative to the upper-left corner. You can do this by changing the position of the clip's anchor point.

4 Double-click the selected layer in the Canvas to open it into the Viewer, and click the Motion tab to reveal its parameters.

5 Look at the Anchor Point parameter—by default it is set to 0,0.

The anchor point is the point around which all motion parameter transformations are centered. As mentioned earlier, the default position of 0,0 defines the center—in the case of the anchor point, this is the center of the selection box that defines the clip's area in the Canvas. If you change the anchor point's position, motion parameter transformations will move the clip, relative to the new anchor point position.

In this case, you want to shrink the clip in track V4, but you want to lock its upper-left corner to the upper-left corner of the Canvas. You can do this by moving its anchor point to that upper-left corner. To determine the position of the corner relative to the center of the frame, you need to do some math based on the frame size of the sequence.

6   In the Browser, Control-click the **Multilayer Animation** sequence, and choose Settings from the shortcut menu.

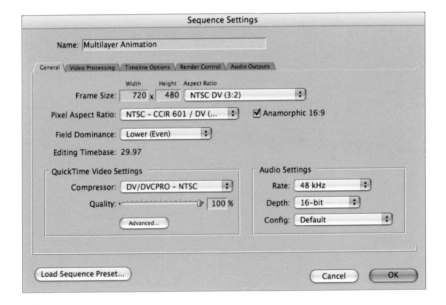

The Frame Size is 720 x 480, even though the image that's displayed in the Canvas is considerably wider. This is because the Anamorphic 16:9 checkbox is selected.

TIP ▶ Anamorphic images are widescreen images that have been scaled into a 4:3 frame. They're designed to be unsqueezed and displayed on a monitor capable of restoring the image to the proper aspect ratio.

To determine the exact position of the upper-left corner, you need to divide both the width and height of the frame size by two. (This is because, according to the Final Cut Pro coordinate system, the upper left corner is halfway up, and halfway to the left of the center of the frame.) These half values are 360 and 240, respectively. According to the Final Cut Pro coordinate system, then, the upper-left corner is –360,–240.

7 Next to the Basic Motion header, click the Reset button to reset the Scale to 100 percent. In the Sequence Settings window, click Cancel.

8 Set the Anchor Point to *–360, –240*.

TIP ▶ After you've entered a new value into the first coordinate field, press Tab to jump to the second field, then press Enter to confirm the change.

9 Drag the lower-right resize handle to resize the clip relative to the corner, so that the Scale parameter reads 50.

NOTE ▶ If you can't get the Scale to be exactly 50, type *50* into the Scale value field and press Enter to confirm the change.

This time the corner of the clip sticks to the corner of the frame. This clip is easier to resize now, and it'll be much easier to animate later.

10 Open the clip in track V3 into the Viewer. (Or, you could double-click its image in the Canvas, now that it's peeking out.)

This time, you want to resize the clip relative to the upper-right corner. Since you've already done the math, all you have to do is to change the appropriate X and Y values from negative to positive to move the anchor point to the correct position.

11 Set the Anchor Point to *360, –240* to move it to the upper-right corner of the frame.

12 Rescale the image to 50 percent so that it sits to the right of the previously rescaled image.

13 Open the clip in track V2 into the Viewer, and set the Anchor Point to *360, 240* to move it to the lower-right corner of the frame.

14 Rescale the clip in track V2 to 60 percent.

Since the clip in track V2 appears underneath two other clips, this lets you crop off some of the headroom above the car without readjusting any other parameters.

15 Open the clip in track V1 into the Viewer, and drag it to the left in the Canvas so that you can see the street butting up against the leftmost edge of the clip with the cable car. (The Center parameter coordinates should be close to −114, 32.)

Now that you've done the hard work of setting up the final scale and position for each clip, you can move on to keyframing the actual animation.

Setting Up the Timeline for Keyframing

Keyframes can be edited in several places in Final Cut Pro. Before you begin creating and editing keyframes, you'll customize the Timeline to display each clip's keyframes directly underneath each video track as they're created. This makes it easier for you to keep track of what you're doing.

1 At the lower-left corner of the Timeline, click the Clip Keyframes control.

This opens the keyframe graph area underneath each track in the Timeline.

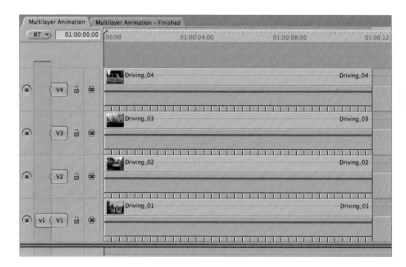

The keyframe graph area is divided into several regions, each displaying information for compositing and effects tasks. By default, three regions are displayed:

▶   The motion bar—a blue strip at the top of the region—indicates the keyframes that have been added to motion parameters.

▶   Underneath the motion bar is the keyframe editor, an open area displaying keyframe graphs, which you'll learn more about later in this lesson.

▶   The speed indicator strip sits at the bottom of each region, with tic marks that show the speed at which a clip is playing. You'll learn more about the speed indicator in Lesson 7.

Next, you'll simplify the keyframe graph area by hiding the keyframe editor and speed indicators.

2   Control-click the Clip Keyframes control, and deselect Video > Keyframe Editor in the shortcut menu to hide the keyframe editor.

The keyframe graph area shortens as the keyframe editor is hidden.

3   Control-click the Clip Keyframes control, and deselect Video > Speed Indicators from the shortcut menu to hide the indicators.

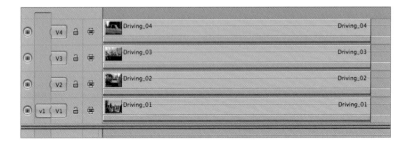

At this point, the keyframe graph area shows only the motion bars. Now you're ready to start adding keyframes.

Animating Motion Parameters by Adding Keyframes

As stated at the beginning of this lesson, keyframes allow you to set specific values for parameters at specific times. When you add two or more keyframes to a parameter with different values, Final Cut Pro automatically changes the parameter values between each pair of keyframes, adding to or subtracting from the parameter's value at each subsequent frame, thereby animating the parameter to move, shrink, grow, or otherwise alter a clip over time.

In this exercise, you'll create keyframes to animate each of the layers you have arranged.

1   In the Canvas or Timeline, move the playhead to 01:00:09;00.

2   With the Selection tool, drag a selection box around all of the clips in the Timeline.

3   In the Canvas, click the Add Motion Keyframe button.

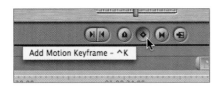

4   Move the playhead to 01:00:02;00 in the Timeline.

You can now see the keyframes that appear on the motion bar for each selected clip.

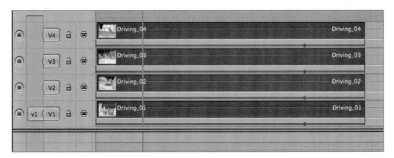

When you clicked the Add Motion Keyframe button, you added a keyframe to every geometric motion parameter for each selected clip in the Timeline, placed at the position of the playhead.

5   Double-click the clip in track V4 to open it into the Viewer, and click the Motion tab to view the motion parameters.

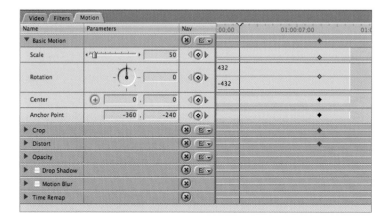

As you can see, the motion parameters that were keyframed by a single click of the Add Motion Keyframe button include Scale, Rotation, Center, Anchor Point, Crop, and Distort. You've keyframed the end state of every motion parameter for each clip you're about to animate—you're already half finished!

You can view keyframes in two areas of the Final Cut Pro interface. The motion bar in the Timeline consolidates all of the motion parameter keyframes at the same frame into a single keyframe. It's a simple way to determine, at a glance, where the motion effect keyframes are in your sequence. The keyframe graph in the Viewer displays individual keyframes for every parameter, providing you with a more detailed view of how each parameter is animated.

Now that the keyframes for the end of this animation have been set, it's time to add the beginning keyframes.

6   With the **Driving_04** clip's parameters open in the Motion tab of the Viewer, change the Scale to 100 by dragging the slider or typing it into the value field and pressing Enter.

After you've made this adjustment, a second keyframe is created at the position of the playhead. When you've added at least one keyframe to a parameter, any other adjustments you make to that parameter at other frames automatically create new keyframes.

Notice also that the Scale parameter's keyframe button is highlighted green.

This lets you know that the playhead is sitting on top of an existing keyframe for that parameter. The gray arrows on either side of this button indicate whether or not there are other keyframes to the left or right of the playhead. In this case, the right arrow is highlighted, because there's another Scale keyframe to the right.

7   Click the right arrow.

The playhead jumps to the next keyframe to the right, which in this case is the last keyframe. Since there are no more keyframes to the right, the right keyframe arrow is dimmed, and the left keyframe arrow is highlighted to let you know there's another keyframe earlier in the clip.

NOTE ▶ If you make an adjustment to a parameter while the playhead is sitting on an existing keyframe, the result is an adjustment to the parameter's value at that keyframe.

8 Press the Home key to return the playhead to the beginning of the sequence, then play the sequence to watch the scale change in action.

The clip starts at 100 percent at the first keyframe, and gradually shrinks towards the upper-left corner until coming to a stop at the last keyframe.

9 In track V3, double-click the **Driving_03** clip to open it into the Viewer, and move the playhead in the Timeline to the position of the first keyframe on track V4.

TIP ▶ If snapping is turned on (use the N key to toggle snapping off and on), the playhead will snap to the position of keyframes in the Timeline and in the keyframe graph of the Viewer.

Viewing the motion bar in the Timeline makes it easier to synchronize keyframed animation across clips. The playhead in the Viewer mirrors the position and timing of the playhead in the Timeline, so lining up the playhead with a keyframe in the Timeline lets you identify where to place a keyframe in a second clip.

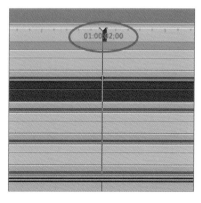

Timeline

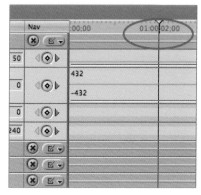

Viewer keyframe graph

10 With the **Driving_03** clip's parameters open in the Motion tab of the Viewer, change the Scale to 100 by dragging the slider or typing it into the value field and pressing Enter.

As in the previous clip, changing the Scale parameter adds a second keyframe. Playing or scrubbing from the first to the second keyframe now shows both clips resizing in tandem.

Animation at frame 01:00:07;00

Now, you'll bring the **Driving_02** clip onscreen by animating its Crop parameter.

11 In the Timeline, move the playhead so that it snaps to the position of the keyframes at frame 01:00:02;00.

12 Double-click the **Driving_02** clip to open it into the Viewer.

With the **Driving_02** clip selected, you should be able to see its wireframe on top of the **Driving_04** clip that's covering it in the Canvas. This enables you to use onscreen controls in the Canvas to make motion adjustments to an image even when it's behind another clip.

13 If necessary, click the disclosure triangle for the Crop parameter group, and drag the Left crop slider all the way to 100.

While you make this adjustment, you can see its effect on the **Driving_02** clip's wireframe. At the same time, you can also see the change that's made to the Crop > Left parameter's keyframe graph.

Playing or scrubbing from the first to the second keyframe shows the top three clips animated together.

14 Scrub the playhead to 01:00:03;00.

If you look carefully at the intersection of all four clips, you should notice a bit of the background black showing through.

You can take care of this by animating the position of the clip on track V1 to cover the hole.

15 Move the playhead in the Timeline so that it snaps to the position of the keyframes at frame 01:00:02;00, and double-click the **Driving_01** clip to open it into the Viewer.

As you can see by the positions of the wireframe showing through the **Driving_04** clip, you left a gap when you moved the clip.

16 Shift-drag the wireframe to constrain its horizontal movement, and move it so that it's right-aligned with the right side of the frame in the Canvas.

After you've made this adjustment, look at the Center parameter in the Motion tab of the Viewer. You can see that a keyframe has been generated.

17 Press the Home key to move the playhead to the beginning of the sequence, and then play through the animation to see it all in action.

Adjusting the Timing of the Animation

The way to adjust the timing of an animated parameter is to change the distance between the two keyframes that define that animation. The farther apart two keyframes are, the slower the animated change will be; the closer the two keyframes are, the faster the animation.

In this exercise, you'll change the timing of the animation by moving keyframes. Then, you'll smooth them to create more pleasing motion.

1   Move the playhead to the beginning of the Timeline and play the sequence.

The animation is a bit slow at the moment. The animation would have more punch if it moved more quickly. To fix this, you'll need to move the keyframes.

2   Open the **Driving_04** clip into the Viewer and click the Motion tab so you can see all of its keyframes in the keyframe graph.

3   If necessary, click the Clip Keyframes control in the Timeline to display the motion bar in the keyframe graph area.

4   Move the pointer to the second keyframe in the motion bar of track V4 in the Timeline, and when it turns into a crosshair, drag the second keyframe to 01:00:04:00. As you drag the keyframe, the Current Timecode field updates to show which frame you're in.

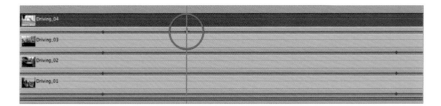

If you look at the Motion tab in the Viewer, you can see that the keyframes for every parameter in that frame have been moved.

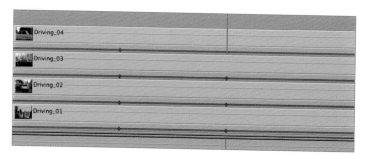

You can use the keyframes in the motion bar of the Timeline to simultaneously move a group of keyframes that are at the same frame.

TIP ▶ Each parameter group in the Motion tab has a similar control in the header bar that appears above the motion graph for each parameter. A solid blue keyframe appears above each group of green parameter keyframes. Dragging the blue keyframe will simultaneously adjust all other keyframes at that frame in that group.

5   In the motion bar of tracks V3, V2, and V1, drag the second keyframe to the same frame (01:00:04:00).

NOTE ▶ Keyframes in the same frame as the playhead may be difficult to see.

6   Play through the sequence, and you'll see that everything moves much more quickly.

At this point, assume you want to have the animation begin later, at frame 01:00:03;00 (which is when the car in the lower-left clip comes over the hill). Instead of moving each individual keyframe to the right, you can simultaneously slide every motion keyframe that's applied to a clip using the motion bar in the Timeline.

7   Move the playhead to frame 01:00:03;00, to help you spot the frame to which you want to move the keyframes.

8   Move the pointer to a section of the motion bar in track V4 of the Timeline without a keyframe so that the pointer becomes a resize arrow.

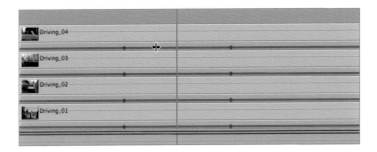

9   Drag the motion bars to the left, moving all keyframes at once until the first keyframe appears at the position of the playhead.

10 Drag the motion bars of tracks V3, V2, and V1 so that all of the keyframes have been moved forward, then play the resulting animation to see the change you've made.

The resulting animation has the right timing, but the motion is a little abrupt. In the next exercise, you'll learn to control keyframe acceleration with smoothing.

Smoothing Animation with Bézier Keyframes

The distance between two keyframes determines the speed of an animated change, but you can also adjust the acceleration of animated change from one keyframe to the next by *smoothing* the keyframes.

Currently, each animated effect you've created uses *corner* keyframes—which produces a constant rate of change from the first to the second keyframe.

The result is a linear change in the parameter, but for some animations this may seem abrupt, as clips go instantly from a still state to full speed, and then immediately stop when the next keyframe is reached. The resulting motion can look mechanical.

To make the motion less abrupt, you can *smooth* keyframes, which adds Bézier handles you can use to adjust the rate of change of an animated parameter.

Bézier handles for smoothed keyframes

By adjusting the Bézier handles, you can accelerate or decelerate a parameter's animation from keyframe to keyframe. This lets you create more organic-looking motion by having a clip slowly ramp up to full speed, and then slow gently to a stop.

Understand that changing the acceleration of an animated parameter does nothing to change the timing. If a parameter change slowly speeds up and then slows down, the parameter moves more quickly towards the middle of the animation in order to pick up time.

TIP ▶ The steepness of the curve in the keyframe graph determines the acceleration at that point in the graph. Steeper curves result in faster parameter changes; shallower curves result in slower parameter changes.

In this exercise, you'll smooth the keyframes so that the animation begins slowly, speeds up, then eases to a stop at the end.

1   Double-click **Driving_04** in the Timeline to open it into the Viewer, and click the Motion tab to see its keyframes in the keyframe graph.

2   Zoom into the keyframe graph by Shift-dragging the right thumb tab of the bottom scroll bar, or by dragging within the Zoom control.

This lets you zoom into the keyframe graph to see sections with multiple keyframes in more detail.

3   Control-click the first Scale keyframe, and choose Smooth from the shortcut menu.

The keyframe turns into a Bézier keyframe, and a handle appears to its right.

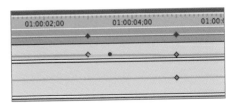

4   Repeat step 3 on the second Scale keyframe.

5   Open **Driving_03** into the Viewer, and smooth both of its Scale keyframes using the same method.

6   Open the **Driving_02** clip into the Viewer. Click the disclosure triangle for the Crop parameter group, zoom into the keyframe graph, and smooth the two Crop > Left keyframes.

This keyframe graph is steep enough so that you can see how the graph has changed from a flat line to a double curve. This curve shows you the rate of acceleration for that parameter.

> **TIP** ▶ The default curves created with the addition of the Bézier handles in this animation are adequate to create a nice smooth effect. When your aim is different, you may click and drag on the end of the Bézier handle (the dark blue dot) to alter the angle of the curve stretching toward the next keyframe.

7   Play through the sequence, and notice how the motion slowly begins, speeds up in the middle, and then comes to a gentle stop.

Synchronizing Keyframe Animation in the Timeline

Now, you'll learn how to display keyframe graphs for different parameters directly in the Timeline, underneath each clip. In the process, you'll see how you can keyframe filter parameters just as easily as Motion settings.

Adding Filters to the Composition

First, you'll be tinting each clip using the Sepia filter.

1   In the Browser, open the Effects tab and drag the Video Filters > Image Control > Sepia filter onto the **Driving_04** clip.

2   Move the playhead to the second keyframe in the Timeline, then double-click the **Driving_04** clip to open it into the Viewer. Click the Filters tab to view the Sepia filter's parameters.

3   Set the Amount parameter to 50 to reduce the degree of tinting in the image.

4   To copy this version of the Sepia filter to the other clips, drag a selection box around the clips in tracks V3, V2, and V1, then drag the Sepia filter from the Filters tab onto the selected clips in the Timeline.

5   In the **Driving_04** clip, click the Tint Color control for the Sepia filter, and choose a light blue color in the color picker. Click OK.

6   Open **Driving_02** into the Viewer, click the Tint Color control, and choose a pale green.

At this point, the image should look like this:

Notice that an additional green filter bar appeared underneath clips in the Timeline after you applied the filters to each clip, just above the motion bar. The filter bar lets you know that a filter has been applied to a particular clip, and shows all of the keyframes that have been applied to that filter's parameters.

Arranging the Timeline Keyframe Editors

You've probably noticed that there's a keyframe graph to the left of the filter parameters in the Filters tab in the Viewer, but you're going to animate each color tint directly in the Timeline using each track's keyframe editor. Before you start keyframing, however, you need to display the keyframe editor.

1   At the bottom of the Timeline, Control-click the Clip Keyframes control, and choose Video > Keyframe Editor from the shortcut menu.

Additional space appears underneath the motion and filter bars in the Timeline.

2   Control-click within the space underneath the clip in track V4, and choose Sepia > Amount from the shortcut menu.

The shortcut menu in the keyframe editor lets you choose any one keyframe graph from any motion or filter parameter for that clip. The keyframe graph appears directly underneath the clip, which allows you to make keyframe changes directly in the Timeline—creating, moving, and snapping keyframes relative to other clips and keyframe graphs in a sequence.

NOTE ▸ Each keyframe editor can only display the keyframe graph for a single parameter.

3   Control-click the keyframe editor for tracks V3, V4, and V5, and choose Sepia > Amount from the shortcut menu for each of them.

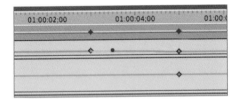

A green keyframe graph appears in each track. Because the graph is not currently keyframed, it's flat at the 50 percent position.

One important advantage of the keyframe editor in the Timeline is that you can stretch the graph vertically to increase the height of the keyframe graph you're working on.

4   Move the pointer to the small vertical keyframe editor resize column to the left of track V4.

5   When the pointer turns into a resize arrow, drag up within this control. A dark bar will stretch up to show how much larger you're making the keyframe editor.

When you release the mouse button, the keyframe editor will be resized.

6   Shift-drag the keyframe editor resize column. This stretches the keyframe editor for every track by the same size.

You can individually or collectively resize the graphs of every track to display the best resolution at which to edit the keyframes for each parameter.

7   If necessary, drag up the seam between the Timeline and Canvas to stretch the Timeline so that you can see all four video tracks.

Animating Parameters in the Keyframe Editor of the Timeline

With the Timeline workspace organized, it's time to start keyframing. You can manipulate the graph in the keyframe editor using the same methods you used to edit opacity and volume overlays in the Timeline—use the Pen tool to add keyframes, and then drag keyframes and segments around the graph to create the desired timing.

1   With the Selection tool, Option-click the keyframe graph in track V4 in the same frame as the first keyframe in the motion bar to create a new keyframe.

> **TIP** ▶ You could also use the Pen tool, but Option-clicking a keyframe graph with the Selection tool has the exact same effect, and saves you from having to constantly switch tools.

2   Move the playhead to 01:00:01;15 to identify that position on the keyframe graph, then Option-click the keyframe graph at the position of the playhead to add a second keyframe.

3   Move the pointer to the keyframe graph segment to the left of the first keyframe. When it turns into a resize arrow, drag the segment to the bottom of the keyframe editor.

As you drag the keyframe graph, a tooltip appears to show you the new value of the parameter. The bottom of the graph is 0, and the top of the graph is 100.

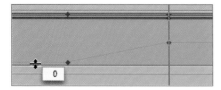

4   Move the playhead to a frame before the first keyframe, and play the sequence.

You can see the clip start completely untinted, and then start to turn blue as the playhead crosses the keyframed part of the graph, maxing out at 50.

You can smooth keyframes in the keyframe editor just as you would in the keyframe graph of the Viewer.

5   Control-click each of the keyframes, and choose Smooth from the short-cut menu.

The keyframe graph should now look like this:

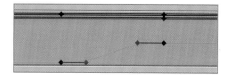

At this point, you might think that the colorization of the top clip starts too soon. Fortunately, you can move the keyframes in the keyframe editor the same way you move keyframes using the motion bar.

6   Move the playhead to 01:00:03;15 to identify that position on the keyframe graph, then move the pointer to the filter bar. When the pointer changes to the resize arrow, drag the filter bar to the right to move the entire keyframe graph so that the first frame sits on the playhead.

Now you're going to use the keyframes you've just placed as a reference to offset the timing of the next pair of tinting keyframes.

7   In the keyframe graph in track V2 (**Driving_02**), Option-click twice to place two keyframes at the same frames as the keyframes in the track V4 keyframe

graph. Drag down the graph segment to the left of the first keyframe to the bottom of the keyframe editor.

8   Control-click both new keyframes, and choose Smooth from the short-cut menu.

9   Drag the filter bar for track V2 to the right, so that the first keyframe in track V2 lines up with the last keyframe in track V4.

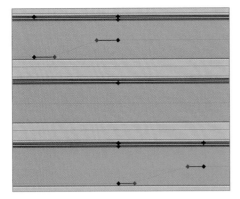

This is a fast way to match the duration of the animated effect in track V4, and then offset the effect so it happens later.

10   Move the playhead to the last keyframe in track V2, and Option-click the keyframe graphs for both tracks V1 and V3 to create keyframes at the position of the playhead.

11   With no clips selected in the Timeline, type *+15* and press Enter to move the playhead 15 frames to the right.

12   Option-click to create keyframes at the playhead in tracks V1 and V3.

13   Drag the graph segments to the left of the first keyframe to 0 and smooth all four keyframes in tracks V1 and V3.

The keyframe graphs for tracks V1 through V4 should now resemble this:

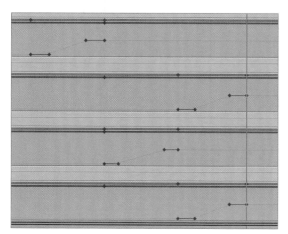

14 Move the playhead to a frame prior to the first motion bar keyframe in the sequence and play it back to observe the quality of the motion.

The result should be an animation in which the layers are geometrically transformed at once, while the color of each clip changes at a different time, one clip after another.

As you can see, the keyframe editor is a good tool to create and edit keyframes when you want to synchronize effects across multiple tracks in time.

Animating Clips Using Motion Paths

Whereas most of the motion and filter parameters you've worked with need to be keyframed in the Motion tab or Timeline, in this next set of exercises you'll create and edit keyframed motion paths in the Canvas by animating a clip's Center parameter. Once created, motion paths can be edited with Bézier handles, enabling you to create any curving path you can imagine.

In the next series of exercises, you'll be creating an animated title sequence for a fictional gardening show.

1   In the 05_Project_Start tab in the Browser, Option-double-click the Exercise 03 bin to open it into its own tab in the Browser.

2   Choose Window > Arrange > Two Up, if necessary.

3   Open the **Image Panning - Finished** sequence into the Timeline.

This is the finished version of a title sequence you'll create by animating a set of graphics using motion paths. The combination of effects in this sequence will probably require you to render the sequence before you can play it in real time.

4   Press Option-R to render the sequence.

5   When the rendering is finished, play the sequence to see the finished product.

Importing High-Resolution Graphics

The first step is to animate the background—a high-resolution still image. Animating large image files is a common technique, which is used to add motion to photographs, stock artwork, and informational graphics such as maps and charts. When you animate an image that's larger than the size of the

Canvas, you create the illusion that the "camera" is panning over a close-up of the image. This lets you visually highlight specific elements.

1   Choose Final Cut Pro > User Preferences.

2   Click the Editing tab.

The duration of all still images imported into a Final Cut Pro project is determined by the Still/Freeze Duration parameter. By default, this value is set to 10 seconds. If you have a different duration, change it back to 10 seconds for this exercise.

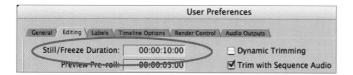

3   Click Cancel. (Or click OK if you had to make any changes.) Open the **Image Panning** sequence.

4   Open the Clips bin in the Browser, and edit the **Garden.tif** clip into the Timeline.

As you can see, the clip is now 10 seconds long—the duration specified by the Still/Freeze Duration preference when the clip was imported. Furthermore, the entire image has been scaled down to fit into the Canvas.

5 Open the **Garden.tif** clip into the Viewer, and click the Motion tab.

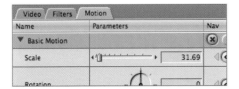

This reveals that the Scale parameter is actually set to 31.69 percent. The image has been automatically scaled down to fit into the frame size of the Canvas, while maintaining its original proportions.

If the image's aspect ratio was taller or wider than the frame size, its larger side would be scaled down so that the height or width of the image matched that of the frame, and there would be blank areas to the sides or at the bottom and top.

6 Change the scale to 100 by clicking the Basic Motion Reset button.

Now you can see the actual size of the graphic. The sides are cut off because it's much larger than the frame size of the sequence.

7   From the View pop-up menu at the top of the Canvas, choose Image+ Wireframe, and then from the Zoom pop-up menu choose Fit All.

> **NOTE** ▶ Zooming does not change the scale of the image. It simply magnifies your work area temporarily.

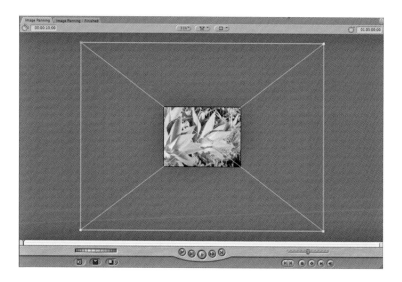

The Fit All command zooms out the Canvas as far as necessary to show the entire composition—including parts of clips that are outside of the visible area of the frame. As you can see by the wireframe, the **Garden.tif** image is quite a bit larger than the 720 x 480 frame size of the current sequence.

Final Cut Pro ignores whatever DPI an image may be set to in its originating application. Instead, when a clip's scale is set to 100 percent, the size of the clip is determined by its native pixel dimensions (the overall width and height in pixels) and is displayed at 72 dpi (video's native resolution).

> **NOTE** ▶ You may be wondering why the image looks soft. The resolution of still images is lowered to facilitate real-time playback and effects, as evidenced by the green render bar above this clip in the Timeline. To see the actual image that will be output, you need to render this clip in the sequence.

Panning Around an Image in the Canvas

In this exercise, you'll animate the clip's Center parameter to pan around the image in the Canvas.

1 In the Canvas, choose Fit All from the Zoom pop-up menu. Drag the image to reveal the lower-right corner in the visible portion of the Canvas.

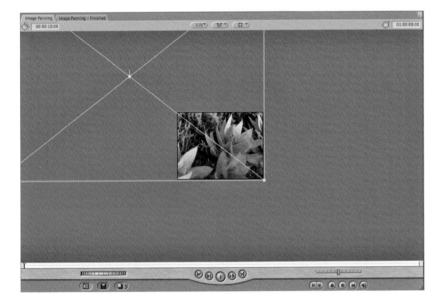

2 Press the Home key, then Control-click the Add Motion Keyframe button, and choose Center from the shortcut menu.

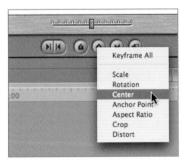

This shortcut menu lets you keyframe a single parameter of the selected clip in the Timeline/Canvas, instead of keyframing everything, as you did previously. If you look at the still-open Motion tab in the Viewer, you can see the keyframe that has been created for the Center parameter.

TIP ▶ The Add Motion Keyframe shortcut menu is a great method to use when you need to set only one keyframe at a time. If you need to set simultaneous keyframes for multiple parameters, but you don't want to set keyframes for all of them, it's better to work in the keyframe graph area of the Viewer.

3   Click the Canvas to make it active, and type *+3.* (+3 followed by a period) to move the playhead 3 seconds forward.

NOTE ▶ Make sure you click the Canvas to make it active. If you type +3. with both the Timeline active and the **Garden.tif** clip selected, you'll move the clip forward.

4   Drag down the clip so you can see the orange flower centered in the screen.

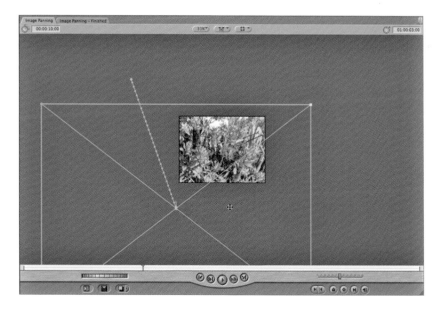

Notice the dotted line that appears in the Canvas. This is a motion path, which traces the progress of a clip's anchor point whenever its Center parameter is animated. Green keyframes indicate the position of the clip at each Center keyframe, and the dotted line connecting them shows the path of motion. The dots running along the motion path represent the speed that the clip travels along this path. Dots that are closer together represent slower motion, and dots that are farther away indicate faster motion.

5   Move the playhead forward 3 seconds.

6   Drag the image to the right so you can see the three succulents in the frame.

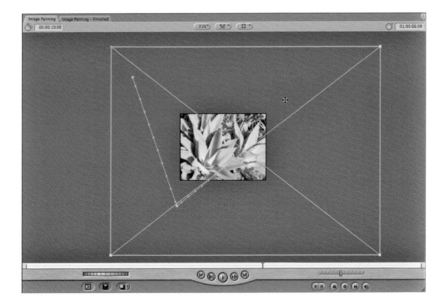

At this point, you can see that the motion path traces a *V* shape as the image moves around the Canvas.

7   Play the sequence.

The clip is animated, but the motion is stiff and angular. You can fix this by smoothing the keyframes of the motion path directly in the Canvas.

Smoothing a Motion Path

Center keyframes are first created as *corner* keyframes, which produce motion that's functional, but not necessarily elegant. You can change the type of the keyframes on the motion path to create curves and changes in velocity similar to the smoothing you already used.

As a general workflow tip, however, you'll probably find it easiest to first set every keyframe in your motion path, then go back later to change the type of each keyframe to create the type of motion you require.

1   Move the playhead to the beginning of the sequence. Control-click each of the three motion path keyframes in the Canvas, and choose Ease In/Ease Out from the shortcut menu.

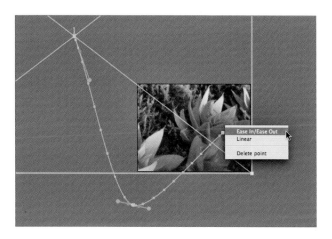

Each point becomes a Bézier curve, with outer handles that control the angle of curvature, and inner handles that control the rate of acceleration of the image to and from that keyframe.

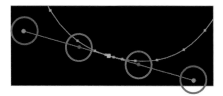

Bézier curve handles (blue circles)
Ease In/Ease Out handles (red circles)

NOTE ▸ Adding Ease In/Ease Out keyframes isn't required to create Bézier handles for your keyframes. Bézier handles also appear for keyframes that are set to Linear. Bézier handles are required if you want the motion path to be curved.

2 Play the sequence from the beginning.

The motion is certainly smooth, but now the graphic appears to start and stop as it slowly accelerates from the start point, and then coasts to a stop at the second keyframe before slowly accelerating and coasting back to a stop at the third keyframe. This starting and stopping is distracting, so you need to change the acceleration of the first and second motion path keyframes to create a more constant movement.

3 Control-click the first and second keyframes, choosing Linear from each keyframe's shortcut menu.

When you set a keyframe to Linear, the Ease handles are placed in a neutral middle position on the Bézier handles so that the clip neither speeds up or slows down as it passes that keyframe on the motion path. By comparison, the Ease handles are located closer to the keyframe when a motion path keyframe is set to Ease In/Ease Out, which causes clips to slow down and then speed back up when passing that keyframe.

TIP ▸ You can customize the rate of acceleration of an Ease In/Ease Out keyframe by dragging the Ease handle along the tangent that connects the motion path keyframe to the outer Bézier handle.

4   Play the sequence again.

Now, the animation starts immediately, continuing at a steady rate of speed before coasting to a stop at the last keyframe. However, the first segment of the animation is still faster than the second. This is because the first segment of the motion path is longer, even though the keyframes are spaced evenly along the Timeline of the sequence. This means that the clip has to move faster along the first segment to arrive within the same duration.

5   In the keyframe editor of the Viewer, drag the playhead to the last keyframe.

6   In the keyframe graph of the Viewer's Motion tab, drag the second Center keyframe to the right approximately 22 frames. (A tooltip appears showing how many frames you're dragging the keyframe.) As you drag the keyframe, watch the dots on the motion path. Results will vary.

7   Play the sequence.

The clip now moves at a fairly constant rate of speed.

Moving keyframes forward or backward in time changes the speed at which the clip will move along each segment of the motion path. The dots on the motion path redistribute themselves as you're making timing adjustments to show the new speed at which the clip will move. As long as the dots along the entire motion path are spaced evenly, the motion will be constant.

The following illustrations show the same motion path keyframe at three different frames in the sequence: to the left (earlier), at a midpoint, and to the right (later).

Fast then slow   Constant speed   Slow then fast

Reshaping the Motion Path

To finish, you'll adjust the handles of all three keyframes in the Canvas to make the overall curve of the clip's path a bit more circular.

1   Drag out the Bézier handles of the first and last keyframes, away from the motion path, to round it out a little more.

2   Play the clip.

With the motion path adjusted like this, a bit of black shows at the right edge of the clip around frame 01:00:00;17 because the clip is moving too far to the left.

3   Move the playhead to the frame in which you can see the most black, then drag the Bézier handle of the first keyframe back to the right until the clip moves all the way to the edge of the frame.

In this way, you can move the playhead to different frames, and make adjustments to the motion path while viewing the resulting change in position of the clip in the frame.

4   Play the sequence from the beginning, and you should have a smoothly animated pan.

NOTE ▶ If, at any point, you zoom the Canvas to 100 percent for a sequence that is interlaced, you'll see the interlaced lines when you create animated motion. Although it may look a bit odd, it's perfectly normal and will look correct when output to video. At any other zoom level, the image is shown deinterlaced. In general, the faster a clip moves, the more exaggerated the interlacing appears.

Adding a Logo with a Second Animated Motion Path

You'll finish up the gardening show opening sequence by animating a second logo graphic flying into the screen and coming to rest at the center of the frame.

This time, you'll draw additional keyframes right on the motion path in the Canvas.

1   In the Browser, open the Clips bin. Edit the **Garden_Logo.tif** clip into the Timeline, superimposing it above the **Garden.tif** clip by creating a new track (V2).

2   Select the **Garden_Logo.tif** clip, and from the Zoom pop-up menu of the Canvas, choose Fit All.

3   Double-click the **Garden_Logo.tif** clip to open it into the Viewer, and click the Motion tab.

As you can see, this clip has been scaled down to 63.38 percent to fit it into the Canvas while maintaining its original shape.

4 In the Canvas, choose Show Overlays from the View pop-up menu to show the Title Safe guides in the Canvas.

With the Title Safe guides showing, you can see that the graphic is too big for broadcast display, as parts of it are extending well beyond the inner Title Safe guide, and the left side of the logo even extends beyond the outer Action Safe guide.

5 Drag the corner handles of the Garden_Logo.tif clip toward the center to shrink the graphic until the *I* of the title touches the inner Title Safe guide.

As a result, the Scale parameter should read approximately 53.

At this point, the logo graphic is centered and scaled to be exactly where you want it at the final frame. As in previous exercises, you create the last keyframes of the animation first, since you've just completed the final lay-out of the animation.

6 At the bottom of the Timeline. click the Clip Keyframes control to reveal the keyframe editor with the motion bars, and move the playhead to the last keyframe displayed along the motion bar of track V1 (at frame 01:00:06;00).

The motion bars in the Timeline are a great way to find keyframes within other clips while you have a specific clip open in the Viewer.

7   With the Motion tab for the **Garden_Logo.tif** clip open in the Viewer, click the keyframe buttons for both the Scale and Center parameters to create keyframes at the current position of the playhead.

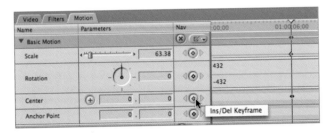

TIP ▶ If the playhead is sitting on top of an existing keyframe, then clicking the keyframe button of that parameter deletes it. You can also delete keyframes by Control-clicking them and choosing Clear from the shortcut menu, or by dragging them outside the keyframe graph until they disappear.

The Motion tab is a great place to set keyframes when you want to add or edit keyframes for several parameters at once. Next, you can begin the animation by moving and rescaling the logo graphic to its initial position.

8   Press the Home key to move the playhead to the first frame of the sequence.

9   Rescale the logo graphic until it's really small (around 13 percent), and then drag it off past the top right of the frame, so that the top of its selection box lines up with the top of the Action Safe guide.

If necessary, select the Canvas and press Command-– (minus sign) to zoom out so you can see what you're doing.

You can see by the presence of the motion path that the clip is now animated.

10 Play the sequence from the beginning.

The clip slowly moves and zooms out. This is a bit boring, so you'll add more keyframes to jazz it up a bit.

Editing a Motion Path with the Pen Tool

To make the flying logo more interesting, you'll add another keyframe to the motion path, and edit the path's curves, all within the Canvas.

1 In the motion bar in track V1 of the Timeline, move the playhead to the second keyframe. In the Motion tab of the Viewer, drag the last Center keyframe to the position of the playhead.

This speeds up the motion, while leaving the Scale intact.

2 Move the playhead back to the first frame of the sequence, so that the selection box is out of the way.

3 Move the pointer to a position on the motion path roughly two-thirds of the distance from the beginning of the clip. When the pointer turns into the Pen tool, click the motion path to create a new Center keyframe.

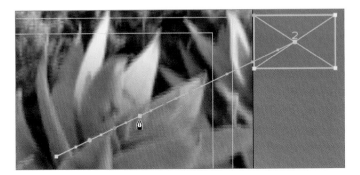

In the keyframe graph for the Center parameter in the Motion tab, you'll see that the keyframe has been created at a frame relative to its position on the motion path. In other words, the keyframe is two-thirds down the center animation keyframes.

4 In the motion graph of the Motion tab, move the playhead to the second keyframe, and then drag the keyframe in the Canvas to a position below and to the left of the keyframe at the end of the motion path. The selection box of the logo graphic should sit in the lower-left corner of the Title Safe guide.

5   Adjust the Bézier handles of this new keyframe so that it creates a nice
     shallow curve.

> **NOTE** ▶ Clicking the animation path instead of the Bézier handle will
> create a new keyframe. To avoid this, notice that the pointer changes
> into the Pen tool when positioned over the path, and it turns into a
> crosshair when positioned directly over a Bézier handle. If you acciden-
> tally set a new keyframe, press Command-Z to undo the action and
> try again.

6   Play through the sequence to see how the motion looks.

     At this point, the logo's motion should occur along a nice steady curve,
     which comes to an abrupt stop in the center of the screen. You can
     smooth out the end keyframe by setting it as an Ease In/Ease Out
     keyframe.

7   Move the playhead to the beginning of the sequence to get the clip's
     onscreen controls out of the way, then Control-click the last keyframe
     on the motion path, and choose Ease In/Ease Out from the short-
     cut menu.

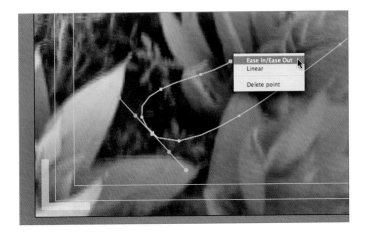

8   Adjust the Bézier handle of the last keyframe to round out the curve even more, so that the clip slides into its final position from the left after the second keyframe.

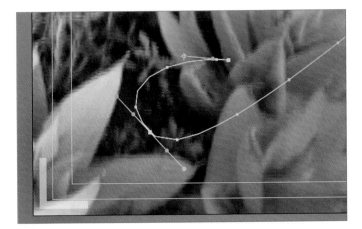

9   Play the sequence from the beginning, and you'll see the clip move gently around a nice smooth spiral, and then slow to a stop.

Setting a Hold Position

At this point, the logo's motion around the Canvas is good, and it zooms continuously from the beginning of the animation until it comes to a stop. To wrap up the animated introduction of the logo, you'll add more keyframes to the Scale parameter to vary its motion.

1 Open the Garden_Logo.tif clip into the Viewer and click the Motion tab, if necessary.

2 In the Motion tab's keyframe graph area, move the playhead to the position of the third Center keyframe, and click the Scale parameter's keyframe button to add a keyframe at that frame.

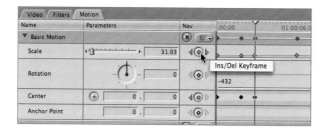

Whenever you create a new keyframe between two existing keyframes, the new keyframe is set to whatever value Final Cut Pro automatically interpolated for that parameter at that frame. You're essentially stamping that value to keep it in place, regardless of any changes you make to other keyframes for that parameter.

Next, you're going to pause the rescaling of the motion by adding a second keyframe a few frames later that is set to an identical value.

3 Select the Scale parameter's value, and press Command-C to copy it.

4 Move the playhead forward to 01:00:04;00, and click the Scale keyframe button to create a new keyframe.

5   Select the Scale parameter's value, and press Command-V to paste the copied value into it. Press Return to confirm the change.

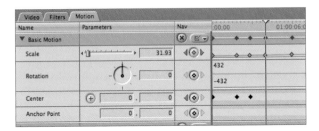

This replaces the new keyframe's previous setting with the same value you copied from the keyframe before it. Whenever you place two identical keyframes adjacent to each other, you pause the animation for that value for the interval between those two keyframes.

6   Play the sequence from the beginning, so you can see the pause you've just created.

7   Control-click the two Scale hold keyframes, and choose Smooth from the shortcut menu. (You may need to zoom into the keyframe graph in the Motion tab of the Viewer to see what you're doing.)

8   Play the sequence again, from the beginning.

Now, the zoom effect coasts to a stop, pauses, then slowly speeds up and coasts to a stop again for its final spurt of growth.

Finishing the Animation
Completing this intro sequence has nothing to do with keyframing, but illustrates how motion graphics projects can benefit from a wide variety of effects to create the end result.

If you look at the **Image Panning - Finished** sequence, you'll see an animated glow interacting with the garden layer. This is simply an animated background that was created in motion, and added as a superimposition using a composite mode to contribute some visual interest to the image underneath.

1   Move the playhead to the beginning of the sequence. Make sure the v1 source control is connected to the V1 destination track in the Timeline, and then place the **Garden_Texture.mov** clip into the **Image Panning** sequence with a Superimpose edit.

   The clip appears in track V2, and the **Garden_Logo.tif** clip has been moved to a newly created track V3. At the moment, the **Garden_Texture.mov** clip is obscuring the **Garden.tif** image.

2   In the Timeline, Control-click the **Garden_Texture.mov** clip, and choose Composite Mode > Overlay from the shortcut menu.

   This blends together the images of the **Garden_Texture.mov** and **Garden.tif** clips, adding a bit of visual interest to the composition. The Overlay composite mode is a bit more render-intensive, however, so you may have to render the sequence to view it at the highest quality.

This also brings up an interesting workflow issue. If you plan your composition's workflow in advance, keeping in mind which elements are more render-intensive than others, you can first work on the elements that can be adjusted and played back in real time, and then add the render-intensive elements in a later step.

> **TIP** ▶ To examine the quality or motion and pacing of motion effects, you don't need to view the entire image. In the Canvas, choose View > Wireframe to play a wireframe outline of your animated sequence—without the images. In Wireframe mode, you can play motion effects in real time, independent of your computer's real-time capabilities. When you're finished adjusting the motion, switch back to the Image+Wireframe mode to see the actual content of your composition.

3   To wrap up, add cross-dissolves to the beginning of the clips in tracks V1 and V2.

You're finished

Creating Reusable Motion Effects with Motion Favorites

In the previous exercise, you manipulated several motion properties in combination to create a final motion effect with which to animate the title logo. As you've learned, creating a well-timed animation can be a time-intensive endeavor. Fortunately, there's a command you can use to save animated motion effects you've created for later use—Make Favorite Motion. Favorite motions are collectof animated parameters, divorced from their original clips. Motion favorites can thus be applied to any clip at all, instantly animating the new clip's parameters according to the motion favorite's preset animation.

In this exercise, you'll save the animated motion you created for the gardening show logo, and apply it to a logo in another program.

Creating Favorite Motions

First, you will create a composition in which multiple images pass through the frame in a seemingly random fashion. But instead of creating each motion from scratch, you will save one as a favorite and use it as a starting point to create varied effects on the subsequent clips.

1   If necessary, open the **Image Panning** sequence you completed in the last exercise, or open the **Image Panning - Finished** sequence.

2   Select the **Garden_Logo.tif** clip, and choose Effects > Make Favorite Motion (Control-F).

This saves the keyframes and values from every single motion parameter—even those that weren't keyframed—into a motion favorite in the Favorites bin.

3   In the Browser, click the Effects tab, and open the Favorites bin to view its contents.

You should see your new favorite, named **Garden_Logo.tif (Motion)**, underneath the ones you've created in previous exercises. By default, new motion favorites inherit the name of the clip from which they were originally derived. This favorite's Type is set to Motion Path, and has a special icon showing it to be a motion favorite.

4   Click the name of the **Garden_Logo.tif (Motion)** clip, then click it again to highlight its name. Rename it *Title Spiral from Right*, and press Return to confirm the change.

As with other favorites you can save, renaming them with something more descriptive is generally a good idea. This becomes more important as you create larger and larger libraries of motion favorites.

Applying a Favorite Effect

After you've saved a motion favorite, applying it to another clip is easy.

1   In the 05_Project_Start tab, Option-double-click the Exercise 04 bin in the Browser to open it into its own tab, and then open the **Motion Favorites** sequence into the Timeline.

    This sequence consists of four clips dissolving together as they play.

2   Open the Clips bin, and place the **Surf_TitleII.tif** clip into the sequence with an Overwrite edit.

    The resulting setup is similar to the previous exercise, with the title graphic just begging to be animated. Fortunately, you've already created an appropriate animated motion effect.

3   In the Browser, click the Effects tab. Open the Favorites bin, and drag the **Title Spiral from Right** motion favorite onto the **Surf_TitleII.tif** clip in the Timeline.

4   Move the playhead to the beginning of the sequence.

    You should immediately notice that, unlike the sequence this motion favorite was saved from, the new logo is sticking into the frame from the right.

Animated parameters in motion favorites are saved verbatim from their source clips. Applying a motion favorite just adds a group of previously saved motion settings and animation timings to another clip. A motion favorite doesn't account for changes in the size or timing of the new clip. Since the surf logo is a different size, its starting point is a little off.

5   Open the **Surf_TitleII.tif** clip into the Viewer, and click the Motion tab to reveal its motion parameters.

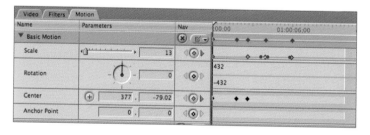

As you can see, the motion favorite simply applied a new set of keyframes and settings to the parameter. Once added, these settings can be customized just like manually-applied keyframes. Oftentimes, motion favorites are just a starting point, and the motion effects are adjusted as necessary to create the desired effects.

NOTE ▸ Because a motion favorite saves every setting from the Motion tab, regardless of whether or not they have been adjusted, be aware that any effects previously set on the Motion tab will be overwritten when a motion favorite is applied.

6 To hide the surf logo, keep the playhead at the beginning of the sequence, select the **Surf_TitleII.tif** clip in the Timeline, and drag the logo in the Canvas to the right until it's off the screen.

7 Play the sequence from the beginning.

It should now be fully animated. Unlike the last sequence, this logo doesn't have any regions of transparency, so it obscures a lot of the action in the background.

8 In the Timeline, Control-click the **Surf_TitleII.tif** clip, and choose Composite Mode > Screen from the shortcut menu.

This composite mode blends nonwhite colors in the logo with the background, with more background showing through progressively darker areas of the logo.

Using Favorites vs. Paste Attributes

Now that you've gotten the hang of favorites, you may be wondering when to use favorites and when to use the Paste Attributes command, which you've used in previous lessons.

One important advantage to Paste Attributes is that you get to choose whether to apply keyframed animation to new clips *without automatically scaling the timing* of the animation to fit the varying duration of the new clip.

To apply animated effects without changing their timing, deselect the Scale Attribute Times option in the Paste Attributes dialog box.

Favorites are often more convenient than Paste Attributes when you want to reuse effects across different projects (and/or when the original clip is unavailable) because favorites are available in the Effects menu at any time; you don't have to have a specific clip with the desired effect open, as you do with Paste Attributes.

Conversely, Paste Attributes is preferable when you want to reuse *only* selective effects from a clip. For example, you can opt to paste basic motion settings independently from Crop and Opacity, whereas favorites saves all of the Motion tab settings and applies them in an all-or-nothing manner.

Moving an Entire Motion Path

Even though the logo is translucent, it's still obscuring a lot of the action. It would be good to move the image up, but ordinarily that would involve adjusting all the other keyframes in the sequence. Fortunately, there's an easy way to move an entire motion path all at once.

1   Move the playhead towards the end of the **Surf_TitleII.tif** clip, at a point where it's at its final size and position in the Canvas, and then click it to select the clip.

2   In the View pop-up menu in the Canvas, choose Show Overlays so that you can see the Title Safe guides.

3   Press Command-Shift, move the pointer to the selected clip in the Canvas so that it becomes a hand, and then drag up the clip to move the entire motion path at once. Don't drag the logo beyond the top Title Safe guide.

4   Play the sequence from the beginning to see the logo move along the new position of the motion path.

Turning on Motion Blur

There's one last thing. You may have been wondering about the Motion Blur parameter in the Motion tab. Motion blur is one of the more render-intensive effects in Final Cut Pro, and it has a very specific effect. Motion blur analyzes keyframed motion, or the moving pixels that occur within a clip itself, and selectively blurs the parts of the image that are moving in the direction of motion, similar to the effect you get when you film a moving subject with a relatively slow shutter speed. The faster a subject moves, the more blurred it becomes.

To see how Motion Blur works, open the **Surf_Title.tif** clip into the Viewer, click the Motion tab, and select the Motion Blur checkbox. Unless you have a very fast computer, chances are that you'll have to render the sequence to see what this looks like.

Two parameters in the Motion Blur group let you adjust the quality of the motion blur effect. The % Blur parameter lets you adjust the maximum amount of blur that's applied to moving images, and the Samples pop-up menu lets you increase or reduce the quality of the resulting blur, as necessary. Higher numbers result in more blur, higher quality, and longer render times.

Animated surfboard with motion blur applied

Lesson Review

1. What is the minimum number of keyframes required to create an animated effect?
2. Identify the four places where keyframes can be edited in Final Cut Pro.
3. How can you keyframe every motion parameter in a clip at once?
4. What does smoothing a keyframe do?
5. What happens if you make adjustments to the parameters of a clip that already has a keyframe for that parameter at another frame?
6. How do you add Bézier handles to a motion path keyframe in the Canvas?
7. What's the difference between the motion path shape created by motion path corner keyframes, and motion path Linear and Ease In/Ease Out keyframes?
8. Which parameter motion graphs can you display in the keyframe graph of the Timeline?
9. How do you create a motion favorite?
10. How do you move an entire motion path at once?

Answers

1. Two.
2. The motion graph of the Viewer, the motion bar of the Timeline, the keyframe editor of the Timeline, and motion paths in the Canvas.
3. Select the clip, and click the Add Motion Keyframe button in the Canvas.
4. Adjusts the velocity with which an animated parameter changes, slowing or speeding the transition at each keyframe.
5. Additional keyframes are added.
6. Control-click a motion path keyframe, and choose Ease In/Ease Out or Linear from the shortcut menu.
7. Motion path corner keyframes create sharp angles on a motion path; motion path Linear and Ease In/Ease Out keyframes create curves.

8. Any motion or filter parameter that has a single value. For example, Center has two values (X and Y) and cannot be shown in the keyframe graph of the Timeline.

9. Keyframe one or more motion effects, select the clip, then choose Effects > Make Favorite Motion (Control-F).

10. Select the clip, then press Command-Shift while dragging the clip and its motion path to another location in the Canvas.

6

Lesson Files Lessons > Lesson_06 > 06_Project_Start

Media Media > Lesson_06_Media

Time This lesson takes approximately 90 minutes to complete.

Goals Edit one sequence into another to create a nested sequence

Use the Nest Items command to convert clips into a nested sequence

Apply effects to nested sequences

Modify individual clips within a nested sequence

Use nesting to work around the Final Cut Pro render order

Mix sequence frame sizes to create scaling effects

Use nesting to manage long-format shows

Lesson 6
Nesting Sequences

When working with complex sequences that involve multiple layers and many clips, you may want to treat a group of clips as a single object. For example, you may wish to apply a single filter to multiple items, or to scale or rotate several clips all at once. To efficiently accomplish such complex tasks, you can take advantage of the Final Cut Pro nesting features.

You can edit any existing sequence into another sequence in exactly the same way you edit any clip into the sequence. The embedded sequence is called a *nested* sequence, and the sequence it is embedded into is sometimes called the *parent* sequence. As well as editing an existing sequence into another sequence to nest it, you can also select a group of clips already in a sequence and combine them into a nested sequence, in place, creating a new nest where the original clips are located within the original sequence.

Nested sequences are useful when organizing clips, but they also allow you to quickly add effects and perform tasks that would be otherwise time consuming. Learning to manage nested sequences will enable you to create powerful effects, as well as improve your overall workflow and flexibility within Final Cut Pro.

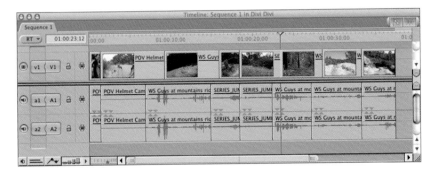

Un-nested

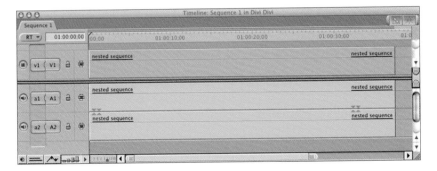

Nested

Basic Nesting

Nesting one sequence inside another is simple. Think of a nested sequence simply as a single clip that contains multiple items.

1   Open Lesson_06 > **06_Project_Start.**

The **Bike Jumps** sequence should be open in the Timeline. If it's not, double-click it in the Browser to open it into the Timeline.

The sequence contains three clips on V1 and a title clip on track 2.

2   In the Browser, double-click **Motocross Sequence.** It opens as a second tab in the Timeline.

3   Activate snapping. In the Browser, select the **Bike Jumps** sequence. Edit it into **Motocross Sequence** by dragging and dropping it into the Timeline as if it were a clip. Place it at the end of the first two clips.

You have now nested one sequence inside of another sequence, with a simple drag-and-drop edit The **Bike Jumps** sequence is the nested sequence, often called simply the *nest*, and **Motocross Sequence** is the main sequence, often called the *parent sequence*. You can see that the new item is a slightly different color than ordinary clips in the Timeline, which helps you identify which items in your sequence are nested

When you play back **Motocross Sequence**, clips nested in the **Bike Jumps** sequence will play just as they were originally edited. Even the title from video track 2 of the **Bike Jumps** sequence will be visible.

Understanding Live Links

The link between a nested sequence and its parent sequence remains live: When you make changes inside a nested sequence, you will see those changes take effect when you play the parent sequence. All editing and effects changes made to any clips or other items inside a nested sequence will automatically be updated in the parent sequence that contains the nest.

1 In the Timeline, click the Bike Jumps tab.

2 Double-click the title clip on track V2 to load it into the Viewer.

3 In the Viewer, click the Controls tab. Type *Motocross Madness!* into the text box and click anywhere outside of the text box to force the text to update in the Canvas.

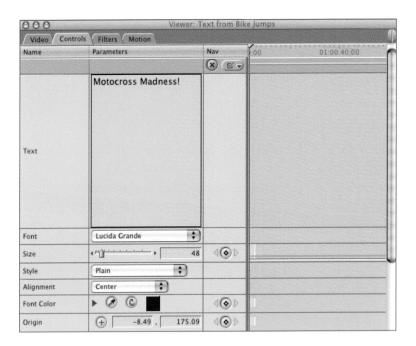

The Canvas reflects the change. If your playhead isn't over the area of the title, drag it there to confirm that the text has been updated.

4 In the Timeline, click the Motocross Sequence tab.

5 Scrub the playhead through **Motocross Sequence** until you see the section where the title should appear. Notice that the text has been updated here as well.

If you make additional changes in the Controls tab of the Viewer for the title clip from the **Bike Jumps** nested sequence, the changes will continue to update live in **Motocross Sequence,** the parent sequence.

Applying Effects to Multiple Clips

You can use nesting to apply a single effect to multiple items at once. This saves time by eliminating the need to apply a filter to each clip individually. If you later decide to change the parameters of the filter, the changes will affect all the clips simultaneously.

In this example, you will tint all of the clips inside the nested sequence red.

1   Be sure that **Motocross Sequence** is open in the Timeline.

2   Select the **Bike Jumps** nested sequence in the Timeline.

3   Choose Effects > Video Filters > Image Control > Tint.

You see the tint effect on every clip in the **Bike Jumps** nested sequence.

The filter affects the image of each clip in the nest, but it is actually applied to the Filters tab of the nest as a whole, and not the Filters tab of each clip inside the nest. To modify filter parameters on a nested sequence, you must open the nested sequence into the Viewer.

Ordinarily, double-clicking a clip in the Timeline opens it in the Viewer. But when you double-click a nested sequence, it opens in the Timeline and Canvas as a new tab, just as a sequence does when you double-click it from the Browser.

4   Select the **Bike Jumps** nested sequence in the Timeline (if it's not already selected).

5   Press Enter, choose View > Sequence, or Control-click the nested sequence and choose Open in Viewer from the shortcut menu.

The **Bike Jumps** sequence is now loaded in the Viewer as if it were an individual clip.

6   In the Viewer, click the Filters tab. The Tint filter controls should be
visible.

7   Set the color of the tint to a pale red by clicking the color selector and
adjusting the color settings.

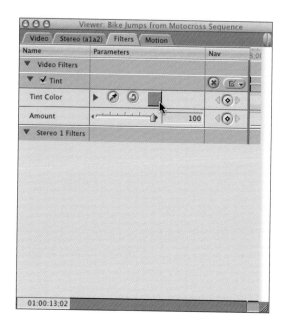

8   Play back **Motocross Sequence.** Notice that the new reddish tint affects the
entire **Bike Jumps** segment.

You could accomplish the same results by applying the tint filter to
each individual clip. If your client decided that he or she preferred a
blue tint instead of red, however, you would then have to open the
clips individually and then modify the filter settings. With nested
sequences, you can modify filter settings and apply those changes to
all items at once.

Applying Complex Geometric Settings

Some effects can be achieved only by using nested sequences. For example, by combining multiple clips into a single element in the Timeline, you can apply geometric attributes such as Scale, Rotation, and Motion to all of the clips as a single unit.

1   In the Browser, double-click the **Split Screen** sequence to open it into the Timeline.

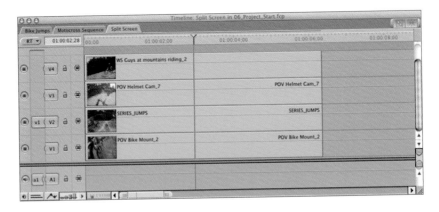

The **Split Screen** sequence contains four clips scaled down to 50% and arranged into quadrants in the Canvas so that all four images are visible onscreen at the same time.

NOTE ▶ If your system is powerful enough, you may be able to play the sequence without rendering. If the Timeline displays a red line in the render bar area, you might not have Unlimited RT selected in the Real-Time Effects pop-up menu in the Timeline. Selecting Unlimited RT and Dynamic quality, instead of Safe RT, will allow you to play many effects in real time.

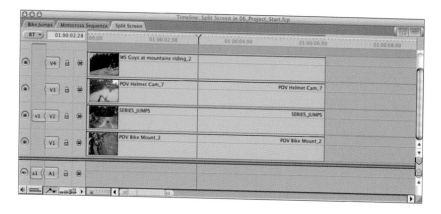

2   If necessary, render your sequence by pressing Option-R.

3   Play the sequence. The four video clips should play simultaneously.

In the following exercises, you will spin the four elements around a single anchor point, and then shrink the whole image to a single point, revealing a new image.

Nest Items in Place

Earlier in this lesson, you created a nested sequence by dragging and dropping one sequence into another. In this exercise, you will create a new nested sequence directly inside an existing sequence, using the Nest Items command.

1   Drag a lasso around the four clips in the Timeline to select them.

2   Choose Sequence > Nest Item(s).

The Nest Items dialog box appears.

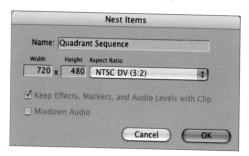

3 In the Name box, type *Quadrant Sequence.* Leave the other settings at their default values and click OK.

Now, instead of four clips on four tracks, the parent sequence contains one item: **Quadrant Sequence.** The image in the Canvas does not change. With rare exceptions, the Nest Items command will not change the visual output of your sequence. It affects only the grouping of the clips in the Timeline.

The Nest Items command automatically puts the new nested sequence on the lowest available track. If a clip already occupies the lowest track, the next available higher track will be used. In some cases, Final Cut Pro will generate a new track to make space for the item. The following screen shots show a case where V2 is the location of a nested sequence created from clips on V1 through V4.

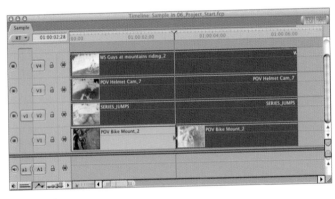

Un-nested

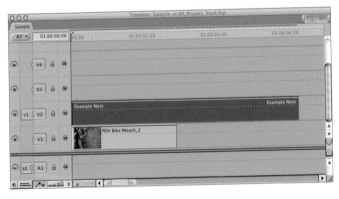

Nested

Nest Items also adds a new sequence icon to the Browser window, representing the nested sequence. You can use this sequence like any other sequence. Any changes you make to the nested **Quadrant Sequence** will modify the parent **Split Screen** sequence.

Apply Motion Parameters

Because the four clips are now inside **Quadrant Sequence,** motion settings applied to the sequence will affect all four of the clips. And because the four clips are geometrically connected, their relative positions will remain intact regardless of changes made to the sequence.

1   Open **Quadrant Sequence** into the Viewer by selecting it in the Timeline and pressing Enter, or by Control-clicking it and choosing Open Item in Viewer from the shortcut menu.

2   In the Viewer, click the Motion tab.

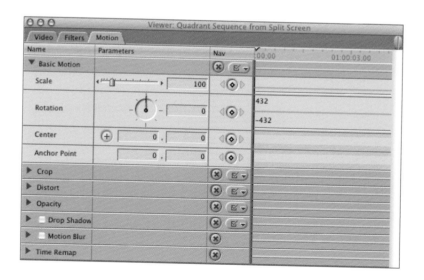

3   Press Home to bring your playhead to the beginning of the sequence in the Viewer.

4   Set a keyframe for the Rotation parameter.

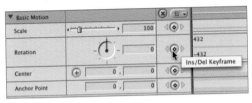

5   Move the playhead 6 seconds into the sequence in the Viewer by typing *+600*. (Or you can type *6* and then type a single period to enter double zeros.)

6   Set the Rotation value to *1440* degrees (four rotations) and press Enter. A second keyframe is automatically added. Switch back to Safe RT mode and render this effect, if necessary.

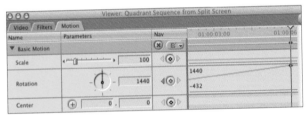

When you play this sequence, the four videos will spin in unison around a common center point. Setting similar Rotation parameters for each clip individually would have resulted in each clip spinning around its own center point.

7   With your playhead on the last Rotation keyframe, in the Motion tab of the Viewer, type *–500* and press Enter to set your playhead to 01:00:01:00. This moves the playhead to five seconds before the second rotation keyframe.

8   Add a keyframe for the Scale parameter (leaving the value at 100).

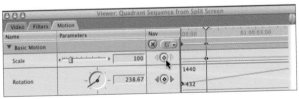

9 Move the playhead forward 5 seconds again so it lines up precisely with the Rotation keyframe.

10 Set the Scale parameter to *0* and press Enter, which will shrink the four clips until they are invisible.

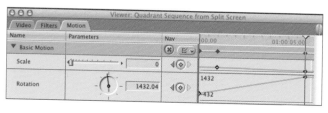

11 Make the Timeline or Canvas active and render the sequence if necessary (Option-R).

12 Play back the sequence.

The four clips spin around a single center point and then vanish into the distance.

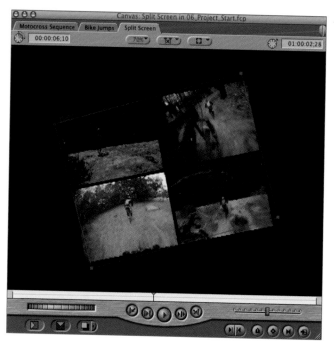

Add a Background Element

At this point, the clips vanish into a black field. You can use this effect as a transition, revealing another clip as the spinning clips disappear.

1   In the Timeline, Shift-drag **Quadrant Sequence** from track V1 onto track V2. Holding Shift as you drag prevents the clip from moving left or right. Alternately, select the clip and press Option-Up Arrow.

2   Drag **Blue Background** from the Browser into the Timeline, dropping it on track V1 directly underneath **Quadrant Sequence.**

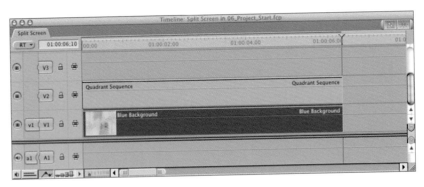

Now when the four clips scale down, **Blue Background** is revealed.

3   Render, if necessary, and play back the sequence.

Adjust the Anchor Point

In the **Blue Background** clip, the bike icon is slightly off center. To integrate the four quadrant clips with the background clip, let's alter the anchor point of the nested sequence so that the clips spin around and vanish into that bike icon.

1 In the Canvas, move the playhead near the end of the sequence and park on a frame where the bicycle graphic in the background is visible. Note the approximate position of the bicycle.

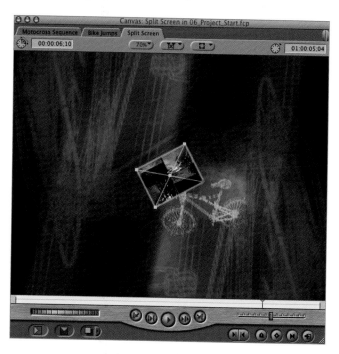

2 Select the Distort tool (D) and then press Home to bring the playhead to the beginning of the sequence.

3 Click the Canvas View button and choose Image+Wireframe from the pop-up menu. Place the cursor over the center point of **Quadrant Sequence** in the Canvas and drag it to the approximate position of the bicycle.

This modifies the clip's anchor point, which is the point around which the object rotates and scales. What you see onscreen may be confusing. Final Cut Pro displays a representation of the change in the motion path, based on the rotation and scaling keyframes you set.

4 Render, if necessary, and play back the sequence.

The clips are now better integrated. To finesse this effect, you can apply a drop shadow or motion blur to **Quadrant Sequence,** smooth out the scaling and rotational movement by applying Ease In/Ease Out settings, crop the black lines at the edges of the clips, or alter the timing of the four clips within so that they reach the apex of their jumps as they scale down and vanish.

Changing the Render Order

Effects are rendered in a specific order in Final Cut Pro. Filters are applied in the order they are listed, from top to bottom, in the Filter tab of the Viewer. Rearranging the render order can change the resulting effect. For example, if you apply a Mask Shape filter after applying a Blur, the edge of the matte will be sharp, but the image behind the matte will be blurred. If you apply the matte first and then add the Blur, the edge of the matte will blur along with the rest of the image.

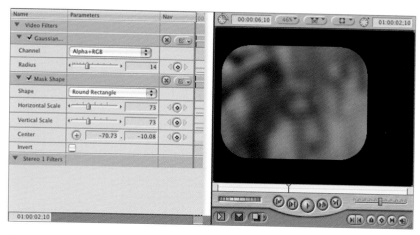

Blur before Mask Shape

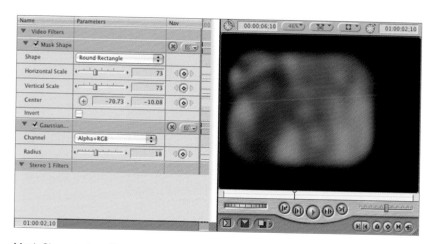

Mask Shape before Blur

Filters affect clips before motion parameters do. This is easy to remember, because the Filters tab appears to the left of the Motion tab in the Viewer. So if you apply a distort filter, such as Wave or Ripple, and then reduce the size of the image, the filter will be applied before the scale operation. The distortion effect is limited to the clip's original size, so the effect may end abruptly at the edges of the clip.

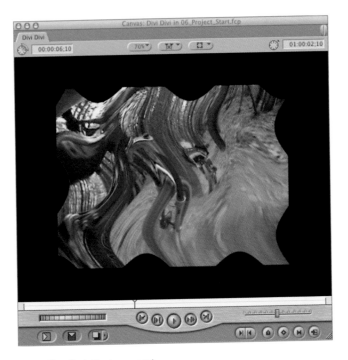

Wave filter first, Scale second

If you scale the clip first and then nest it within another sequence, applying this filter to the nested sequence will produce the desired effect.

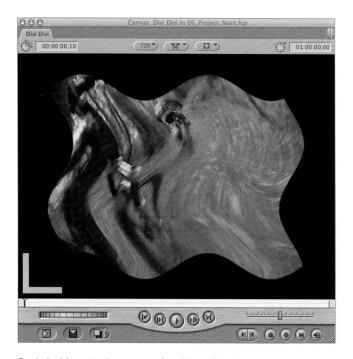

Scale inside nested sequence first, Wave filter the nested sequence second

In the next exercise, you will use a nested sequence to work around the Final Cut Pro render chain.

1   Create a new sequence and call it *Render Order*. To make the effect more visible, set the Canvas background color to white using the Canvas View pop-up menu. Be sure the Selection tool is active.

2   Edit the clip **POV Bike Mount_2** into the new **Render Order** sequence.

3   With the Canvas in Image+Wireframe mode, drag one of the corner points with the Selection tool and scale the clip down to approximately 80 percent of its original size.

4   Double-click **POV Bike Mount_2** and select the Motion tab in the Viewer.

5   Select the Drop Shadow parameter box.

6   Select the clip in the Timeline and choose Sequence > Nest Items, or press Option-C.

7   Name the new sequence *POV Bike Mount Nested Sequence* and click OK.

8   Select the nest in the Timeline, then choose Effects > Video Filters > Distort > Ripple to apply a ripple effect to the nested sequence.

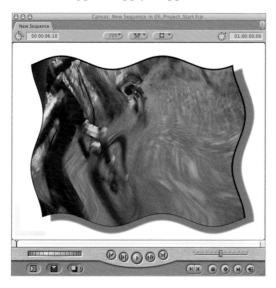

Applying the filter to the nested sequence allows the filtering effect to be processed after the motion parameters are applied. In this case, you can see how the drop shadow is distorted along with the image itself.

Reordering Motion Effects

You can also use nesting to reorder effects within the Motion tab. In an earlier exercise in this lesson, you changed an anchor point that affected both scaling and rotation. Now let's change the anchor point for the scaling, but leave rotation alone, by applying a second nesting operation.

1   Open the **Split Screen 2** sequence.

This sequence is just like the **Split Screen** sequence you modified earlier. The rotation has already been applied to **Quadrant Sequence,** but the Scale and Anchor Point settings have not yet been modified.

2   Select **Quadrant Sequence** and choose Sequence > Nest Items.

3   In the Nest Items dialog box, name the nested sequence *Rotating Quadrant Sequence* and set its frame size to *1140x760.*

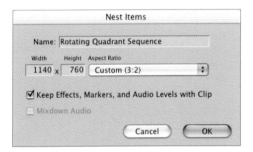

Making the nested sequence frame size larger allows the clips plenty of room to rotate in virtual space without bumping into the edge of the frame.

4   Click OK.

Although **Quadrant Sequence** is already a nested sequence, you can nest it again. There is no limit to the number of times you can nest a sequence.

5   Load **Rotating Quadrant Sequence** into the Viewer (using any of the three methods you have learned earlier in this lesson) and click the Motion tab.

6   Set a keyframe value of *100* in the Scale parameter at 01:00:01:00.

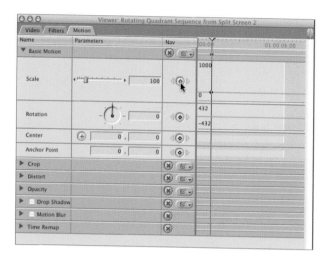

7 Set a second keyframe at 01:00:06:00 with a value of *0*.

8 Temporarily set the opacity for V2 to 20%, so you can see where to drag the anchor point.

9 Press Home or drag the playhead to the beginning of the sequence.

10 Select the Distort tool and drag the center point of **Rotating Quadrant Sequence** to the approximate position of the bicycle.

11 In the Motion tab of the Viewer, set Opacity back to 100%. Render, if necessary, and play back your sequence.

The sequence will rotate around the center point of the four quadrants, but when it scales down, it will vanish into the center of the bike logo.

Mixing Sequence Sizes

The Nest Items dialog box allows you to modify the frame size for newly created nested sequences. Making use of variable frame size further expands the creative possibilities of nesting.

For example, if you want to build a background that comprises multiple video images and then pan across that background, you can construct a sequence with a large frame size, and then nest it into a standard NTSC-sized sequence.

1 Open the **Stacked** sequence from the Browser.

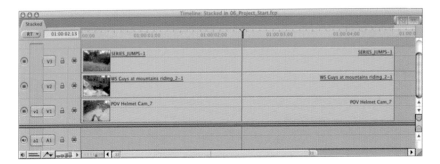

This sequence contains three clips that are stacked one on top of another. All are full-frame, standard DV resolution.

2 Select the three items and choose Sequence > Nest Items.

3 In the Nest Items dialog box, set the Aspect Ratio pop-up menu to Custom, then define the new frame size as *2160x480*. This is three times the width of a standard NTSC DV frame.

4   Name the new sequence *Wide Sequence* and click OK.

5   Double-click **Wide Sequence.** A new Timeline tab appears.

The Canvas displays the wide sequence, reduced to fit into the viewable area, so that you can see your nonstandard frame size.

6   Set your Canvas background back to Black and then set the Canvas view to Image+Wireframe mode.

7   With the Selection tool, select the clip in track V3 in the Timeline. In the Canvas, drag it to the left.

8   Now select the clip in track V2 in the Timeline. Again, in the Canvas, drag this selected clip to the right of the frame. Press Shift to constrain the lateral movement.

All three clips now appear side-by-side in the Canvas window.

9   Open a new text generator from the Generator pop-up menu in the Viewer.

10 Target track V3 and place the Timeline playhead in the center of the clips. Drag the Text clip from the Viewer to the Canvas and drop it as a Superimpose edit. This places the text on a new track above the existing clips.

11 Double-click the text from track V4 in the Timeline to open it into the Viewer. It has now updated to the sequence size.

12 In the Controls tab in the Viewer, change the text to *Motocross*.

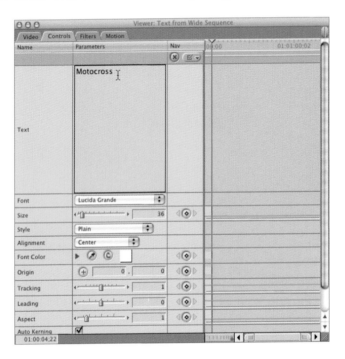

13 Set the text color to your liking. Set the font Size to *100*.

The Canvas updates to reflect your changes.

14 In the Controls tab in the Viewer, use the Origin control to adjust the text so that it is centered across the three images.

15 In the Canvas, click the Stacked tab. Currently, the **Wide Sequence** is scaled down to view the entire sequence in the 720x480 frame size. Open the **Wide Sequence** into the Viewer and scale to 100 percent under the Motion tab.

16 Set the Canvas Scale pop-up menu to Fit All so that you can see the entire wireframe boundary box of the nested sequence inside the **Stacked** parent sequence.

It may help to think of this view as looking through the standard-sized window of the **Stacked** parent sequence into the wider nested sequence below.

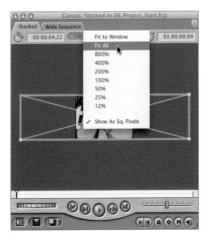

17 In the Canvas, drag the wireframe for the nested **Wide Sequence** to the right, until its left edge aligns with the visible area of your sequence.

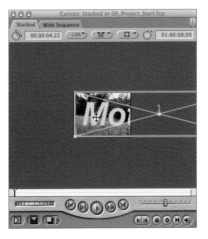

18 Press Home to move the playhead to the beginning of the sequence. Then, with the nest still selected, add a keyframe by clicking the Add Keyframe button in the Canvas, or by pressing Ctrl-K.

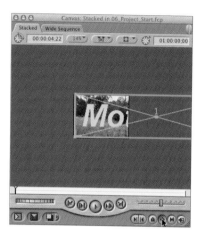

The wireframe for the nest turns green to indicate that a keyframe has been created.

19 Move the playhead to the last frame of the sequence.

20 In the Canvas, drag the nested sequence to the left until the right edge of the visible image aligns with the right edge of the boundary box.

A new keyframe is automatically added, and a motion path appears in the Canvas.

21 Set the Canvas back to Fit to Window. Render, if necessary, and play the sequence.

Using Nesting as an Editing Tool

Although Final Cut Pro doesn't prevent you from building hours of program material in a single sequence, it's not the most efficient or practical way to work. When editing long format shows such as TV programming or feature films, most editors break the program into sections (often called scenes, reels, or segments) and treat each one as a separate sequence. When individual segments are complete, they can be edited into a single main sequence for viewing and output.

To help you keep the terminology of nesting sequences straight, notice that when editors nest a scene or program segment into a longer main sequence, some will often call the main sequence a *master* sequence, instead of a *parent* sequence, and sometimes call the nested sequence a *subsequence* instead of a *nested* sequence. The differences in terminology are strictly a matter of preference. In Final Cut Pro, a master sequence is identical to a parent sequence, and a subsequence is identical to a nested sequence. Since the terms are often used interchangeably in everyday industry practice, we will use them interchangeably in this section, to help you get used to the terminology.

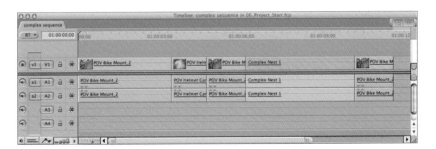

Nesting allows you to quickly rearrange entire segments so that you can experiment with scene order. You can manipulate the sequences as if they were a series of clips, trim nested sequences using the trimming tools, and add transition effects using In/Out points and Bézier handles. Nesting facilitates flexibility because you can modify individual scene sequences, and the master sequence will update to reflect the latest edits. You'll do some of these things now, starting with creating the master sequence.

1   Create a new sequence named *Master Sequence* and open it.

2   Drag the **Stacked** sequence from the Browser directly into the Timeline.

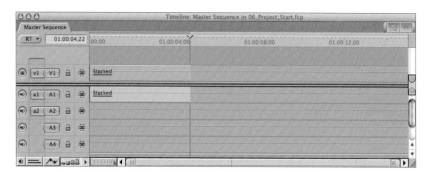

The **Stacked** sequence is now nested in the master sequence.

Mark a Sequence with In and Out Points

By setting an In or Out point in a sequence before you nest it, you define which portion of the sequence will be included in the master sequence. Just like with editing a single clip, the portions of the sequence you want to nest that fall outside the In and Out points become handle frames, to accommodate transition effects, such as a cross dissolve, or close trimming of the edit points in the Timeline.

1   Double-click the **Bike Jumps** sequence to open it in the Timeline.

2   Set an Out point at the end of the title on track V2.

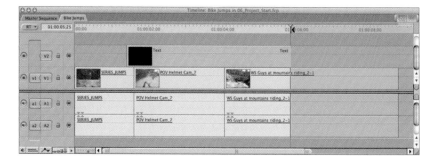

3   In the Timeline, click the **Master Sequence** tab to bring it to the fore-
     ground. Press the Down Arrow or End key to make sure your playhead is
     at the end of the sequence, one frame past the nested **Stacked** subsequence.

4   Edit **Bike Jumps** into **Master Sequence** by dragging it from the Browser to
     the Canvas or Timeline.

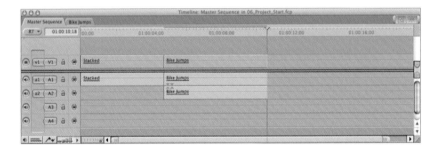

Now the master sequence contains two subsequences: **Stacked** and **Bike
Jumps.** Since nested subsequences follow all the standard rules of three-
point editing when edited into master sequences, the **Bike Jumps** sequence
ends in its master sequence at the Out point you designated inside the
Bike Jumps sequence.

Editing Within the Nested Sequence

Imagine these are the first two scenes of the finished program. You can continue to make editorial changes to clips inside the individual subsequences,
and the master sequence will be updated automatically.

1   Place the playhead at the end of **Master Sequence.**

2   Press M to add a sequence marker.

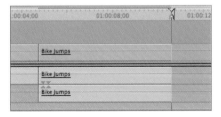

This marker will be used to illustrate how the editing changes in the nested sequences affect the parent sequence.

3   Double-click the **Stacked** sequence in the Browser to open it into its own Timeline tab.

4   Drag the clip **SERIES_JUMPS** from the Browser and edit it in at the end of **Wide Sequence**.

5   Switch back to **Master Sequence.**

When you added the clip to **Stacked** as an Insert edit, the master sequence was affected. In order to make room for the new clip, the sequence rippled to the right, and the entire master sequence became longer, as you can see by the marker you added.

If you add, delete, or trim the individual clips (or even another nested sequence) inside a nested subsequence—*that has no In or Out points set in it*—the master sequence will ripple to the right or left, making the master sequence shorter or longer. Again, the editorial changes you make within the nested subsequences are automatically updated in the parent, as long as you have no In or Out point set in the nested subsequence.

An Alternate Behavior

However, you should know that contrary to the behavior of nested subsequences with no set In or Out points, if you set an In or Out point in the nested subsequence *either before or after editing it into the master,* you will achieve somewhat different results.

1   Open the **Bike Jumps** sequence into the Timeline.

2   Drag the **SERIES_JUMPS** shot from the Browser into the Timeline to add it to the end of this sequence.

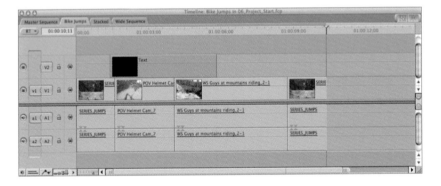

Although this action makes this subsequence longer, the Out point set earlier will still define the nested sequence's length within the master sequence.

3 Bring **Master Sequence** to the front. Notice that nothing in **Master Sequence** has changed. Of course, you can manually ripple the nested **Bike Jumps** subsequence in the master, just like any clip, to reveal more of its content.

4 Using the Selection tool in the master sequence, drag the right edge of the **Bike Jumps** subsequence to make it longer.

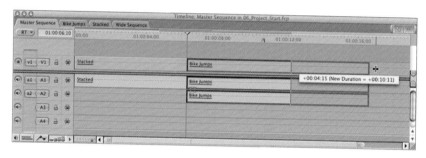

The additional content in the subsequence is now visible in **Master Sequence.**

Editing the Content of a Subsequence

In all of the examples so far, you have been nesting several clips and treating them as a whole to add effects or edits to a group of clips at one time. Occasionally, you may need to perform a reverse technique to un-nest individual items within a nested sequence. This is necessary when making an edit decision list (EDL), which is a text list of all of the In and Out points for all of the clips in your sequence. If your master sequence contains a nested sequence comprising multiple clips, the EDL will mistakenly represent that nested sequence as a single clip. This may cause serious problems if you are using the EDL to re-create your sequence on another system.

1 Close all of your open sequences by closing the Canvas window.

2   Double-click **complex sequence** in the Browser.

This sequence contains a series of clips, as well as a nested sequence.
Nested sequences are a different shade than other clips in the Timeline.

The nested sequence **Complex Nest 1** is also located in the Browser. You
will replace **Complex Nest 1** with the clips that comprise it, in its parent
sequence.

3   Make sure snapping is enabled (N).

4   Select the **Complex Nest 1** sequence in the Browser and drag it over the
Timeline. Position it directly over the exiting instance of the same nest,
but do not release the mouse yet.

5   Press and hold the Command key.

The Timeline overlay identifies the individual clips within the sequence.

6   Make sure you are performing an Overwrite edit (not an Insert) by placing the cursor in the lower section of the Timeline track. Release the
mouse to drop the five clips originally edited into **Complex Nest** *1* as an
Overwrite edit.

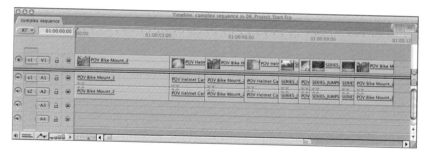

The nested sequence has been replaced by its original clip contents. You
have un-nested the sequence, and your EDL will accurately reflect all of
the individual clips used to build the master sequence.

NOTE ▶ After you complete this operation, there is no live link between
the sequence and the individual clips. From this point forward, changes
made to one clip will not affect the others.

Nesting is incredibly versatile. For audio-intensive projects, you can use nesting to combine groups of sounds to approximate the bussing features of audio-specific tools. For example, you might make a nest of different sound effects tracks, and then control the overall volume with a single slider. Or use nesting to output a sequence with Timecode Print filters applied to nests so that both sequence and source timecode are burned in on output to tape. As you become more adept at nesting, you will find countless ways to put it to use. Nesting is one of the fundamental tools for exploring the true depth and flexibility of Final Cut Pro.

Lesson Review

1.   What are two ways of nesting a sequence?

2.   Can you apply filters to a nested sequence?

3.   If you adjust the Rotation parameter of a nested sequence with four composited layers, what happens to those layers?

4.   If you edit three sequences within a fourth and change the In and Out points of each nested sequence, what happens if the overall duration of one of the sequences you nested changes?

5.   If you edit three sequences within a fourth without setting their In and Out points, what happens if the overall duration of one of the sequences you nested changes?

6.   How do you edit the content of a sequence into a Timeline without nesting it?

Answers

1.   Edit a sequence inside of a second sequence, or select one or more clips in the Timeline and choose Sequence > Nest Items.

2.   Yes. Filters affect every clip within a nested sequence to which they're applied.

3.   The layers all rotate together as if they were a single clip.

4. Nothing. Setting the In and Out points of a nested sequence locks its duration.

5. The nested sequence with the changed duration gets longer or shorter, rippling the position of the other nested sequences that come after it.

6. Drag a sequence into the Timeline, and before you release the mouse button, press the Command key. When the edit points between each clip in the sequence appear, release the mouse button.

7

Lesson Files
Lessons > Lesson_07 > 07_Project_Start

Lessons > Lesson_07 > 07_Project_Finished

Media
Media > Lesson_07_Media

Time
This lesson takes approximately 60 minutes to complete.

Goals
Apply basic speed manipulations to clips

Learn to read the speed indicators in the Timeline

Use the Time Remap tool to add and manipulate keyframes

Manipulate time keyframes in the motion bar

Customize the Clip Keyframes control for different uses

Create freeze frames using variable speed controls

Make part of a clip play backward

Smooth speed keyframes to create gradual changes

Save a speed setting as a favorite

Lesson 7
Variable Speed

Speed effects are one of the most common and versatile effect types available in Final Cut Pro. Basic speed changes, such as slow motion, can be employed for dramatic effect, and increasing playback speed can simulate time lapse. The real fun happens when you employ variable speed effects (often called *time ramping*) to vary a clip's speed throughout playback. For example, a shot can begin playing in slow motion, speed up, and then return to another playback speed at the end of the shot. A speed-varied shot can slow to a freeze frame, or play back in reverse. Final Cut Pro displays time remapping data in several different ways. Learning how to read time controls is essential to mastering the variable speed tools.

Basic Slow Motion

Before delving into variable speed effects, it's important to review how Final Cut Pro handles constant speed changes such as slow motion.

1   Open Lesson_07 > **07_Project_Start.** The sequence **Golfer 1** should be open in the Timeline. Play the sequence.

2   Select clip **6E_1** (the third clip) and choose Modify > Speed.

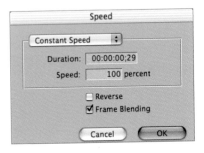

3   Select the Frame Blending box if it's not already selected. Frame blending generates new frames by blending the surrounding frames. This creates a smoother slow motion effect.

4   Set the Speed to 50 percent and click OK.

In the Timeline, you can see that slowing down the clip rippled it to the right and made it longer.

5   Click the Clip Keyframes control to turn on clip keyframes.

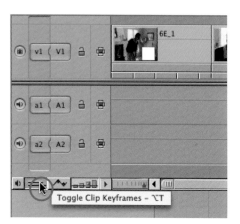

The Clip Keyframes control turns on the speed indicators beneath clips in the Timeline. Notice that the tic marks beneath **6E_1** are farther apart than they are in the surrounding clips. The distance between the tics indicates the speed of the clip. The farther apart the tics, the slower the clip will play back.

6   Render and play your sequence.

> **NOTE** ▶ If you play the sequence using Unlimited RT instead of rendering, you can preview the effect, but frame blending will not be applied until you render.

You may notice that even with frame blending enabled, **6E_1** still appears to have a strobe or stuttering quality. The fourth clip (**6F_3**) was photographed in slow motion. You can compare the difference between the two clips. Creating slow motion in-camera will always produce a smoother result than applying an effect in post-production.

If you must slow a clip in post-production, adding Motion Blur can often improve the effect.

7   Double-click **6E_1**, the third clip in the **Golfer 1** sequence, to open it into the Viewer.

8   Click the Motion tab.

9   Turn on Motion Blur and click the disclosure triangle to reveal its settings.

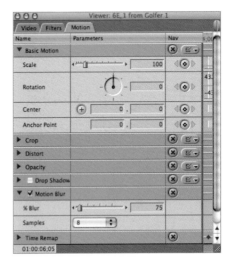

10   Set % Blur to *75* and Samples to *8*.

11   Render and play your sequence.

Motion Blur uses frames before and after the current frame and combines them to create an effect similar to the natural blur that occurs in-camera when shooting in slow motion. The Samples setting equals the number of frames both before and after the current frame that are used to create the effect. % Blur sets the amount of blur applied to these sampled frames. Because of this, Motion Blur is a render-intensive effect. Higher settings will take longer to render. Remember, a little bit goes a long way with motion blurring.

Variable Speed Effects

Slowing only a portion of a clip is accomplished by using a variable speed effect.

1   Double-click the **Golfer 2** sequence to open it into the Timeline.

    This clip contains a single clip of the golfer swinging his club.

2   Select the clip, play the sequence, and set a marker just as the golfer begins the downward motion of his swing.

Marker

3   Select the Time Remap tool from the Tool palette.

4   Click the clip at the frame where you added the marker.

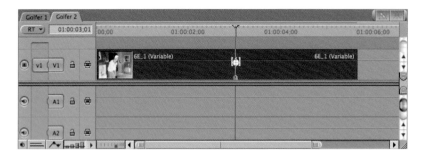

Setting this keyframe prepares the clip so that the speed changes you make will affect the clip from this point forward. The word *Variable* appears next to the clip's name in the Timeline to indicate that speed keyframes have been applied.

5   Click and hold the Time Remap tool near the right edge of the clip. Turn off snapping (N) if necessary. You might see the tool turn into an arrow near the right edge, but if you click and hold, a tooltip appears.

6   Drag the Time Remap tool to the left until the tooltip indicates that Speed Left equals approximately 50%.

The clip should play at normal speed until the golfer begins his swing (where you set the first keyframe), and then switch to slow motion for the duration of the swing.

7   In the Timeline, click the Clip Keyframes control.

Notice that the tic marks in the speed indicator spread out during the section of the clip that is in slow motion. Also, the blue motion bar indicates where keyframes have been set.

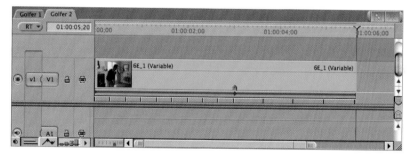

Creating a Freeze Frame

Variable speed effects can be used to make a clip play at normal speed, and then stop and hold on a particular frame. This is sometimes used in title sequences and trailers to introduce characters.

1   Double-click the **Character Intro** sequence to open it into the Timeline.

2　Play the sequence and stop when the girl is visible full frame, from head to toe (approximate timecode 01:00:11:10).

3　Select the Time Remap tool and click at the playhead position to add a single speed keyframe.

4　Type +3. (three followed by a period) to move your playhead forward 3 seconds.

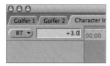

5　Add a new keyframe by clicking with the Time Remap tool at the playhead position.

The clip still appears to play at normal speed, but you've prepared it to create the freeze-frame effect.

6 Turn on Clip Keyframes.

The Clip Keyframes control aids in performing keyframing operations in the Timeline. In addition to displaying speed indicators and a motion bar, a keyframe editor also appears and can display speed keyframes for manipulation directly in the Timeline.

Although the Clip Keyframes control itself simply turns the visibility of controls in the Timeline on and off, you can make it more useful by customizing the controls it displays and which keyframes are visible.

7 Control-click the Clip Keyframes control and deselect Video > Filters Bar in the shortcut menu. Leave the other three selections selected.

8 Control-click the Clip Keyframes control again and choose Audio > Select None.

Now the variable speed effects settings are the only ones visible in the Timeline tracks.

9 Control-click the blue motion bar under the clip and choose Hide All from the shortcut menu.

By default, keyframes for all parameters are visible. After you choose Hide All, no keyframes will be displayed in the motion bar.

This menu allows you to choose which keyframes will be displayed in the motion bar. You can have multiple parameters displayed simultaneously, but you will not be able to tell them apart by looking at the motion bar. In this case, you want to view only speed keyframes.

10 Control-click the blue motion bar and choose Time Remap > Time Graph from the shortcut menu.

Now only speed keyframes will be displayed in the motion bar.

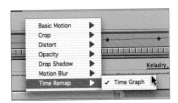

11 Control-click the area between the blue motion bar and the speed indicator, where the keyframe editor appears, and then choose Time Remap > Time Graph from the shortcut menu.

This shortcut menu allows you to choose which keyframe graph will be displayed in the Timeline's keyframe editor. You can only view one parameter graph at a time. Graphs for all parameters are always visible in the Motion tab of the Viewer.

When the keyframe editor is visible, a small new control appears at the right edge of the track headers: This thin bar controls the height of the keyframe graph.

12 Click the thin, vertical black bar and drag it upward to increase the height of the graph, which will give you more room to manipulate the Time Remap keyframes.

Now you will set the second speed keyframe to the same frame as the first to create a freeze-frame effect.

13 Position your playhead at the first keyframe. (Turn snapping back on [N], if necessary.)

14 Choose View > Match Frame > Master Clip, or press F.

This loads the source clip into the Viewer, parked on the identical frame. You'll use this as a visual reference for setting the speed keyframe.

15 Make sure snapping is turned on. Using the Time Remap tool, click and hold on the position of the second keyframe in the Timeline. Do not click in the keyframe graph; click the clip itself.

The tooltip appears.

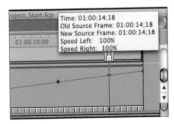

The Canvas displays the frame assigned to the place in time where you clicked. As you drag the Time Remap tool, the Canvas updates to display the new frame you are assigning to that time position.

16 Drag the tool to the left until the frame in the Canvas matches the exact frame displayed in the Viewer. As you drag, match the number on the Source Timecode Overlay in the Canvas to the Current Timecode position in the Viewer.

The keyframe graph and speed indicator can also assist you in identifying when you have achieved the freeze frame. The keyframe graph will display a horizontal line, and the speed indicators will not contain any tic marks for the duration of the freeze.

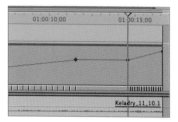

To finalize the effect, you must set the remaining portion of the clip back to regular speed.

17 Click the Time Remap tool on the last frame of the clip and drag it to the left until the tooltip reads Speed Left: 100%.

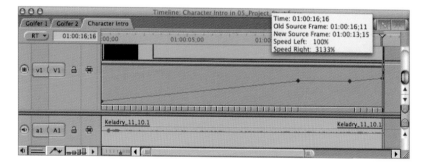

Ignore the Speed Right value because none of those frames will be played. If you have trouble setting the speed value to a precise number, you can use the keyboard modifiers Shift and Command to restrict the movement of the Time Remap tool.

18 Click and hold the last frame with the Time Remap tool.

19 Press Shift to constrain movements to 10 percent increments, or press Command to restrict movements to 1 percent increments.

This allows you to set precise values for speed effects.

20 Play your sequence and view the freeze-frame effect.

21 Using the text generator, create a title, identifying the actor as *Kel*.

22 Set the duration of the text generator to 3:00.

23 Edit the text clip onto V2 beginning at the first speed keyframe.

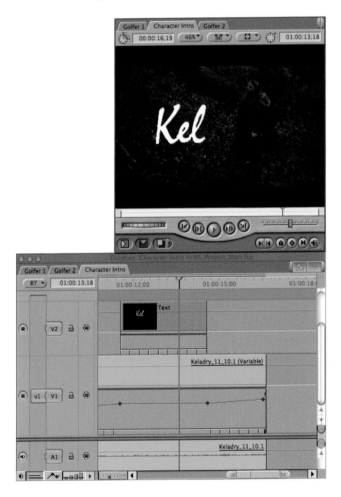

Modifying Existing Speed Keyframes

Once you've applied speed keyframes, you can modify their position in time to alter the variable speed effect. For example, you can alter speed to play in fast motion leading up to the freeze frame.

The Time Remap tool normally does what its name implies: it remaps, or moves, a particular clip frame to the current position in sequence time where you click the tool. It then speeds up or slows down intermediate frames in front of and behind that particular frame to execute this remap.

When you Option-click with the Time Remap tool, however, you move the current frame to a different position in time. Frames speed up and slow down on either side of this repositioned frame to compensate for the move.

To reflect this difference, a tooltip displays the Old Time and New Time, rather than the old and new Source Frame. In both cases, you are modifying the speed of the clip, so the Speed Left and Speed Right information is still visible.

1   Use the Time Remap tool to Option-click the clip at the first keyframe position. A tooltip appears.

NOTE ▸ Clicking or Option-clicking the clip with the Time Remap tool sets a new keyframe if there was not one there already. When adjusting settings for an existing keyframe, activate snapping to aid precision.

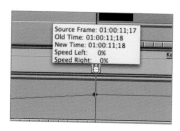

2   Drag the keyframe to the left until New Time reads approximately
01:00:04:20.

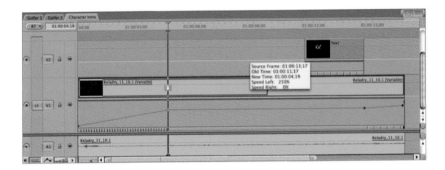

As you can see, using the Option key with the Time Remap tool allows you
to extend this freeze frame for about 6 additional seconds. To accomplish
this, the beginning frames that were playing normally are now squeezed
together in time to play back at approximately 250%. This is reflected in
the Timeline by the speed indicator, which shows the tic marks very close
to each other. Now, however, the title no longer lines up with the effect, so
you need to fix that.

3   Change back to the Selection tool (press A) and drag the entire clip on V2
so it begins at the same time as the freeze frame.

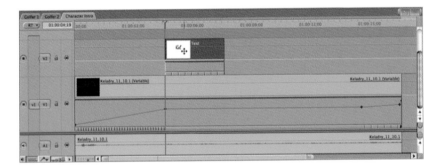

4   Option-drag the second speed keyframe (where the freeze frame ends)
with the Time Remap tool, or simply drag the keyframe point in the graph
to line up with the end of the title.

Before the effect is complete, you must reset the speed between the last two keyframes so the clip will play back at 100% speed.

5 Option-click the last frame of the clip with the Time Remap tool and drag to the left until Speed Left equals 100%. Make sure you are adjusting the existing keyframe, not adding a new keyframe. Zoom in to the Timeline and use snapping if necessary.

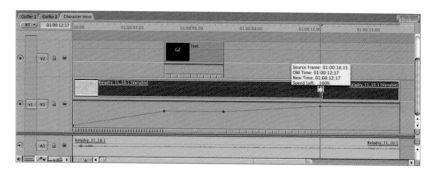

Due to the original duration of the sequence, a few extra frames remain at the end of the shot.

6 Using the Selection tool, drag the right edge of the clip until it lines up with the last keyframe.

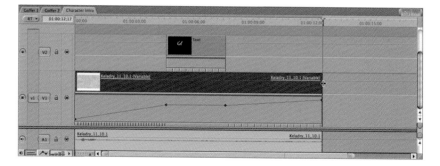

7 Play the sequence.

When creating freeze frames, you need to check how the output looks on an interlaced, external monitor to be sure no field artifacts are visible in the frozen frame. If you select a frame that contains fast, horizontal movement, the freeze frame might look good on your computer screen, but it will flicker when displayed on a TV monitor.

If you see flicker in the freeze frame, choose a frame that doesn't contain such lateral movement. If you must choose a frame that contains movement, eliminate the flickering effect by applying the De-Interlace filter to the range of the clip that has the freeze frame. Be aware, however, that removing the interlacing from the clip can have a negative effect on slow-motion effects, amplifying the strobe or stutter effect discussed earlier in the lesson.

Complex Speed Effects

Once you have mastered the basics of variable speed effects, you can make increasingly complex effects using many keyframes. You can even switch between forward and backward play.

1   Close all of your open sequences and then open the **Head Turn** sequence and watch it once.

In preparing for his golf swing, the actor makes an interesting, somewhat comical head roll.

2   Identify the frame where the actor begins his head roll.

3 Set a keyframe at that point by clicking the clip with the Time Remap tool.

4 Control-click the keyframe graph and choose Time Remap > Time Graph from the shortcut menu.

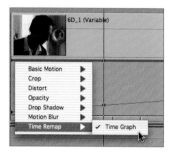

5 Find the frame where the head movement ends.

6 Option-click that frame and drag it to the left, compressing the time between the two keyframes to approximately 200%.

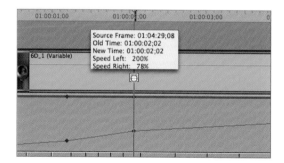

7 Move the playhead 1 second to the right of the last keyframe. Click and drag to the left with the Time Remap tool (do not hold down the

Option key) to create a new keyframe with a Speed Left value of
approximately –155%.

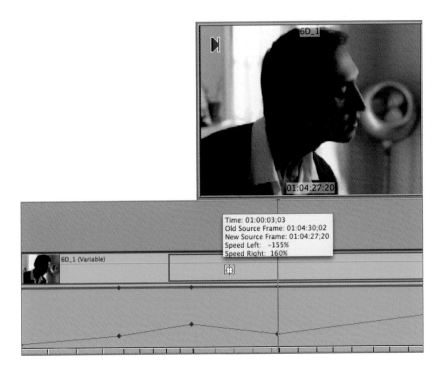

You have just set the clip to play backward between the second and third
keyframes. The speed indicator displays red tic marks for the duration of
reverse playback. Notice that the keyframe graph displays a downward
slope.

8   Move the playhead forward 2 seconds beyond the third keyframe
     and click-drag to the left with the Time Remap tool (no Option key).
     Watch the Canvas and stop when the last frame of the head movement
     appears.

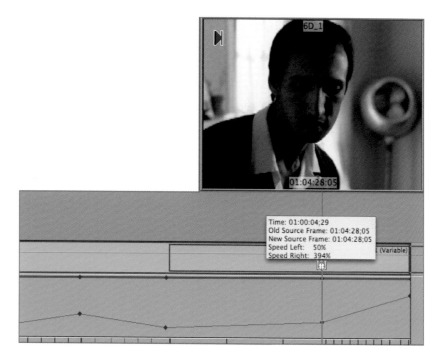

This adjusts the speed between keyframes three and four to about 50%.

9   Play your sequence.

You can continue adding additional keyframes to extend that short head turn for great comic effect.

Gradual Speed Changes

The speed effects you have created thus far transition abruptly from one speed to another—the clip plays at 100% until it reaches a new keyframe and then suddenly switches to 50% speed. This creates dramatic effects, but you can further improve your speed effects by controlling the ramping velocity of the speed changes.

1   Control-click the second keyframe in the keyframe graph and choose Smooth from the shortcut menu.

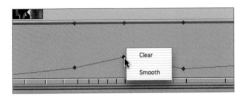

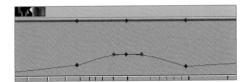

The transition from forward to reverse speed now occurs gradually, creating a subtle and natural-looking effect. The Bézier handles that appear when you choose Smooth allow further manipulation of the transition.

Be careful when manipulating these handles. Small movements can have dramatic effects and completely alter the subtlety of the speed settings you just established.

2   Zoom in to get a closer look at the keyframe you are about to manipulate. You can also enlarge the track height.

3   Drag the Bézier handle points towards the keyframe to reduce the duration of the transition. Be careful to keep the handles completely horizontal. By default, moving one handle automatically moves the other.

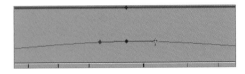

Lengthening the handles adds time to the transition between speed settings. Experiment with different settings to find the transition that feels most natural to you.

Once you smooth a keyframe, the Speed tooltip reports the Speed Left and Speed Right as Variable.

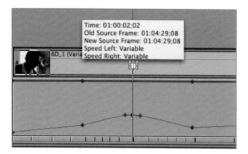

This makes it impossible to apply additional changes to the keyframe values. For good workflow, do not apply smoothing to your keyframes until speed value changes are final. Of course, you can always Control-click the smoothed keyframe and set it back to a corner point, if necessary.

4   Apply the smoothing effect to all keyframes in the sequence. You don't need to adjust Bézier handles, because the default settings provide adequate smoothing.

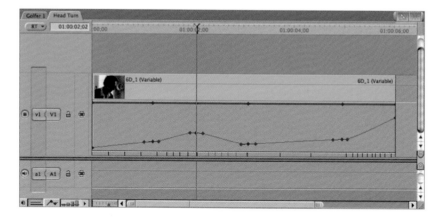

5   Play the finished sequence.

Using the Motion Viewer

The speed effects and controls used in the Timeline are also visible in the Time Remap section of the Motion tab in the Viewer.

1   Still in the **Head Turn** sequence, double-click **6D_1** with the Selection tool to open it into the Viewer.

2   Click the Motion tab. Toggle open the Time Remap parameters.

The graph displayed here is identical to the graph visible in the Timeline. Viewing this graph in the Motion tab allows you to compare it to keyframes applied in other motion parameters.

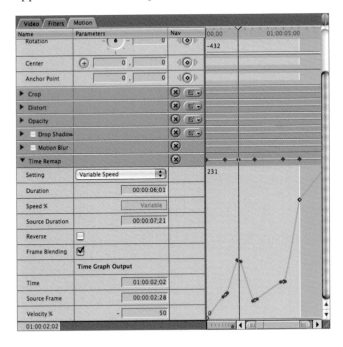

The primary disadvantage to making changes in the Motion tab is that, unlike when you use the Time Remap tool in the Timeline, you cannot view the frames interactively as they update in the Canvas.

The most useful control in the Motion tab is the Reset button that removes all speed keyframes applied.

3   Click the Reset button for the Time Remap section of the Motion tab.

Copying and Saving Speed Effects

Speed effects are recorded in the Motion tab, so you can copy or save a clip's speed settings just as you can with any motion setting.

1   Open the **Copy Clip** sequence.

2   Play back the sequence.

The first clip has a variable speed effect applied to it, and the second clip plays at regular speed.

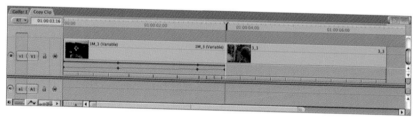

3   Select the first clip and choose Edit > Copy (or press Command-C).

4   Select the second clip and choose Edit > Paste Attributes (or press Option-V).

5   Select the Speed box and click OK.

If you are pasting attributes to a clip of a different length, selecting the Scale Attribute Times box will scale your keyframes to fit the length of the new clip.

You can save the speed settings so that they're available to use on other clips.

6   Select the first clip and choose Effects > Make Favorite Motion.

Make Favorite Motion stores all motion settings (Scale, Distortion, Drop Shadow, Speed, and so on) that are currently applied to the clip in the Motion tab.

7   In the Browser, click the Effects tab and open the Favorites bin.

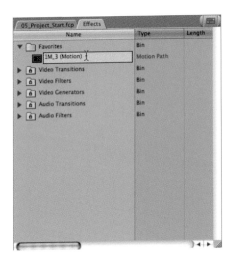

8   Rename **1M_3 (Motion)** to *My custom speed effect* and press Enter.

The custom effect also appears in the Effects > Motion Favorites submenu.

You can now apply this speed setting to any selected clip in any sequence.

Lesson Review

1. How can you make simple, linear changes to the speed of a clip?
2. How can you make variable speed changes to a clip in the Timeline?
3. What's a good way to soften the strobing that happens in a slow motion clip?
4. How do you identify a clip's speed using the speed indicators?
5. How can you make a change from one speed to another more gradual?
6. Can you save a speed effect as a favorite?

Answers

1. Select the clip, and choose Modify > Speed, and specify the percentage at which you want the clip to play.
2. Use the Time Remap tool, or turn on the keyframe graph in the timeline, reveal the time graph, and keyframe your speed changes.
3. Turn on Frame Blending.
4. Tic marks that are farther apart indicate slow motion; tic marks that are closer indicate fast motion; and no tic marks means a freeze frame.
5. Choose the Smooth command in a keyframes shortcut menu in the Motion tab or the keyframe graph of the Timeline.
6. Yes.

8

Lesson Files   Lessons > Lesson_08 > Project_Start

Media   Media > Lesson_08_Media

Time   This lesson takes approximately 60 minutes to complete.

Goals   Use basic text generators to create titles

Customize text generators

Create a lower-third title

Use the Timecode Generator and Timecode Reader filters

Lesson 8
Adding Text to a Sequence

Although Final Cut Pro lacks many of the extremely flexible text customization and animation features of Motion, it has several standard tools you can use to quickly add still and animated text to your sequences.

Text is created inside Final Cut Pro using generators, found in the Generator pop-up menu at the bottom of the Viewer's Video tab. Final Cut Pro comes with six built-in text generators, located within the Generator pop-up's Text submenu, each of which creates a different still or animated text effect. Each of these generators has custom parameters located in the Controls tab, which work similarly to those found within various filters. These parameters can be modified and animated to create many different titling effects.

The lessons in this chapter focus on how to add and customize many of the text generators available in Final Cut Pro to create basic titles, lower-thirds, scrolling credits, and other text effects. You will also learn how to use two of the text generating filters, the Timecode Generator and Timecode Reader filters, to create timecode window burns.

Using Generators to Create a Title

In the following exercises, you will create a simple title page by combining an animation clip created in another application with generators created within Final Cut Pro.

1   Open Lessons > Lesson_08 > **Project_Start**.

2   Option-double-click the 01 - Opening Title bin.

This opens the bin as another tab in the Browser, maximizing screen real estate and maintaining an orderly desktop. This bin contains the one clip used in this exercise as well as the sequence containing a finished version of the composition you are about to create.

3   Double-click the **Opening Title - Finished** sequence.

4   In the View menu at the top of the Canvas, verify that Show Overlays is turned off to hide the Title Safe overlays.

The title you are about to create consists of three layers—a background clip on track V1, a gradient generator on track V2, and a text generator on track V3.

5 Double-click the **Opening Title - Beginning** sequence, in preparation for the next exercise.

In a typical workflow, you may receive numerous background graphic elements from a motion graphics designer for a show you are editing. For many programs, the edit can change so often that that it doesn't make sense for the designer to spin out new graphics every time a title needs updating. (Documentaries or news programs are two good examples.) In these circumstances, creating the actual text within Final Cut Pro makes more sense, so that it's easily changed to match any re-edits that occur.

Assembling the Basic Composition

As always, putting together a graphics effect begins with assembling the basic clips used in the composition within the Timeline.

1 Double-click the clip **Text_Background.mov** to open it into the Viewer.

This is the background clip you'll be using as the basis for your title.

2 Play the clip in the Viewer.

This animated clip is a particle effect that was created and output using Motion.

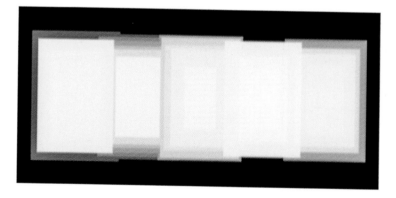

TIP ▶ The **Text_Background.mov** file was output using the DV/DVCPRO NTSC codec. A better way to export clips for project exchange would be to use the Uncompressed 8-Bit 4:2:2 codec. This is a good format to output clips that you want to use as design elements within Final Cut Pro because it produces extremely high-quality clips. For maximum flexibility, you can also edit a Motion project directly into a Final Cut Pro sequence. For more information, see the Motion documentation.

3   Press F10 to edit the background clip into the Timeline.

Next, you're going to superimpose some text over the background that has just been added.

4   Click the Video tab in the Viewer, and from the Generator pop-up menu at the bottom of the Viewer, choose Text > Text.

By default, the text generator displays the words *SAMPLE TEXT* as white text against a black background. Before editing this generator into the sequence, it's a good idea to change a few of its basic parameters to better suit your compositional needs.

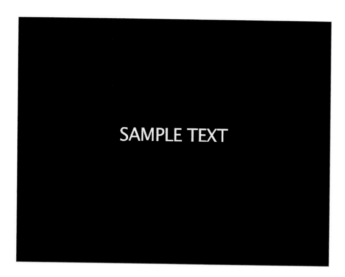

5 Move the playhead to the beginning of the sequence in either the Timeline or the Canvas, then press F12 to perform a Superimpose edit.

The text generator now appears on track V2 in the Timeline.

Notice that the new text you added appears perfectly superimposed over the background layer in the Canvas. This is because text generators automatically create their own alpha channels, so that the black background is transparent.

NOTE ▶ If the text appears to be jagged, it may be because the Canvas Zoom pop-up menu is not at 100 percent. At 100 percent, the text generators should appear perfectly smooth, which is how they look when output from Final Cut Pro. At any other Canvas or Viewer zoom level, text may appear jagged because of the fast rescaling that occurs within the Canvas and Viewer.

Customizing the Text Generator

Now that the basic elements are assembled, it's time to further customize the text generator you just added in order to make the text better fit into the composition.

The Controls tab that allows you to customize each generator is found in the Viewer, so changing a generator's parameters and seeing the results at the same time is difficult. For this reason, you may want to edit a text generator into a sequence first, then reopen it into the Viewer as a sequence clip. If you keep the playhead over the generator in the sequence, you can edit the generator's parameters in the Controls tab of the Viewer and see the results immediately in the Canvas.

1   In the Timeline, double-click the text generator to open it into the Viewer. Keep the playhead over the generator in the Timeline.

2   In the Viewer, click the Controls tab.

The Controls tab contains all the parameters you can use to customize a generator. In this case, the Controls tab is displaying all of the parameters for the text generator. You can edit these as you would edit any other group of parameters in Final Cut Pro.

3   Click the Text field once. Immediately, both words are selected. Type *extra* (with all lowercase letters) to replace the previous text.

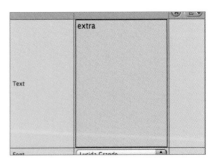

4   Click the Font Color control to change its color. The color picker appears.

Since the background is so bright, you need to darken the text so that it will stand out.

5   In the color picker, drag the Intensity slider so that it's halfway down to select a 50 percent gray color.

When you've finished, click OK.

Now it's time to edit your newly modified text generator into the Timeline.

6   From the Font menu, choose Times New Roman.

TIP▸ When choosing a font for a title that's going out to an interlaced video format, avoid fonts that are too thin—especially fonts with one- or two-pixel horizontal lines. Thin fonts appear to vibrate as the video plays because they're thin enough to be caught on single lines of video, each of which only appears onscreen for half the duration of a frame. Another way to avoid this problem is to increase the size of the fonts you use.

7 Set the Size parameter to *70*, either by moving the slider or typing into the value field. If you scrub through the sequence, you may notice that the background layer consists of five pulsating regions. Since there are five characters in the title, each letter can be cleverly lined up with a corresponding region in the background using the Tracking parameter. The Tracking parameter controls the spacing between each character of text in the generator.

8 Change the Tracking parameter to *40*.

The letters are now spaced like the background, but their position is mis-aligned. You could modify the Center parameter in the Motion tab, but each text generator also has a parameter, called the Origin parameter, that controls where the first line of text is drawn in the frame.

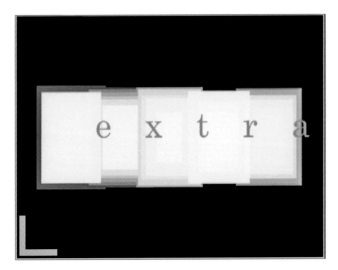

The Origin parameter's X value positions the text based on the setting of the Alignment parameter. If the Alignment parameter is set to Left, then it sets the leftmost edge of the text. If it's set to Right, it defines the right-most edge of the text. The Origin parameter's Y value defines the point at which the bottom of the text sits.

There are two ways you can use the Origin parameter. You can click the crosshairs button and then click or drag within the Canvas to move the text to a new position, or you can change the coordinates numerically using the value fields.

9 In the Origin parameter of the Controls tab, roughly position the text by clicking the crosshairs button, and dragging within the Canvas until the letters of the text appear to line up with the background regions.

10 If necessary, refine this change numerically so that the Origin parameter is set to -80, 15.

Each character of text is now aligned with a corresponding background region.

Adding Another Generator to the Composition

The title is looking good, but now that the characters of the text are spread out and lined up, the letters almost get lost amid all the motion of the background. Fortunately, you can easily remedy this oversight without changing the design of the background by adding a second generator to use as a backdrop for the text—a gradient generator.

Final Cut Pro has many kinds of generators besides the text generators: bars and tone generators for every format of video, shape generators that provide ovals and rectangles for you to use as design elements and compositing tools, and render generators.

Render generators are dynamic and can create many different effects. Some are even animated, like the particle generator. One of the most versatile, however, is the gradient generator, which you'll use in this next exercise.

1   In the Viewer, click the Video tab.

2   From the Generator pop-up menu, choose Render > Gradient.

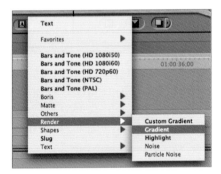

The Viewer fills with the image of a grayscale gradient (sometimes referred to as a *ramp*), which is white at the left and fades to black at the right.

You can customize the colors and orientation of the gradient using the parameters in the Controls tab, but it just so happens you can use this generator exactly as is.

3   Move the playhead back to the beginning of the sequence, and press F12 to edit the current gradient generator into the Timeline with a Superimpose edit.

Notice that the video source control is still connected to the V1 destination control, so the newly superimposed gradient generator has been edited into track V2, and the previously superimposed text generator has been moved up to track V3, so that it's still the frontmost layer. Clever!

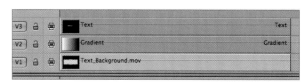

Unfortunately, the full-screen gradient you just added is now obscuring the background layer, so you need to crop it to the necessary size using its Motion parameters.

4   In the Timeline, double-click the Gradient generator clip to open it into the Viewer as a sequence clip.

5   Click the Motion tab to reveal its motion parameters.

Generators possess the same motion parameters as any other clip in Final Cut Pro, and you can geometrically transform them using the same methods.

6   Click the Crop disclosure triangle to reveal the individual Crop parameters.

7   Move the Top slider to 42 to crop the top to fit the Text layer. Then move the Bottom slider to 44 to crop the bottom to fit the Text layer.

Now the gradient appears as a strip directly underneath the text.

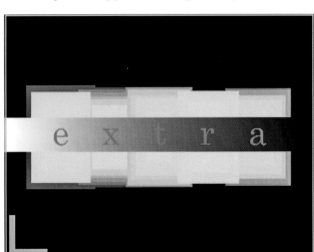

The Gradient layer looks good, and serves its purpose of making the text pop out more, but its dark color doesn't really fit with the rest of the composition. You can quickly change this by setting the generator to use a different composite mode.

8   In track V2 of the Timeline, Control-click the Custom Gradient layer, and choose Composite Mode > Screen.

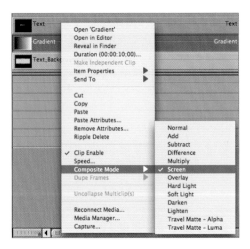

This last step creates a bright transparency effect for the gradient by turning increasingly darker areas of the image more and more transparent. This effect also interacts with the brightness of the animated background layer to create a slightly more dynamic effect than a simple reduction to the opacity setting would.

As you've seen, Final Cut Pro's Generators can be edited, transformed, and composited just like any other clip. In addition, they have control parameters of their own, which you can use to create customized text and graphics elements right from within Final Cut Pro.

Creating a Lower-Third Title

In the following exercises, you will create a simple lower-third title using the Lower 3rd generator.

1   In the 08_Project_Start tab, Option-double-click the Exercise 02 - Lower Thirds bin.

This opens the bin as a tab in the Browser. This bin contains the interview clip you'll be identifying with a lower-third title, as well as the sequence containing a finished version of the composition you are about to create.

2   Double-click the **Lower Third - Finished** sequence.

This title is even simpler than the one in the previous exercise. However, it uses a single generator to create one of the most fundamental titling elements you'll use.

In many shows, primarily documentaries, corporate communications videos, and newscasts, new speakers are typically introduced with a lower-third title (a title located in the lower third of the screen), which typically identifies the name of the speaker and his or her title.

Final Cut Pro has a dedicated generator that serves this purpose, with numerous customization options you can use to match the look of your lower-third titles to the graphic style used by the rest of your sequence.

Assembling a Lower-Third Composition

As always, putting together a graphics effect begins with assembling the basic clips used within the composition.

1   In the Browser, double-click the **Lower Third - Beginning** sequence to open it.

    This sequence contains the background clip you'll be using as the basis for your title.

2   Play the sequence in the Viewer.

    It's a typical talking head.

Next, you're going to superimpose a Lower 3rd generator over the interview clip you just added.

3 In the Viewer, click the Video tab, and choose Text > Lower 3rd from the Generator pop-up menu.

The first thing you can see is that, unlike the text generator you used previously, the Lower 3rd generator has two text fields, and sure enough, they're located in the lower third of the video frame.

4 From the View pop-up menu at the top of the Viewer, choose Show Overlays, then choose Show Title Safe, if necessary.

No matter what video format your sequence is set up to use, the Lower 3rd generator automatically respects the Title Safe overlay. For now, turn off the Title Safe overlay.

Sample Text 1
Sample Text 2

Because it's difficult to change a generator's parameters while also viewing the results, you should edit this generator into the sequence first, then open it back up in the Viewer as a sequence clip.

5   Move the playhead to the beginning of the sequence, then press F12 to edit the Lower 3rd generator into the sequence.

6   In the Timeline, double-click the Text generator to open it into the Viewer. Make sure to keep the playhead over the generator in the Timeline.

By default, the Lower 3rd generator displays the words *Sample Text 1* and *Sample Text 2* as white text against a black background. Clearly, this needs to change.

7   In the Viewer, click the Controls tab to expose the Lower 3rd generator's parameters.

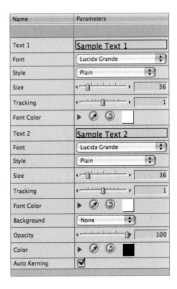

8   Click the Text 1 field. Type *Charlene Piralta* to replace the previous text.

Typically, the Text 1 field contains the speaker's name.

9   Click the Text 2 field, and type *Novice Dive*r as the speaker's title.

After you've made these changes, the text updates in the Canvas.

The resulting title is functional, if ugly. Next, you'll customize some additional parameters to make this look more professional.

TIP ▶ Press Return to make the text update immediately after you type something new into one of the Lower 3rd generator's Text fields.

Customizing the Lower-Third Generator

One of the guiding principles of design is to create interesting contrast between different elements within a composition. Leaving both titles the same size makes the title unclear because neither piece of information has priority. Styling the name and title a little differently adds this much-needed design contrast between both items of information, in this case making the name jump out at the viewer as the more important piece of information.

1 Set the Font parameters of both Text 1 and Text 2 to Futura.

TIP ▶ Futura is an excellent font to use for titling. It's bold and easy to read, with no thin lines to cause noise.

2 To make the name stand out as the dominant title, set the Style parameter to Bold, leave the Text 1 Size parameter at 36, and set Tracking to 6.

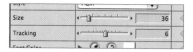

3 Change the color of Text 1 by clicking its Font Color control.

4 In the color picker, set the color to a light gray by dragging the Intensity slider about one-fourth of the way from the top. Click OK.

5 To maintain the visual contrast between the name and title, set the Text 2
Size parameter to 29, and set its Tracking parameter to 6.

To add further contrast, leave the title text the default color of white.

Next, you'll add a translucent background using the Background, Opacity,
and Color parameters.

6 Turn on the Lower 3rd's background by choosing Solid from the
Background pop-up menu.

A solid rectangle appears behind the Lower 3rd text, with a default color
of black. In this case, the solid background is distracting, but you can minimize this effect by making the background translucent using the Opacity
parameter.

7 Set Opacity to 35.

8   Click the Color control. In the color picker, select a deep, dark blue by clicking the edge of the blue area in the Hue control and then moving down the Intensity slider near the bottom of its range.

9   Click OK.

Now this title is a more typically styled lower third. Unfortunately, the letterboxing in the clip is running into the bottom of the title.

You can use the Center parameter in the Motion tab to move the title up.

10 In the Viewer, click the Motion tab, and change the Center parameter to *0,* *–36* to move up the Lower 3rd generator.

Now that the appearance of the lower third title is complete, the last thing to do is change the title timing so it appears and disappears at the appropriate times.

It's an accepted convention to wait until an individual has been onscreen for a few moments before giving their name in a title, so the first thing you'll do is to trim the In point of the title.

11 Play the **Charlene_Interview.mov** clip to find the beginning of the word "Experience." Then park the playhead at that frame in the Timeline, which makes it easy to snap the In point of the Lower 3rd title to that frame.

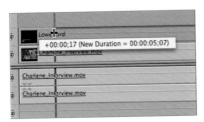

Next, you want to find a good Out point for the title.

TIP One method for determining a good duration for a title is to time how long it takes you to read it quickly three times.

12 With the playhead at the beginning of the title's new In point, play through the clip until you determine a good Out point.

In this example, the end of the word "Jamaica" seems to be a good place for the title to stop.

13 Stop the playhead at an appropriate place, and trim the Lower 3rd title's Out point to match it.

Lastly, it'll add polish to make the title fade in and out, as opposed to cutting. You'll do this by using the Opacity overlays in the Timeline.

14 Click the Clip Overlays button to display the Opacity and Level overlays in the Timeline.

15 Move the pointer directly over the Lower 3rd generator's Opacity overlay in track V2, and press the Option key down so that the pointer turns into the Pen tool. When the Pen tool appears, while still pressing Option, click the overlay to create keyframes.

Create two keyframes at the beginning of the title (with about 12 frames between the first and second frames), and two more at the end. Then drag the first and last keyframes all the way to the bottom (the Opacity tooltip should read 0) to make the clip fade in and out.

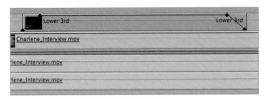

You're finished! Play the clip to see your title in action.

There are many other ways you could customize a Lower 3rd generator to suit the needs of your program, including using other generators or imported graphics as a background, instead of the built-in background controls, adding filters for different looks, or animating them to bring them on and off the screen.

Creating Subtitles

In the next few exercises, you'll use the outline text generator to create subtitles. In the process, you'll learn how to create subtitles that read well against any background; create a title template clip you can use as a basis for creating a large number of subtitles; and optimize a title's quality when manipulating its Motion parameters.

By now, you've probably guessed that the way to create subtitles in Final Cut Pro is by superimposing text generators above the clips with the corresponding dialogue. The outline text generator is ideal for this purpose, because a black outline around white text ensures your subtitles are legible regardless of the lightness or darkness of the image in the background.

1   In the 08_Project_Start tab, Option-double-click the Exercise 03 - Subtitles bin to open it into its own tab in the Browser, and then double-click the **Subtitles - Beginning** sequence to open it into the Timeline and Canvas.

A clip named **diving_interview.mov** has already been edited into the sequence. This clip contains two lines of dialogue for which you'll be creating subtitles.

2   Play through the clip, locating and placing markers for the two lines the diver speaks ("That was amazing" and "It really was").

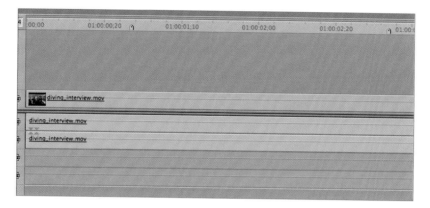

3   In the Viewer, click the Video tab, and choose Text > Outline Text to create a new title.

Next, you'll edit this title into the sequence so, while you make changes, you can see the subtitle superimposed against the video.

4   In the Timeline, move the playhead to a frame between the two markers you placed in step 2.

5   Press Control-A, or choose Mark > Mark to Markers to define In and Out points that match the duration of the first line of dialogue.

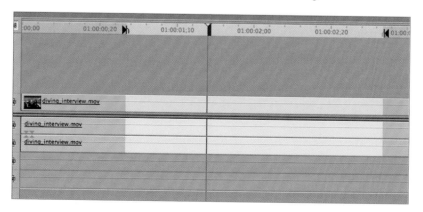

6   Press F12 to edit the title into the Timeline with a Superimpose edit.

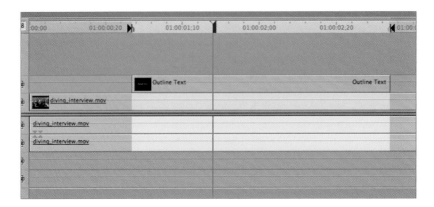

7   Double-click the text generator you just edited into your sequence to open it into the Viewer as a sequence clip. Click the Controls tab, and in the text field, type *That was amazing*.

By looking at the Canvas, you can instantly see that this title is too big. Next, you'll edit the outline text generator's parameters to make it fit properly into the frame.

8   Open the title into the Viewer, and click the Controls tab to open the outline text generator's parameters.

9   Set Size to *30*, and Line Width to *5*.

The text now looks more like a traditional subtitle, but you still have to reposition it at the bottom of the frame.

10   In the Canvas, turn on Image+Wireframe in the View pop-up menu.

11   Click the Canvas to select the top layer (in this case, the outline text generator). Hold down the Shift key to constrain the layer's movement vertically, and drag the clip down to the bottom of the frame, just above the bottom letterbox.

Now that you've defined a style for the first title, you'll want to save this style as a template to use in subsequent titles.

Saving a Title as a Template

You can save multiple variations of Final Cut Pro's title generators as templates for future use. For example, if you were subtitling a conversation between two people, you could save two versions of the outline text generator: one with a white text color for the first speaker, and one with an orange text color for the second speaker. You could then edit copies of each one into the sequence as necessary so that the audience would know which speaker was talking.

In this exercise, you'll save the outline text generator you customized in the preceding section and reapply it for the next line of dialogue.

1   Drag the outline text clip from the Timeline or Viewer to the project tab in the Browser.

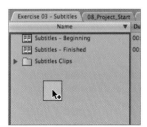

This has no effect on the outline text generator in your sequence, but it creates a copy of it as a new Browser clip. This copy is affiliated with the original generator clip, so changing the name of the duplicate will change the name of all other instances of that clip. However, each affiliate generator clip can have its own Controls parameters.

2   Click the name of the outline text, and change it to *Subtitle*.

Now anytime you need that particular configuration of the outline generator, you can customize and edit the Subtitle clip into your sequence. You'll go through this process to create the second subtitle.

> **TIP** ▶ You can copy text from a word processing program and paste it directly into the text field of any text generator.

3   Double-click the **Subtitle** clip to open it into the Viewer, and click the Controls tab to reveal its parameters.

4   In the Text parameter, replace the previous text with *It really was*.

5   Move the playhead to the end of the first **Subtitle** clip in the Timeline, and set an In point. Play through the clip to find the end of the line, "It really was," and set an Out point there.

6   Press F12 to edit the duplicated **Subtitle** generator clip from the Viewer into your sequence.

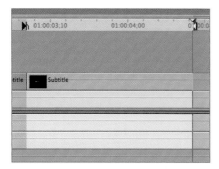

7   Play the sequence to see the subtitles play with the diver's dialogue.

In this way, you can continue playing through a sequence, customizing duplicates of the Subtitle clip in the Browser, and editing them into your program to subtitle it.

Fine-Tuning the Position of Text

Text that looks good in the Canvas but appears soft when output to video may be suffering from improper positioning. There are three reasons why this might be happening.

First, text may look soft in the Viewer or Canvas because the viewing scale is not set to 100 percent. At 100 percent, your text should look crisp and sharp. At any other percentage, your text is rescaled on the fly, and the results are not representative of the final output.

Second, your text may look poor when output to a broadcast display. Text almost always looks good on high-resolution, progressive-scan computer monitors. However, on an interlaced scanning television screen, text can be blurry or display artifacts because the chosen font is either too thin, too small, or has too much fine detail.

Finally, text you've repositioned using the Center parameter of the Motion settings may be softened as a result of Final Cut Pro's subpixel rendering. When repositioning text, you need to make sure that the Y field (the second field) that controls the clip's vertical positioning is a whole number (for example, 116 rather than 116.325).

Before signing off on any final text or subtitles, you should always evaluate it on an external video monitor.

Creating Window-Burned Timecode

In this exercise, you'll add a more utilitarian form of titling to a sequence: window-burned timecode. Window burns refer to the process of placing (or "burning") a small window of timecode over individual clips or over an entire edited program. This window is usually centered in the lower third of the frame, and it serves as a reference for all manner of postproduction activities.

Traditionally, window-burned timecode served as a reference to match sections of offline tapes with their online equivalent. Although Final Cut Pro has automated the offline/online workflow, and also has numerous other timecode display tools (the Timecode Overlays in the display pop-up menu of the Viewer and Canvas) that make this less important, there are still times when you need to output window-burned timecode to tape or DVD.

For example, if you're handing a copy of your project to a composer or sound designer, they typically want a window-burned timecode that they (and you) can use as a reference while synchronizing their work to your sequence. Unfortunately, the timecode overlays display timecode only in the Viewer and Canvas, and they don't output timecode to movies you export from Final Cut Pro, whether as a movie file or when printing or editing to tape. However, the Timecode Reader filter allows you to create a window burn that is output along with your program.

1   In the 08_Project_Start tab, Option-double-click the Exercise 04 - Timecode Burn bin.

    The bin opens as another tab in the Browser. This bin contains a sequence used in this exercise.

2   Double-click the **Edited Program** sequence.

3   If the entire sequence isn't immediately visible, click the Timeline window and press Shift-Z to fit all the clips in the sequence to the width of the Timeline.

4   In the View menu at the top of the Canvas, choose Show Timecode Overlays so you can see the timecode in each clip.

If you scrub around the sequence, you can see that this is a simple sequence of 11 clips, each with embedded timecode. In the following exercises, you'll learn two methods for adding window-burned timecode to a sequence in preparation for output.

Adding a Window Burn to Display the Timecode of Individual Clips
In this exercise, you'll use the Timecode Reader filter to display the timecode of each individual clip in your program. This process is useful if you need to have a reference of the source tape for each individual clip, and it's especially useful when you're outputting a reference tape for an online conforming project.

1   In the Browser, select the **Edited Program** sequence, and press Option-D to duplicate it.

2   Double-click the newly duplicated sequence (now named **Edited Program Copy**) to open it in the Timeline and Canvas. If necessary, press Shift-Z to fit its entire duration into the current width of the Timeline.

3   In the Browser, click the Effects tab and open the Video Filters bin by clicking its disclosure triangle.

4   Open the Video bin.

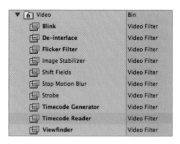

This is where the Timecode Reader and Timecode Generator filters are located. To create a timecode window burn that displays the timecode of each clip in a program, you need to apply the Timecode Reader filter to each clip in its sequence.

5   Double-click the Timecode Reader filter to open it into the Viewer without applying it to a clip.

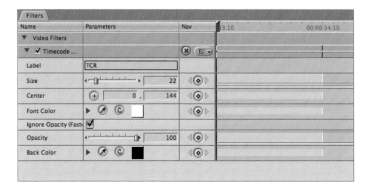

Despite its numerous parameters, the Timecode Reader filter is pretty simple. The most important parameters allow you to change the location of the timecode window (if your program is letterboxed, for example, you might use the Center parameter to move down the timecode in order to get it completely out of the way of the image) or to customize the way it looks. In general, the default settings are fine. It's hard to get more legible than white text on a black background, and leaving the background color solid makes the filter fast to render.

If anything, you might consider changing the Font Color to a light gray, so that it's not so bright in a dark screening or editing room, but that's a matter of personal preference. If you are going to change any of the settings, make changes to a blank filter opened into the Viewer, and then add the modified filter to all the clips in the sequence.

6 In the Filters tab, click the Font Color control.

7 In the color picker, drag down the Intensity slider about a quarter of the way to make the color slightly gray.

8 In preparation for applying this filter, select all of the clips in the sequence. (With the Selection tool, drag a bounding box over every clip in the sequence.)

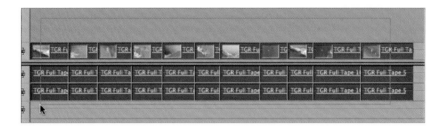

9 To add the modified version of the Timecode Reader filter, drag it by its name from the Viewer onto any of the selected clips in the sequence.

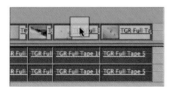

The filter is now added to each clip of the sequence. Scrubbing through the sequence should reveal a timecode window at the bottom of each clip. Notice that at each edit point, the displayed timecode changes to match the timecode of each clip. With the timecode overlays turned on in the View menu of the Canvas, you can also see that the timecode window being generated by the Timecode Reader filter matches the timecode of each clip.

At this point, you can output this sequence as a QuickTime movie in preparation for burning to DVD, or to tape using the Print or Edit to Tape commands.

Adding a Window Burn to Display the Timecode of a Sequence

In this exercise, you'll use the same Timecode Reader filter to display the time-code of the program itself. This is useful if you need to provide a copy of your program so that a composer, sound designer, or effects artist can reference your program's overall timing.

This method involves nesting your program's sequence inside another sequence, expressly for the purpose of adding the Timecode Reader filter to the sequence itself.

1   Click the 08_Project_Start tab in the Browser and press Command-N to create a new sequence.

2   When the new sequence appears in the Browser, rename it *Window-burn Output*, and press Return.

3   Double-click the *Window-burn Output* sequence to open it into the Timeline and Canvas.

4   Drag the **Edited Program** sequence from the Exercise 04 - Timecode Burn
    bin to the beginning of the **Window-burn Output** sequence. Make sure that
    the In point of the nested sequence is at the very beginning.

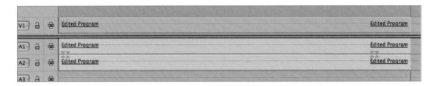

5   In the Browser, click the Effects tab. The Video bin should still be open.

6   Drag the Timecode Reader filter onto the **Edited Program** nested sequence
    in the Timeline.

7   Turn off the timecode overlays in the Canvas so you can see the unob-
    structed timecode window.

    Scrubbing through the Timeline should now show a window burn in the
    Canvas that mirrors the timecode of the entire sequence, regardless of
    which clip is at the current position of the playhead.

TIP You can also use the Timecode generator filter to display new timecode values and to change the format of the newly displayed timecode. The format of the timecode displayed by the Timecode generator can either be drop or non-drop, or even feet and frames. This timecode is generated by the filter and has no connection to the timecode in your sequence.

As long as you don't change the In or Out point of the nested sequence, it will grow or shrink as you re-edit the original sequence. As a result, you can continue to use the **Window-burn Output** sequence to output a window-burn version of your program regardless of what changes are made to the original sequence.

Lesson Review

1. What is one way to create a new generator?
2. Where are the parameters located for customizing each generator?
3. What are the two ways you can move the text in a text generator?
4. What's a good way to determine the duration for a title?
5. What makes a font good for use in a video title?
6. Which generator is good for use as a subtitle?
7. Which filter can be used to create window burns?

Answers

1. Choose one from the Generators pop-up in the Viewer.
2. The Controls tab in the Viewer.
3. Change the Origin parameter, or move the entire generator with the Center parameter in the Motion tab.
4. Time yourself reading the title three times fast.
5. Video fonts should be fairly bold, with no thin lines, and no fine details.
6. The Outline Text generator.
7. The Timecode Reader filter.

9

Lesson Files   Lessons > Lesson_09 > 09_Project_Start

Media   Media > Lesson_09_Media

Time   This lesson takes approximately 60 minutes to complete.

Goals   Identify good footage for keying

Use the Chroma Keyer filter to create a transparent matte

Modify the Chroma Keyer filter parameters over time

Combine a foreground and background to make a composite

Fine-tune a key through thinning, softening, and enhancing edges

Apply color smoothing to DV footage before keying

Apply spill suppression to eliminate unwanted remnants

Eliminate unwanted edge elements with a garbage matte

Lesson 9
Keying

The Color Key is one of the most powerful and most commonly used tools in your compositing arsenal. It allows you to isolate (or *matte*) a foreground subject from its background and combine it with a different shot (often referred to as a *plate*). The key effect works by identifying all of the pixels of a certain color and making them transparent, so only the remaining pixels are visible. This is how Superman can appear to fly, or how a dinosaur can appear in the same shot as real actors.

The color used for keying is typically green or blue. This is because the most common subject is a human being, and human skin color falls on the opposite side of the color wheel from green and blue. But a key can be created from nearly any solid color. For example, if you were shooting a product shot of a green car, you might place it against a solid red background. Because there is nearly no overlap between green and red, Final Cut Pro would easily isolate all of the red pixels, leaving the green car to be composited onto a mountaintop, inside a volcano, or wherever you desire.

Identifying Good Source Footage

Keying is a very specialized craft. You can produce good results only when you start with shots that have been photographed against a solid background of a particular color expressly for the purpose of *pulling* a key. Although Final Cut Pro's keying tools are robust, it takes a properly shot source image to extract a clean matte and pull a successful key.

If the background color is inconsistent for some reason (such as improper lighting or a mix of paint types) or if it doesn't completely surround the subject, it may be impossible to pull a proper key. In these cases, the only solution is to painstakingly paint the matte by hand, frame by frame, in a rotoscoping tool such as Shake or Commotion.

Good source footage

Bad source footage

Well-shot footage for keying (sometimes referred to as green screen or blue screen footage) must also be shot and captured on a tape format with extremely high color fidelity. Unfortunately, standard DV does not qualify. One of the ways that DV compresses images is by throwing out a great deal of color information. This works great in most situations because our eyes are far more sensitive to gradations of light and dark than they are to nuances of hue. But when Final Cut Pro examines each pixel to identify whether it is green (and therefore part of the background) or not green (and so part of the subject), DV's true colors (or lack thereof) come out.

Formats that are adequate for creating a good key include the following:

- ▶ Uncompressed Standard Definition (SD) video
- ▶ High Data Rate M-JPEG compressed analog video
- ▶ DVCPRO-50
- ▶ HDCAM
- ▶ DVCPRO-HD

Formats that don't lend themselves to a good key include the following:

- ▶ MiniDV
- ▶ DVCAM
- ▶ DVCPRO-25

If you try to key footage shot in one of these formats, you will find that the edges of the key are prone to jagged edges and aliasing.

 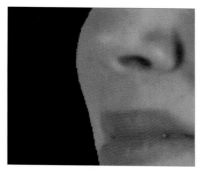

Basic Keying

When working with good source footage, performing a basic key in Final Cut Pro is very easy.

1   Open Lesson_09 > **09_Project_Start**.

2   The sequence **Cave Key** should open in the Timeline. If it doesn't, double-click it in the Browser to open it.

3   Select the clip **CU K Looks Back D_18_6B_8** and choose Effects > Video Filters > Key > Chroma Keyer to apply a Chroma Key filter.

Although nothing appears to change, the filter has been applied.

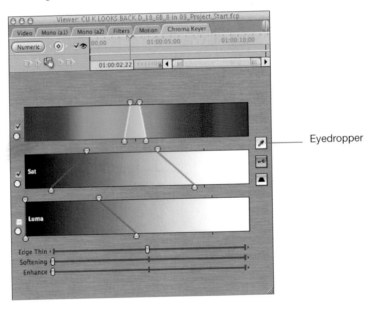

Eyedropper

4   Open the clip into the Viewer, click the Chroma Keyer tab, and choose the eyedropper at the right of the window.

5 Use the eyedropper to select a green spot in the Canvas. Click just one spot—don't drag.

Before   After

Immediately you should see that any area in the picture with the same color as the one you selected automatically becomes transparent and appears black. If there are still significant areas of green that need to be keyed, add to the selection as follows.

6 Choose the eyedropper again.

7 Press Shift and choose another green spot in the Canvas.

When you press Shift, a tiny + appears next to the eyedropper cursor. You can Shift-click as many times as necessary until nearly all of the green has been selected.

Alternatively, you can adjust the Color, Sat, and Luma bars in the Chroma Keyer filter. The diagonal lines across the bars indicate what areas will be keyed.

By dragging the button at the top of the line, you adjust the range of color, saturation, or luminance that will be keyed. By adjusting the bottom of the bars, you modify the softness, or tolerance, with which the effect is applied. Be careful not to include any areas of the subject in your selection.

If the edges of your key are still green or jagged, don't worry. You'll continue to clean up and finalize the effect now.

Tools for Finessing the Key

Final Cut Pro has several tools that help you clean up your rough key. Two of them are the Key icon and the Invert button.

1   Click the Key icon on the right side of the Chroma Keyer window (below the eyedropper).

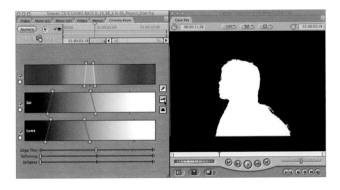

A black-and-white image appears in the Canvas. This image is the matte information. Black areas are transparent, and white areas are opaque. The Key icon itself changes color to a black-and-white icon to let you know you are looking only at the matte.

2   Click the Key icon again.

The Key icon now turns blue. This indicates that the keying effect is temporarily disabled so you can view your original source image.

3   Click the Key icon a third time.

This returns you to the starting state, which shows your final output. The matted area is transparent, and the subject is opaque.

4   Click the Invert icon (directly below the Key icon).

The Invert icon temporarily makes the transparent area opaque and the opaque area transparent. This can be helpful for viewing the matte edge when the subject is complex or blends with the background.

5   Click the Invert icon again to return to the normal state.

6   In the Canvas, choose View Options > Checkerboard 1.

Now, the Canvas background displays a checkerboard pattern, which will help you identify the matted area for clips where part of the subject is black. You can also set the background to white or an alternate checkerboard pattern.

Keyframing the Chroma Key Filter

Remember that all video images change over time. You may generate a perfect key on one frame, but 5 seconds into the shot, a shadow may appear that changes the background and requires different key settings. Fortunately, like all filters in Final Cut Pro, the Chroma Keyer filter can be keyframed.

1   Click the Numeric button in the Chroma Keyer tab.

    This brings the Filters tab to the front.

2   Toggle open the filter parameters by clicking the disclosure triangle at the left of the filter name.

Each of the controls in the Chroma Keyer window is represented here numerically. To keyframe individual parameters, you must first decide which parameters will need to be changed in your video to improve the key.

3   To add keyframes for each individual parameter, click the Insert/Delete Keyframe button to the right of each parameter name.

Or, if you are unsure which individual parameters need to be keyframed, you can keyframe all of the parameters simultaneously from the Chroma Keyer window.

4   Click the Visual button to return to the Chroma Keyer window.

In the upper-left corner of the window, there is a single Insert/Delete Keyframe button. This adds a keyframe to every filter parameter at the current playhead position.

Adding a Background

It's impossible to judge the quality of your key until you see how the foreground image works against the intended background. How convincingly the effect works will depend on many factors. Is the lighting the same in the two shots? Does the camera angle match? A successful key effect depends on the care and craft the production team uses when shooting the green screen shot and the corresponding plate.

Still, you can do your part by fine-tuning the key effect to best match the two shots together.

1   Drag **CU K LOOKS BACK D_18_6B_8** from track V1 in the Timeline up to V2.

2   Drag **background clip** from the Browser window and drop it onto track V1 directly beneath **CU K LOOKS BACK D_18_6B_8**.

You should immediately see the Canvas update, replacing the transparent areas with **background clip**.

3   In the Canvas, click the View Options button and choose Image+Wireframe.

4   Choose 25% from the Canvas Zoom control menu.

5   Select the background layer on track V1 in the Timeline.

6   In the Canvas, scale the background clip up by dragging one of the corners outward until the wireframe enclosing the cave image is larger than the screen. Dragging a corner without holding down any keys scales an image proportionately.

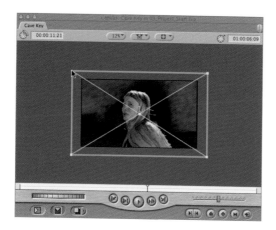

The wireframe in the Canvas has a number in the center to help identify which layer is selected. In this case, the clip on V1 is selected, so the number is 1.

7   Move the background clip to the left so that the right edge of the clip aligns with the right edge of the wireframe.

8   Park the playhead at around 01:00:05:20 and then select the clip of the actor in the Timeline, on track V2.

9   In the Canvas, move the clip to the right so the subject's shoulder is near the right edge of the frame. Note also that the wireframe now shows the number 2 in the center, since a clip on V2 is selected.

At this point the background and foreground are in approximately the right positions. But the lighting conditions are different. The foreground has a much cooler feel than the background, due to the different color temperature of the lighting used in each scene.

10 Apply a tint filter to **background clip** by selecting it and choosing Effects > Video Filters > Image Control > Tint.

Although this makes the clip black and white, you can adjust the filter's settings to bring some color back into the image so that it better matches the foreground.

11 Open **background clip** from the Timeline into the Viewer window and click the Filters tab.

12 Set Color to a very dark blue and set the Amount slider to about 70.

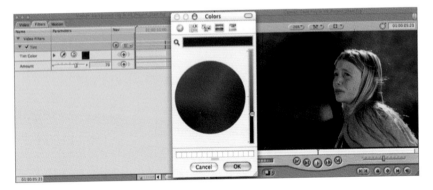

Finessing the Edges of the Matte

Now your key is almost complete. All that remains is fine-tuning the edges of the matte. There are several controls that allow you to make fine adjustments to the edges of your keyed matte, including edge thinning, softening, and enhancement.

1   Double-click **CU K LOOKS BACK D_18_6B_8** in the Timeline to load it into the Viewer.

2   Click the Chroma Keyer tab to bring it to the front.

At the bottom of the Chroma Keyer window are three sliders. The first is the Edge Thin slider. Edge thinning shrinks or enlarges the matte slightly by working only on the gray pixels at the edge of the matte, making them more or less transparent. As you experiment with these three sliders, turn the Saturation and Luma Limit controls on and off to get a feel for how these parameters all interact.

3   Drag the Edge Thin slider to the right.

If you drag too far, the edges of your subject will get too sharp.

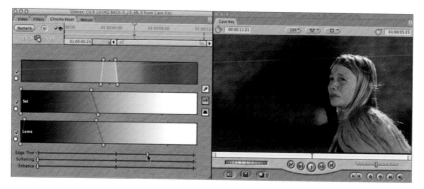

Once you get the edge of the matte as close to the subject as you can without edging into the subject itself, you may want to add a small amount of softening to blur the edges of the matte. If Softening is set too high, it can destroy the keying effect, but a tiny amount of blur may help the foreground blend into the background.

4 Click the tiny arrow on the right side of the Softening slider to add a subtle blur. Generally, one or two clicks are sufficient.

The third slider is Enhance. This effect controls the color of the semi-transparent pixels within your key. Typically, after the initial keying settings have eliminated nearly all of the key, a slight green halo remains around the subject. If you try to remove it with edge thinning, you may eat into the subject, and if you try to remove it through softening, the halo blurs but remains green. Enhance turns any semitransparent pixels in your matte the opposite color of the key color, to help cancel out the color of the key that may remain in any edges.

5 Drag the Enhance slider slightly to the right. Again, a little goes a long way.

Dragging it a small amount will have the effect of desaturating those areas of your matte. Dragging too far will add the opposite color. This is usually undesirable.

Using Spill Suppression

Sometimes the color of the background from the green or blue screen may reflect (or *spill*) onto shiny surfaces in the subject. This will not be affected by the Enhance slider because the pixels are not semitransparent. This spill color can be removed with the Spill Suppressor filter—choose Effects > Video Filters > Key > Spill Suppressor – Green.

Be sure to apply the Spill Suppressor filter *after* you apply the key filter, so the Spill Suppressor filter works on the end result of the keying process, not on the raw source image. In this lesson, the clip you have been manipulating does not have any visible spill, so this filter is not needed for this example.

Applying Color Smoothing

If you must attempt to pull a key with DV footage, you can improve the results of your key by using the Color Smoothing 4:1:1 filter.

This filter applies a slight horizontal blur to the color channels (leaving the luminance unmodified) to help smooth out difficult stepped edges in the color data, to make pulling a successful key easier.

Here is an example of how to use color smoothing to improve the keying of some DV footage.

1   Open the **Color smooth** sequence by double-clicking it in the Browser.

2   Select **Source.mov**. (This is a DV clip.)

3   Choose Effects > Video Filters > Key > Color Smoothing-4:1:1.

This filter has no parameters. (The 4:2:2 filter is for formats such as Motion JPEG, DVCPRO 50, HDCAM, or DVCPRO HD.)

4   Next, apply the Chroma Keyer filter.

It is very important that you apply the Color Smoothing filter before the Chroma Keyer, so that the Chroma Keyer works on the smoothed color edges.

5   After applying the Color Smoothing and Chroma Keyer filters, you can then create the matte, following the steps in this lesson from the beginning through the "Finessing the Edges of the Matte" section.

Notice how color smoothing improves the stair-stepping artifact that normally occurs when keying DV footage.

Without color smoothing   With color smoothing

Adding a Garbage Matte

Some footage requires the use of an additional matte to eliminate elements from the scene that are not part of the subject and cannot be removed through the Chroma Keyer filter alone.

Final Cut Pro's two Garbage Matte filters are designed to hide this "garbage" so that it will not be included in your final composite.

1   Open the **LS Key** sequence.

At the top of the frame, the edge of the green screen stage is visible.

2   Select **MS K STANDS_18_1B.4** in the Timeline.

3   Apply an eight-point garbage matte by choosing Effects > Video Filters > Matte > Eight Point Garbage Matte.

Numbered tags appear in the Canvas window, indicating the eight control points for the matte.

4   Open **MS K STANDS_18_1B.4** into the Viewer from the Timeline and click the Filters tab to bring it to the front.

Each of the eight control points is represented in the Filters tab. You can use all eight points to create a shape. Anything outside of the shape will be treated as transparent.

5   In the Filters tab, click Point 1.

View Mode	Preview	
	Corners	
Point 1	⊕	−960 ,	−540
Point 2	⊕	0 ,	−540
Point 3	⊕	960 ,	−540
Point 4	⊕	960 ,	0

6   In the Canvas, select a location in the green area near the upper-left corner.

The Canvas updates to show the change. The background clip is now visible in the upper-left corner.

7   In the Filters tab, click Point 2.

By default, Point 2 in the Canvas is midway across the top of the frame.

8   In the Canvas, click near the top center, in the green area, but safely above the girl's head.

If you click and hold, you can drag the new point around and see it update. Once you release the mouse, you will need to reselect the point control in the Filters tab to set a new point in the Canvas.

9   In the Filters tab, click Point 3.

By default, Point 3 in the Canvas is positioned at the upper-right corner of the frame.

10 In the Canvas, set the new position for the third control point near the upper-right corner, in the green area.

Your garbage matte is now complete.

11 The Chroma Keyer filter has already been applied to this clip. Activate the Chroma Keyer filter by checking its box in the Filters tab. (The necessary settings have already been applied.)

12 Hide the point controls in the Canvas by going to the Garbage Matte controls in the Filters tab in the Viewer and setting View Mode to Final.

The key for this clip is now complete. In this example, the order of the Chroma Keyer and Garbage Matte filters in the Filters tab do not affect the final composite. However, as you use garbage mattes for other effects, such as blurs, the order of the filters does matter. Experiment with the filter order to see what works best for you.

The Garbage Matte filters offer additional controls in case the shape you need to matte out is more complex. Additionally, you can keyframe the Garbage Matte parameters in the event that the shape of the object that needs to be matted out changes over time.

Going Beyond the Basics

This lesson covered simple keying with only one foreground subject and one background plate. However, you can also easily combine many different elements, each photographed separately, into a single composited scene in Final Cut Pro. The software has several other keying and matting tools designed for specific compositing needs.

If there is any camera movement during the shot, keying gets a lot more complicated. If the camera movement can be recorded using a motion-control camera rig, the same movement can be applied to each shot, and you can key and composite the elements in Final Cut Pro just like you would with a static shot. Alternatively, tracking marks can be applied onto the green screen, and then using a tool like Apple's Shake you can record the movement and apply it digitally to a new computer-generated background element. Of course, the tracking marks also have to be manually removed from the green screen using a series of garbage mattes.

The power of keying is one of the most dazzling of all special effects. It is used commonly in major motion pictures to allow people to appear to frolic with dinosaurs or ghosts; training and educational films use keying to describe complex machinery; and television newscasts routinely show their weather forecasters standing in front of weather maps keyed with green screens.

As you master the various keying and matting tools in Final Cut Pro, you will undoubtedly come up with many new uses for this powerful effect.

Lesson Review

1. Describe the keying process.
2. When is keying most successful?
3. When keying, how do you adjust for visual changes in a scene?
4. How do you reduce stair-stepping artifacts?
5. Name tools used to refine a matte in Final Cut Pro.
6. How are unwanted elements removed from a scene?

Answers

1. Keying involves applying the Chroma Keyer filter to mask a foreground subject from the background.
2. Keying is most successful when the source footage is filmed against a solid background, such as a green screen or blue screen.
3. Add keyframes to the Chroma Keyer parameters in the Filters tab to accommodate changing lighting and shading conditions that occur across multiple frames.
4. Use the Color Smoothing key filter to compensate for the stair-stepping artifact that occurs when keying DV footage.
5. Fine-tune the matte using the Edge Thin, Softening, and Enhance controls.
6. Create a garbage matte to eliminate unwanted elements from a scene.

Color Correction

10

Lesson 10
Evaluating Video Images

Color correction, the process of evaluating and enhancing the color and brightness of an image, is one of the final stages of post-production. A well-corrected sequence looks good, provides continuity from shot-to-shot and scene-to-scene, supports the direction and mood of the sequence, and meets certain brightness and color requirements to be suitable for broadcast. Poorly corrected images not only look bad, they are unsuitable for broadcast and can even bleed into the audio signal of the program, creating distortion.

In this lesson, you will learn the most fundamental skill required for color correction: how to evaluate a video image. You'll learn the three main ways to evaluate an image: a quick method known as range checking, a detailed evaluation using the Final Cut Pro video scopes, and an old-fashioned reality check—viewing the image on an external monitor. You'll spend the most of your time learning the video scopes, since they're the most useful tools for detailed image analysis.

Later, in Lessons 11 through 14, you'll use the various color-correction tools available in Final Cut Pro, but always in conjunction with one or more video scopes.

Identifying the Attributes of a Video Image

Start out by taking a look at the information you use to assess a video image. Final Cut Pro displays two types of information about a video image: luminance and chrominance.

Luminance

The *luminance* of a video image describes the brightness levels of the pixels that constitute the image. These levels range from the darkest black through various shades of gray to the brightest white.

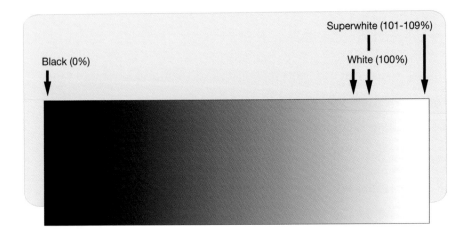

In Final Cut Pro, the range of possible luminance levels from black to white is represented by a percentage on a scale, with pure black at 0 percent and pure white at 100 percent. Additionally, there is a small range of bright whites, known as superwhite, which ranges from 100 percent up to 109 percent. When you read luminance levels in a video scope in Final Cut Pro, every pixel that makes up the image is represented as a percentage somewhere on this scale.

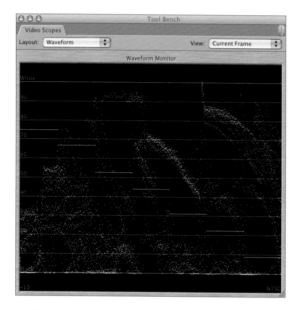

Luminance levels represented in the Waveform Monitor

Chrominance

In Final Cut Pro, color information is usually represented using a color wheel model. The color wheel can be found in the color-correction filters, the OS X color picker (used to assign color for various generators, including text), and even, in abstract form, in the video scopes.

The color wheel is simply a circular representation that is capable of displaying every possible color.

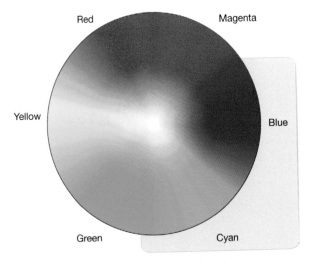

A color wheel shows the range of possible colors.

The main benefit of the color wheel model is that it is an objective way to describe color. When referring to color, people tend to use fairly subjective words. For instance, you may say that something is a *warm red* or *navy blue*. These references may have different meanings to different people. The color wheel, on the other hand, provides a consistent, quantifiable way to describe virtually any color in the spectrum.

Chrominance is the term used to describe the color of an image, and it can be broken down into two parameters: hue and saturation.

Hue

Hue is what we think of as an actual color, such as red or blue. It is represented on a color wheel as a location somewhere *around* the wheel. Any color hue can be represented as an angle on this wheel.

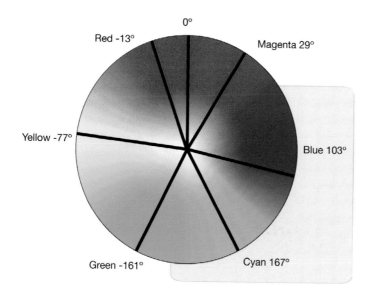

Saturation

Saturation describes the intensity of the color, whether it's bright or pale. It is represented on a color wheel as a point along a radius, from the center of the wheel to the outer rim.

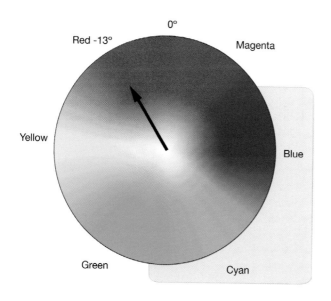

The closer to the outer rim of the wheel, the more intense, or saturated, a color is. The closer to the center, the paler it becomes. For example, if the angle (hue) of a color is red, then different levels of saturation include everything from light pink to bright red. At the very center of the wheel is no color at all—no hue or saturation.

Keeping Brightness and Color "Legal"

Video images need to meet certain brightness and color requirements to be suitable for broadcast—this is referred to as being *broadcast legal*. For example, images that are too bright, or have colors that are too saturated, may exhibit undesirable artifacts when played back or broadcast using equipment that doesn't support such high levels.

As a result, if an image falls outside of these standards, it may be rejected by a network or broadcast facility. Even if you do not plan on broadcasting your program, you should still adhere to these broadcast standards.

Final Cut Pro provides several methods of monitoring the levels of luminance and chrominance of the images in your sequences. In the Waveform Monitor, which displays a graph of the luminance levels in an image against a numeric scale, 100 percent is often labeled simply as White and 0 percent as Black.

> **TIP**   Check with the intended broadcast facility for its specific standards.

When you color correct in Final Cut Pro, you keep the luminance *legal* by keeping the darkest black levels no lower then 0 percent and the brightest white levels no higher than 100 percent. If pixels of white appear in the superwhite range (above 100 percent), they are considered unsafe for broadcast.

Remember that within Final Cut Pro, all images are digital. As a result, all video signals are displayed by the Final Cut Pro video scopes using a digital

scale, from 0 to 100 percent. As a result, the basic principle of keeping all luminance levels between 0 and 100 percent is appropriate regardless of whether
your video originated via a digital or analog format, and regardless of whether
it's NTSC or PAL. In all cases, the proper black level to set when working
within Final Cut Pro is 0 percent.

When you go back out to the analog world, such as when you output to a video
format like Beta SP or 3/4-inch, it becomes important to know that NTSC has
a black level standard of 7.5 IRE, and PAL has a black level standard of 0 IRE.
(In an interesting twist, NTSC in Japan has a black level standard of 0 IRE
also.) Typically, the analog black level that's output is determined by the video
interface you happen to be using. (Many are switchable, although some are
not.) Regardless of the source or destination format, in Final Cut Pro, black
is represented by a digital value of 0 percent.

> **NOTE** ▶ IRE is a measure of voltage in the video signal. This is a term
> used in the analog world to evaluate the luminance levels of the video.
> This term is not used in Final Cut Pro, because only luminance level
> percentages are used for digital readings.

Although monitoring luminance as you work is extremely important, there
are also broadcast-legal considerations for color saturation. As you explore the
Vectorscope later in this lesson, you will learn more about the standards for
legal color.

Using Range Checking

When you need only a quick check of whether a video is broadcast legal, Final
Cut Pro gives you a great option: Range Check. Available as an overlay in the
Viewer or Canvas, these graphical notes tell you at a glance whether there are
any problems with luminance levels or saturation.

When you need more detailed information about the image, that's where the
Final Cut Pro video scopes come in. You start out by examining the Range
Check option, and then go into more detail about the image by looking into
the video scopes.

Range Checking Luminance

As you learned earlier in this lesson, broadcast facilities set the maximum legal luminance at 100 percent. The superwhite range of luminance between 100 percent and 109 percent might just as well be called *illegal white*, because white levels in this range are not broadcast safe.

In this exercise, you will spot-check your image for problem white areas—areas that are too bright for broadcast. You'll notice that the Range Check option flags these areas with green or red *zebra stripes* as an overlay in the Canvas or Viewer.

NOTE ▶ The Range Check option will display its zebra pattern at the current playhead position when the clip is paused or stopped. Scrub your playhead to different areas within the clip to view how your white levels change.

1   Open Lesson_10 > **10_Project_Start.**

2   Control-click the Timeline ruler.

At the bottom of the shortcut menu is a list of Timeline markers. Choosing a marker's name from this menu is a quick way to jump to that spot in the Timeline.

3   Choose **cu face** from the shortcut menu to navigate to this clip.

This clip is a good one to look at first because its luminance levels are already broadcast legal.

4   Make sure the Canvas or Timeline window is active, then choose View > Range Check > Excess Luma. A new overlay appears in the Canvas—a green circle with a checkmark.

> **NOTE ▶** You can choose different Range Check settings for the Viewer and the Canvas, depending on which window is active when you choose an option from the Range Check submenu.

The green checkmark in the Canvas indicates that there are no brightness levels above 90 percent in the image. It is broadcast legal, with room to spare.

5   Control-click the Timeline ruler and choose the clip **marginal luminance** from the shortcut menu.

Now you should see two new overlays. Near the top of the image is a green circle with a checkmark and a tiny arrow.

This overlay indicates that the image is broadcast legal and all luminance levels are below 100 percent. Additionally, it indicates that the brightest areas of the frame are between 90 percent and 100 percent.

You should also see zebra stripes, which are much like the diagonal stripes you find in many camera viewfinders that can check exposure. In this case, the zebra stripes are green, indicating that these areas of the video are between 90 percent and 100 percent.

6   Control-click the Timeline ruler and choose **excess luminance** from the shortcut menu.

Two new overlays appear: a yellow triangle with an exclamation point, and red zebra stripes.

The red overlays indicate that the video is not broadcast legal and that the values in the overlapping areas of the picture are above 100 percent. The green zebra patterns indicate areas of the image that are hovering between 90 and 100 percent. You will always see the red zebra pattern and the yellow exclamation point together, an indication that there is a problem and that the video is not broadcast safe.

Range Checking Saturation

In addition to range checking luminance, you can range check for saturation levels to see if any colors are too saturated for broadcast.

Choosing View > Range Check offers three options:

▶   Excess Luma: Checks for luminance levels that are above broadcast-legal standards

▶   Excess Chroma: Checks for saturation levels that are above broadcast-legal standards

▶   Both: Enables the checking of both luminance and chrominance levels that are above broadcast-legal standards

Excessive saturation is a particular problem in NTSC video, where red and yellow tend to bleed into surrounding colors, as well as produce a color ringing or buzzing effect when viewed on an external video monitor.

The Excess Chroma overlay is similar to Excess Luma; it also uses a yellow warning indicator and red zebra stripes—only this time, the indicators call out areas in the image that are above the broadcast-legal limit for saturation.

1   Control-click the Timeline ruler and choose **excess luminance** from the shortcut menu.

2   Choose View > Range Check > Excess Chroma.

Interestingly, the Range Check symbol changes to a green circle with a checkmark. Although this clip has unsafe luminance levels, it does have legal chroma levels. When you are range checking chroma, the green checkmark represents safe saturation levels.

3   Navigate to the clip **excess chrominance** in the Timeline.

This clip has a yellow caution icon, indicating that the clip has overly saturated areas and is not suitable for broadcast.

Although they may be difficult to see, red zebra stripes on the faces of a group of people in the center-left of the screen indicate that this is where the offending saturation levels lie.

To summarize, a green circle with a checkmark means the image is legal. The yellow warning icon and red zebra stripes mean the image contains illegal luma or chroma levels. If an image contains illegal levels of luma or chroma, you need to color correct it before you can submit it for broadcast.

Using the Video Scopes

Final Cut Pro has four video scopes, each with a specific purpose. In general, however, they are used to obtain a more objective view of the video image than the human eye provides. Having this impartial viewpoint is essential for adjusting the image to meet broadcast specifications, and for creating consistency in the visual texture, or *feel,* of the video when you're comparing different images and matching scenes.

The four video scopes in Final Cut Pro are the Waveform Monitor, the Vectorscope, the Parade scope, and the Histogram. Each scope displays different information about the video image—either its luminance, its chrominance, or a combination of the two.

Take a moment to open the Video Scopes window and look at the different scopes. One way to open the Video Scopes window is to choose from one of the window arrangement presets.

1   Move the playhead back to the clip **cu face**. (Control-click the Timeline ruler and choose **cu face** from the shortcut menu.)

2 Choose Window > Arrange > Color Correction.

The video scopes open as a tab in the Tool Bench window, and the other windows in Final Cut Pro automatically rearrange themselves to make room. Within the Video Scopes tab of the Tool Bench window, all four video scopes are displayed by default.

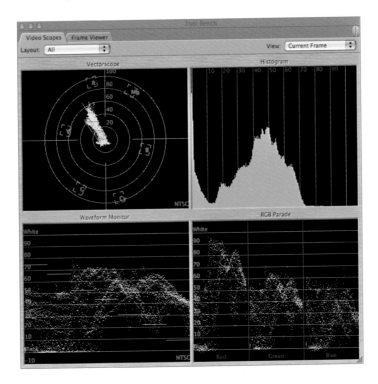

NOTE ▶ You can also open the video scopes display by choosing Tools > Video Scopes, although this option will not automatically rearrange the other windows.

3   In the Video Scopes window, make sure that the View pop-up menu is set to Current Frame. This ensures that the video scopes are reading the current image in the Canvas.

Notice the overlay of the various colored dots in each of the graphs in this window.

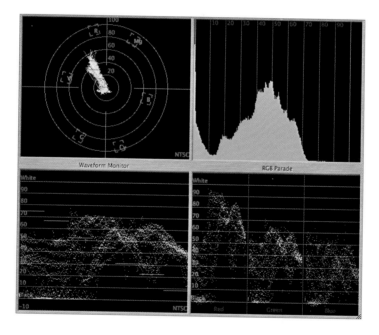

These dots constitute graphs in each of the video scopes, each of which represents the digital values of pixels from your image in a different way. Despite the differing representations, each represents the luminance (brightness levels) or chrominance (color levels) in your images.

4   Move your cursor over the four displays.

Notice that that in each one, a yellow line follows the cursor as it moves. A small window in the upper-right corner of each scope displays the percentage of luminance or chrominance that corresponds to the location of the cursor.

Once you learn to understand these scopes, you will use the cursor to quickly spot specific luminance and chrominance values in areas of the image.

Using the Waveform Monitor

Two of the Final Cut Pro video scopes, the Waveform Monitor and the Vectorscope, are used primarily to evaluate luminance and saturation to determine whether a video image is within broadcast standards.

Checking Luminance Levels with the Waveform Monitor

In this exercise, you will learn how the Waveform Monitor displays luminance levels and how to check an image to see if it falls within acceptable ranges.

1   In the Video Scopes window, choose Layout > Waveform to show just the Waveform Monitor.

2   Control-click the waveform display and make sure that Saturation is *not* selected in the shortcut menu.

3   From the View pop-up menu in the Video Scopes window, choose None.

Now you have an unobstructed view of the scale along the left of the Waveform Monitor. The effective range of the scale spans from –10 percent to 110 percent—in other words, below darkest black to superwhite. Look along the left side of the Waveform Monitor to view this scale. At 0 percent is a line labeled Black, and at 100 percent is a line labeled White.

NOTE ▶ There is a small range on the left side of the scale from 0 to –10 percent. For our purposes—checking luminance levels—0 percent is the bottom of the scale, and no blacks should fall below this line.

4   From the View pop-up menu in the Video Scopes window, choose Current Frame. The dots in the screen will reappear.

Although one of the primary goals of color correction is to make sure that blacks are at 0 percent and whites are no brighter than 100 percent, the scopes reveal much more information than that. In this image, you should notice that the dots in the graph rarely rise above 70 percent.

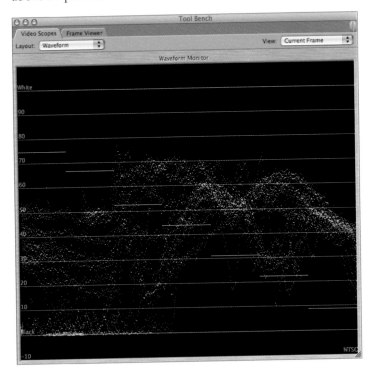

This makes sense because the image is not very bright, with diffuse shadows and no hot spots or reflections from direct sunlight. You may or may not have picked out this shot as a candidate for improved contrast based on the image itself, but the Waveform Monitor reveals that you have ample headroom in which to make such a correction.

Next, you'll see how the Waveform Monitor's display corresponds to a video image.

5   With the Timeline window active, press the down arrow key twice to go to the next clip in the Timeline, **Gradient**.

In the Canvas, the gradient clip has a clear transition from white to black, from left to right. Notice how the corresponding graph in the waveform display is a line that stretches diagonally from white to black, from left to right, matching the luminance of the image in the Canvas.

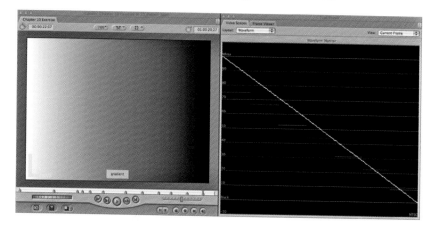

As you can see, the graph within the Waveform Monitor represents the digital percentage of luminance in an image, as scanned from left to right.

6   Control-click the Timeline ruler and choose **cu highlights** from the shortcut menu.

7   Turn off Range Check, and observe the spike at the right of the luminance graph.

8   Press the left arrow key for 30 frames, pausing briefly between each key-
stroke to let the Waveform Monitor update as you move backward in the
Canvas.

Notice how the spike corresponds to highlights on the right side of the
woman's face, and how the graph moves in unison with the camera's pan.
When the side of the woman's face goes off the frame, the rightmost spike
in the Waveform Monitor also disappears.

Binoculars

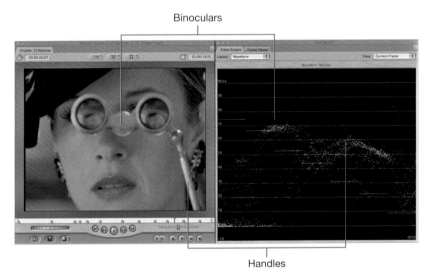

Handles

9   While looking at this frame, move the cursor over what is now the topmost dot in the Waveform Monitor to check the luminance level of the
highlight in the woman's binoculars.

A line follows the cursor up and down in the display. Look at the top right
corner to see the corresponding percentage level.

You can see that, although it's near the top, the brightest spot of this video falls just at 100 percent, safely within the broadcast standards for NTSC.

10 Move the cursor down to check the luminance levels of the darkest part of the frame, which in this case correspond to her dark black hat, which dips to the left of the frame, and the black earrings hanging from her right ear.

Notice that this is one of the darkest parts of this video frame, and nothing dips below 0 percent (black). When looking at only luminance in this scale, anything that should be black should be represented at this line. If the darkest part of the hair were higher than 0 percent, then what should be black would only look like a muddy gray.

11 Control-click the Timeline ruler and choose **winner** from the shortcut menu.

12 Move your cursor over to the top right corner of the Waveform Monitor at the spot of the highest luminance values. These white values top out at around 105 percent. You can use the cursor to pinpoint any parts of the image in this way.

These values represent the sky showing through the passageway, as you can see by comparing the image with the graph in the Waveform Monitor. In this case, the sky is above 100 percent in the Waveform Monitor and is not legal for broadcast.

13 Control-click the Timeline ruler and choose **clock** from the shortcut menu.

14 Move your cursor over the Waveform Monitor. Notice that the brightest area of this clip falls at about 91 percent, well under the legal maximum.

Further examination reveals that this clip has another issue that will be problematic when the video is played. The black levels of the image sit well above 0 percent. Visually, you will notice that the darkest areas of the image are "mushy" or grayish, instead of providing rich, deep tones.

Since the highlights are still relatively bright compared to the shadows, it might not be apparent that the shadows aren't at ideal levels simply by looking at the visuals. Once again, the Waveform Monitor shows that there's plenty of room for improvement, as most of these shadow areas are around 20 percent. To achieve the richest, deepest colors, the darkest parts of the image should hover just at 0 percent.

In order for the blacks in the `clock` clip to look more natural, they should be color corrected (in this case, darkened). Later, you will use the Waveform Monitor while color correcting to ensure that blacks are at 0 percent.

Using the Vectorscope

The Final Cut Pro Vectorscope is useful in a number of ways. One important function is monitoring the colors of the video primarily to determine whether saturation levels are broadcast legal.

The Vectorscope is a graph that represents information about the chrominance in the video. Using the Vectorscope, you can read the hue and saturation of the various elements of the frame. This information is handy when you're trying to match colors in different scenes. You can also use it to evaluate flesh tones to determine whether people appear realistic and natural, which can be tricky with the eye alone.

Reading Hue and Saturation in the Vectorscope

The first step in using the Vectorscope is getting to know how it correlates to the video image.

In this exercise, you will look at a test image to see how it is represented in the Vectorscope. This will familiarize you with how a video image is displayed in the Vectorscope; the test image will also serve as a guide to understanding broadcast standards for saturation levels.

1 In the Video Scopes window, choose Layout > Vectorscope.

2 Control-click the Vectorscope display and make sure that Targets is selected in the shortcut menu.

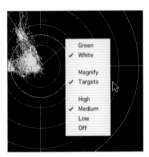

Before reading a video image, you should get familiar with this display. The circular shape is akin to the color wheel. You will also see six small, labeled pink boxes. These are *targets*, and they represent six hues in the wheel. The different mixes of these six colors represent the extent of the color palette with which you have to work.

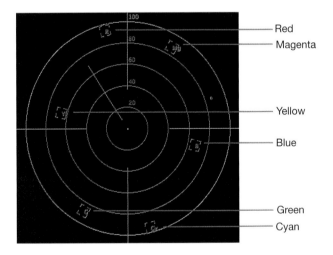

Colors in the video image are plotted on this circular graph. In a moment, you will study a test clip of color bars—but first, a little introduction on how to read color in this display. A color's location on the wheel depends on its hue and saturation. An orange color, for example, would be located in the Vectorscope somewhere between yellow and red, as orange is a mixture of those two.

3   Control-click the Timeline ruler and choose **Bars and Tone** from the shortcut menu to navigate to this clip in the Timeline.

The Vectorscope shows a number of crisscrossing lines. These lines, called *traces*, represent the colors in the sample image's color bars. Notice that they intersect in the six targets.

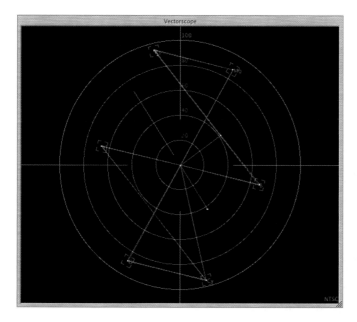

These traces all point to the center of the target boxes. Each trace intersects in the middle of its respective target. This particular test image is accurate, as the colors in the bars have an accurate hue (a specific angle around the wheel) and are as saturated as can be within broadcast-legal levels. If the traces were any farther outward (that is, closer to the perimeter), the color would be too saturated for broadcast.

4   Look at the colors of these bars on your monitor, preferably an external interlaced monitor.

These are as intense as colors should get in the video image. As you should notice, even broadcast-legal colors have issues when they are adjacent to other saturated colors. The edges between colors seem to vibrate. Although colors can be this vibrant, stay well under this color intensity, especially when vibrant colors are adjacent to one another, to avoid the harsh display that you see in this test image.

> **NOTE** ▶ The previous step refers specifically to viewing on an external NTSC or PAL monitor (or TV). The computer monitor is not subject to the limitations of NTSC or PAL video and, therefore, doesn't accurately display those video formats. In other words, an image that looks good on a computer monitor may not display properly on an interlaced NTSC or PAL monitor. If one of those video formats is your intended medium, always preview your work on an NTSC or PAL monitor. Also note that PAL uses a slightly different color bar test pattern, so the examples in this chapter are primarily applicable to NTSC monitors.

5   Control-click the Timeline ruler and choose **bad bars** from the shortcut menu to navigate to that clip.

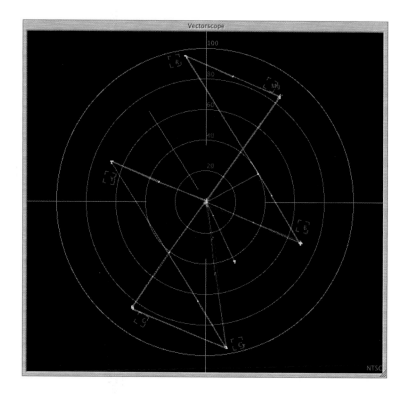

In the Vectorscope, these traces do not intersect in the target boxes as they did for the previous color bars image. Instead, they miss their respective targets. This indicates that these hues are out of phase. They do not accurately display the colors that they are supposed to represent.

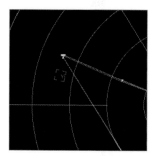

Checking Saturation Levels for Broadcast

The targets of the Vectorscope not only identify specific colors but also serve as a guide to ensure that saturation does not exceed broadcast standards. Just as you use the Waveform Monitor to check for legal luminance values, you can use the Vectorscope to check for legal chrominance.

Remember, the closer a color is to the perimeter of the color wheel, the more saturated it is. As a rule of thumb, video is legal as long as no color's saturation extends beyond the center of any color target.

1   Control-click the Timeline ruler and choose **excess luminance** from the shortcut menu.

Notice that no values extend beyond any of the color targets, although some traces come close to the red target. The traces that extend the farthest represent the yellow/orange coat.

2   Move the cursor over the Vectorscope to see an approximation of how close the saturation values of the red dress are to the closest color target, red. A circular line follows the cursor as you move it around the Vectorscope.

3   Move the cursor next to the dot that is the farthest away from the center. The dot will be between the yellow and red targets. This clip is marginal

for broadcast because the dots extend just past the nearest color target—in this case, yellow.

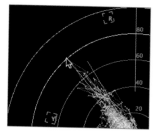

4   Control-click the Timeline ruler and choose **excess chrominance** from the shortcut menu.

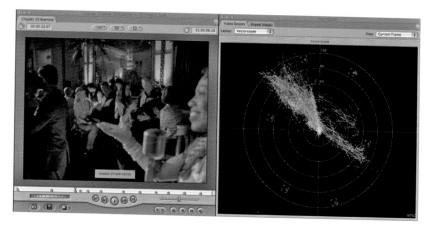

As the marker name indicates, this clip has values that extend not only beyond the closest target (red) but go well beyond the outer ring of the Vectorscope scale. This clip is far too saturated for broadcast and should be corrected to diminish the intensity of the color.

Identifying Individual Colors

So far, you have seen that a color is represented by an angle in the Vectorscope, and that the intensity of the color (saturation) is displayed as a distance from the center of the color wheel. Now you're going to look at how individual colors in a frame are represented in the Vectorscope. The following technique, which uses cropping to isolate parts of the frame, shows how you can evaluate individual elements of the frame. This technique is used throughout subsequent lessons on color correction to help identify and manipulate colors.

1   Control-click the Timeline ruler and choose **horse race** from the shortcut menu.

   The image has a wide variety of colors in the frame. The colors most readily identifiable in the Vectorscope are the greens of the grass at the top of the frame, and the browns of the horses and racetrack, clumping near the center of the Vectorscope and angled up towards the red target.

   The other colors in the jockeys' uniforms fall all over the place, so you may find it hard to pick out a specific color value you may want to use as a reference to make a correction.

   To get a sense of how to spot a particular color in the Vectorscope, you can use cropping to exclude everything from the image except the image you want to analyze.

2   In the Canvas, choose View > Image+Wireframe.

3   In the Canvas, click the image to select it. The wireframe overlay appears in the Canvas.

4   Select the Crop tool.

5   Crop the sides of the image until only the pink/magenta portion of the middle jockey's shirt is shown. To crop two sides at once, drag a corner of the wireframe.

6   In the Vectorscope, the relatively few spikes that remain now represent only the top of the shirt, and that the angle (hue) is a range of values between red and magenta, with the more saturated part of the shirt leaning slightly closer to red.

In other words, the top of the shirt is a little closer to red, even though it appears more magenta to the naked eye. The Vectorscope clarifies color distinctions that aren't immediately obvious.

Without cropping, you could see the whole picture. The traces for the single shirt were hidden in the overall display of the image. With cropping, you can get a fix on any part of the frame. As you continue, you will use this technique to help identify different elements of a frame and determine how an image should be color corrected. This technique can be especially handy when evaluating skin tone (color) in images with many similar values in the frame that make it difficult to discern the color of the skin itself.

Identifying Flesh Tones in the Vectorscope

One of the most important functions of the Vectorscope is to show you whether or not the flesh tones of people in the frame are colored realistically. Not surprisingly, people are extremely sensitive to the hue of skin, and even slight deviations can result in an image that is unsatisfactory.

For this reason, the Final Cut Pro Vectorscope has a special target, a line, that indicates the proper hue of people's skins. In this exercise, you'll learn to identify skin tones against this target.

1   Control-click the Timeline ruler and choose **gradient** from the shortcut menu.

There's only a single trace at the middle of the Vectorscope. This is because there's no color in the gradient. With no color, there's no saturation, and no graph in the Vectorscope.

You'll also notice that there's a target that appears as a diagonal line, falling between the yellow and red targets. This is the Flesh Tone line.

2   Control-click the Timeline ruler and choose **cu face** from the shortcut menu.

When the woman's face appears in the Canvas, you'll immediately notice a cluster of color values that fall about the Flesh Tone line.

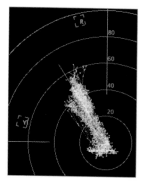

As you can see, this image is pretty much right on the money when it comes to the color of her face. The dominant colors all fall around the Flesh Tone line, with other minor spikes in the direction of yellow (the binoculars), red (her lipstick), and green (the background).

3   Control-click the Timeline ruler and choose **spectators** from the shortcut menu.

This image has substantially more variation in the frame, but there are many, many faces as well. If you look in the Vectorscope, a few things pop out. The first is a spike in towards the red target. This, most likely, corresponds to the woman's red dress, since it's the reddest thing in the picture.

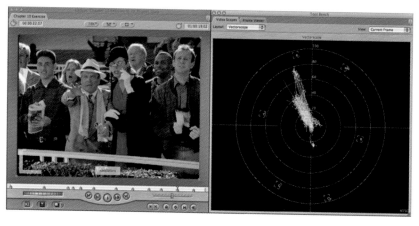

There's another large cluster of values that appears around the Flesh Tone line, and we can surmise from the number of faces in the frame that they probably correspond to the faces of the people in the stands. To prove this, you'll crop in on one of the faces to verify that the skin tones have the correct hue.

4 Click the image in the Canvas to select it. The wireframe overlay appears in the Canvas.

5 Select the Crop tool.

6 Crop the sides of the image until only the face of the man wearing the hat and scarf (to the left of the woman in red) is shown. To crop two sides at once, drag a corner of the wireframe.

As you can see in the Vectorscope, the remaining parts of the graph in the Vectorscope do indeed lie over the Flesh Tone target, and it appears correct.

Understanding the Histogram

The other two video scopes in Final Cut Pro, the Histogram and the Parade scope, are most useful when making comparisons, either between two or more images or between the different areas of an individual shot.

The Histogram displays the distribution of brightness, or levels of gray, in a video image. When two images are compared using the Histogram, you can identify major differences between them. This is helpful when you have to match different shots to one another.

When color and brightness vary too much between two shots that are supposed to have been taken at the same time under the same conditions, it can be distracting to the viewer. In other words, different angles within a scene shouldn't *feel* like they are substantially different from one another. There shouldn't be an unnatural change in the lighting as you cut from one image to another within the same scene.

The Histogram is a handy way to detect and correct differences in contrast.

Evaluating the Brightness of an Image

In this exercise, you will get familiar with the Histogram and learn to interpret its displays.

1   Control-click the Timeline ruler and choose **winner** from the shortcut menu.

2   In the Video Scopes window, choose Histogram from the Layout pop-up menu.

3   Control-click the Histogram display and make sure that Include Black is selected.

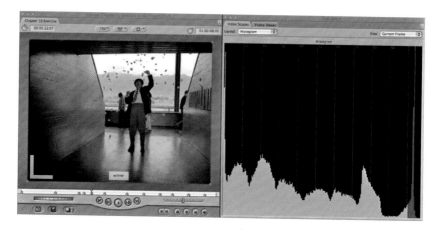

The Histogram is a bar graph representing luminance values of your clip from 0 to 110 percent. This luminance scale is similar to that of the Waveform Monitor—but similarities to the Waveform Monitor end there.

TIP ▶ With Include Black turned on, the height of the graph in the Histogram is scaled down to accommodate the highest spike in the graph, even if that spike represents black. Although this is not one of the video scope's more frequently used options, you can turn off Include Black to exclude black when automatically scaling the height of the Histogram graph, which can make it easier to see spikes for other brightness values in an image.

4   Move the cursor across the Histogram from left to right. Notice that a line follows the cursor, and an indicator shows the brightness percentages wherever the cursor is positioned.

The height of the bar represents the number of pixels in the image with that particular luminance value. The horizontal position of the bar indicates the luminance value of those pixels.

5   In the Histogram display, take note of which bars spike, and how high. Each spike indicates that there are a lot of pixels in that range of brightness.

The highest spike appears at 0 percent, showing that there is an abundance of black in the image. The next highest spike is at 103 percent, showing that there are also plenty of whites (many of which are above broadcast legal). The next two biggest spikes are at 21 percent and 76 percent, which tells you without even looking at the image that there are plenty of values across the entire scale.

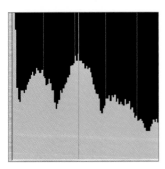

Looking at the wide range of values across the graph on the whole shows you that there's a lot of detail visible at every brightness level in the image. The large spikes at the bottom and top of the graph also show that the contrast between darks and lights in the image is high. (You can also see that part of the whites are spiking up into the super-white range.)

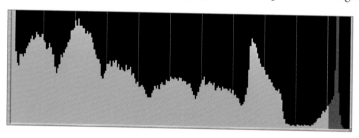

However, you can also tell just from looking at the graph that the image is weighted slightly towards the blacks. Depending on the look you wanted to achieve, there are probably some adjustments you can make to the midrange values of this image (being careful to leave the whites and blacks alone) to brighten the subject of the shot.

Comparing the Contrast of Two Images

Next, you will compare this image with a lower-contrast image.

1   In the Timeline, press the Down Arrow key to navigate to the **clock** clip.

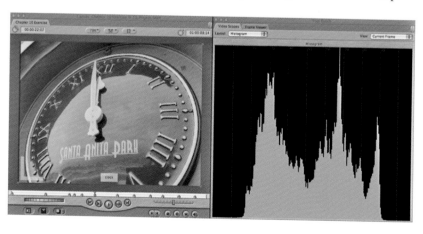

The close-up shot of the clock has lower contrast. As you can see, there are no values below 18 percent, resulting in muddy-looking blacks. Neither are there any values above 90 percent white. In fact, this image is nearly the opposite of the previous image, as the majority of its brightness values appear in a clump in the middle of the Histogram graph (the area representing the midtones).

By evaluating the Histograms of two clips, you immediately can determine how the distribution of their luminance levels differ. Next, you will navigate back and forth between the two clips of fruit in the Timeline, and observe any differences as they appear to the eye and in the Histogram.

2   Press the Up Arrow key to navigate back to the **winner** clip.

3   Play this shot and continue to the next one, the clock. Notice that the transition from one clip to the next has a disturbing visual discontinuity. Somehow, it doesn't quite feel as though the two clips were shot together at the same time of day. Although you can tell that there's a problem by simply watching the clips play, using the Histogram, you can determine exactly what the problem is.

Evaluating Color Balance Using the Parade Scope

The Parade scope, also known as the RGB Parade, is a modified Waveform Monitor. In a Waveform Monitor, the brightness values of the entire image are shown on the same display. However, on the Parade scope, the red, green, and blue components of the image are broken down and shown on three separate waveform displays.

The Parade scope is used for monitoring and comparing the relative red, green, and blue levels between shots. In this exercise, you'll evaluate the color balance of individual images to determine whether there is a neutral color balance or any color tint in the scene.

1   Control-click the Timeline ruler and choose **ms winner** from the short-cut menu.

2   In the Video Scopes window, choose Layout > Parade.

The Parade scope displays the luminance levels of the red, green, and blue color channels separately.

In this particular clip, the values of the three channels are somewhat uneven, with the green channel a little stronger then the red channel, and the blue channel appearing the strongest of all. Without even looking at the image, you can tell that the scene's color balance is tilted towards the blues, although the white shirt appears fairly neutral.

3   In the Timeline, navigate to the clip, **winner.**

Visually, this clip has a noticeable color change. Exactly how it is different can be determined by looking at the Parade Scope.

In this clip, the whites in the red channel are much brighter, which is seen as a reddish overall tint.

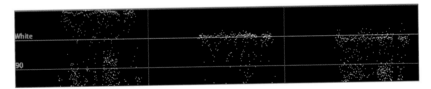

Generally, one of the primary goals when color-correcting a scene is to create a similar look for all the clips in that scene, so there is a more natural feel when cutting between them. The Parade Scope makes this task much easier, as it helps you to measure exactly how the colors in each shot differ.

> **NOTE** ▶ While working with the various video scopes, you have examined one frame from each clip. It is important to mention that looking at only one frame gives you a snapshot of just that single moment. A scene can change quickly and dramatically. During your evaluation of images, scrub though each clip to look for changes in luminance and color shifts across many frames.

Using an External Monitor

If your intended output is NTSC, PAL, or SECAM—in other words, some format of standard video displayed on a television or high-end video monitor—then you should be evaluating the images in the next several lessons with the best external NTSC or PAL monitor you can afford.

The video scopes are analytical, but it's also important to see an approximation of how the video will look to your eventual audience. Because there are so many variables in the setup of consumers' televisions, and because it is hardly feasible to go to everyone's house to set up their televisions for them, you will just have to use some predetermined standards as well as a little intelligent guesswork.

> **NOTE** ▶ Lessons 11 through 14 assume you are viewing images on an external NTSC monitor rather than a computer monitor. All directions for the exercises are directed at a video image as it is viewed in NTSC, whether that is a high-end monitor or a television. If you do not have an external monitor, you can still follow the lessons. Use color correction to approximate the final look, and practice the techniques. It is more important that you have an external monitor when color correcting real projects that are meant for broadcast.

Monitor or TV?

Should you use a high-resolution monitor or a standard television? Preferably both. The monitor has precise controls for helping to obtain a neutral setup. Additionally, the monitor may have more lines of resolution.

However, professional monitors do not represent how the video will look displayed on a home television set, which has a more limited range of color and luminance latitude. And like it or not, most programs will ultimately be displayed on that standard television.

So, if you have access to a high-resolution monitor, use it to perform color corrections. And having a standard TV available gives you added information when making decisions while color correcting.

Setting Up the External Monitor

> **NOTE** ▸ This section is applicable to NTSC monitors. Setting up a PAL monitor requires a different process, using a different color bar test pattern.

To set up the external monitor or TV, you'll use a test image. This will make sure the TV accurately represents the color and luminance of the video. For example, if your external monitor's saturation is turned up too high, colors will appear more saturated than they actually are.

1   Navigate to the clip of **Bars and Tone** in the Timeline. This is the same video generator available by choosing Effects > Video Generators > Bars and Tone (NTSC).

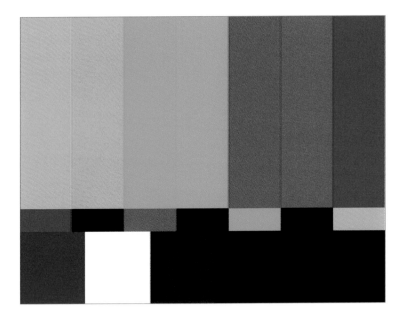

2   Choose View > External Video > All Frames to turn on external video to send an image to your output device. Hook up your external monitor to a FireWire device or capture card. (For these lessons, FireWire is appropriate, as the material is conformed to the DV format.) The **Bars and Tone** clip in the Timeline should now be visible on the external monitor.

3   On your external monitor, dial Chroma (also called Color) all the way down. The bars should now be only shades of gray, with no color.

4   Increase the monitor's Brightness setting until you see three gray bars in the lower-right corner of the screen.

NOTE ▶ These three bars are visible only when viewing to the external monitor or TV. If you look in the Viewer or Canvas, you will see only one bar.

These three bars are called the PLUGE (picture line-up generating equipment) bars. The one on the left is blacker than video black, often referred to as superblack. The middle one is video black. The one on the right is brighter than black. These are set up correctly when only one of the bars is visible.

5   Lessen the Brightness control on the monitor until the bar on the right is still just visible, but the two bars on the left are not. This bar lines up directly underneath the red bar to the right.

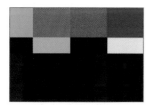

NOTE ▶ The red bar currently has no color. If you are unsure which bar is being referred to, temporarily turn up the color to see. Once you have identified the red bar, turn the color back down.

The black and darker-than-black bars are now indistinguishable from one another, constituting just a single bar.

6   Dial up the Contrast control on the monitor (sometimes called Picture) to increase the intensity of the large white bar on the bottom left of the color bars. Brighten until the white starts to bloom, or bleed into the surrounding bars. Then dial down a little on the contrast until it isn't blooming.

7   If you are using a TV, skip to Step 9.

8   If you use a monitor that has a blue-only setting, turn it on. The monitor now displays just shades of blue and black.

Set Chroma (color) until the bars on both the left and the right (light gray and blue) match the sub-bar beneath each of them. Then set Hue (tint) until the cyan and magenta bars (bars 3 and 5) match the brightness and color of the sub-bars beneath them. When you are finished, all blue bars match their sub-bars, and all that you'll see is solid blue bars.

At this point, you can turn off the blue-only setting. The monitor is now calibrated.

9   If you do not have a blue-only switch on your monitor, you will have to
set up the Chroma and Hue (color and tint) by eye. As a guide, the colors
from left to right should be light gray (no color), yellow, cyan, green,
magenta, red, and blue.

Lesson Review

1.   What is the fastest way to see if the luminance or chrominance is too high,
without using the video scopes?

2.   What is the broadcast legal range in which image data is represented in the
Waveform Monitor, Parade Scope, and Histogram?

3.   What IRE is black within Final Cut Pro?

4.   Which video scopes are most useful to measure the brightest and darkest
things in an image?

5.   Which video scopes are most useful for measuring the color in an image?

6.   How can you tell that an image has whites that are above the legal broadcast limit using the Waveform monitor or Histogram?

7.   What's the order in which you make the following adjustments to your
broadcast monitor: chroma, brightness, and contrast?

Answers

1.   Use the Range Check options in the Viewer or Canvas, available from the
View menu.

2.   0 to 100 percent.

3.   Trick question. IRE has no meaning inside of Final Cut Pro, it is only used
to measure the black level of analog output.

4.   The Waveform Monitor and Histogram.

5.   The Vectorscope and the RGB Parade scope.

6.   Parts of each scopes graph extend above 100 percent.

7.   You adjust brightness first, then contrast, and finally chroma.

11

Lesson Files Lessons > Lesson_11 > 11_Project_Start

Media Media > Lesson_11_Media

Time This lesson takes approximately 60 minutes to complete.

Goals Break down a video image into its components

Incorporate video scopes in the grading process

Use the Color Corrector 3-way filter

Modify the contrast of an image

Understand the terms contrast, blacks, mids, whites, highlights, and grayscale

Lesson 11
Controlling Contrast

Color correction is a process for enhancing a video image. It is sometimes called *finishing*, because it's the last step in finalizing the image. A color-correction artist, or colorist, is charged with molding raw, photographed images into something fantastic. In some cases, color correction involves using broad strokes to dramatically change the look of a film. Other times, it's used for more subtle tasks, such as smoothing variations in exposure and lighting, or fixing the occasional mistake. Color correction means different things depending on the project, but its success always depends on the skill of the colorist. In good color correction, the colorist's work may not even be noticeable in the final product.

Professional colorists spend years honing their skills and their eye for color. It's essential to learn to really *see* the video image—to grasp subtle color nuances and appreciate the subconscious effects of manipulating color balance and contrast.

There are fundamental principles that you will learn to apply to correct the first shot of any scene. In this lesson, you'll begin with the first and most essential task of all: controlling the contrast.

Understanding Contrast

The term *contrast* is thrown around a lot and means different things to different people. For the sake of simplicity, consider that contrast represents the number of steps from the darkest to the lightest tone in your image.

Regardless of the colors involved, an image can range from deep, solid blacks, through varied mid-gray tones, and to light, pure whites.

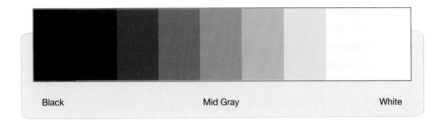

Black   Mid Gray   White

In this exercise, you'll examine the contrast in two different images, with the help of the Final Cut Pro video scopes.

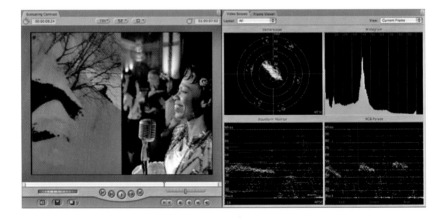

Getting Started

1   Open Lesson_11 > **11_Project_Start.**

If your workspace isn't already set up to include the video scopes in the Tool Bench window, you should do this now.

2   Choose Window > Arrange > Color Correction to open the Video Scopes tab.

3   From the Layout pop-up menu, choose Waveform to switch to that view of the window.

4   In the right of the window, make sure that the View pop-up menu is set to Current Frame.

5   Press the Option key and double-click the Exercise 01 - Evaluating Contrast bin to open it into its own tab in the Browser.

6   Open the **Evaluating Contrast** sequence.

Evaluating the Values in an Image—Highlights vs. Shadows

You first need to break the image down into shadows, midtones, and highlights. In the Final Cut Pro color-correction controls, these regions are referred to as *blacks*, *mids*, and *whites*.

This may sound obvious, but learning to perceive which color values of an image fall into which of these zones is the basis for all the color correction work to follow, and it is a valuable skill to develop.

1   Scrub through the first clip in the **Evaluating Contrast** sequence.

To focus on the brightness levels in the image, you can eliminate the color.

2   Select the **Dance_Club.mov** clip, then choose Effects > Video Filters > Image Control > Desaturate.

The image is *desaturated*. In other words, the chrominance of the image has been eliminated, conveniently leaving the luminance for your evaluation.

3   Scrub through the desaturated image, and pay careful attention to the darkest and lightest areas of the image.

The different levels of brightness should really leap out at you. In particular, notice how some areas that may have seemed darker because of their colored tint, like the almost sepia glow in the windows and interior highlights, are now revealed to be very close to white.

Judging Contrast Ratios

For purposes of color correction, one of the most important characteristics of an image is its *contrast ratio*: how much difference there is between the blackest black and the whitest white. You can quickly judge the contrast ratio by looking at the height of the graph displayed in the Waveform Monitor.

1   Scrub through the desaturated image again, this time watching the graph in the Waveform Monitor.

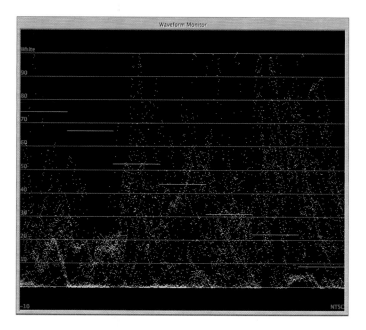

As you can see, there are large portions of the image that fall into the blacks down around 0 percent, but there are also numerous graph spikes up in the whites, at 100 percent luminance. This is the widest possible contrast ratio, and accounts for the crispness of the image.

2 Move the playhead to the **Skier.mov** clip, and play through it to get a sense of the colors and brightness.

3 Select the **Skier.mov** clip, and choose Effects > Last - Desaturate.

Since the Desaturate filter was the last one you applied, it appears at the top of the Effects menu in case you want to apply it again.

4 Locate the playhead to 01:00:04:11, and look at the Waveform Monitor.

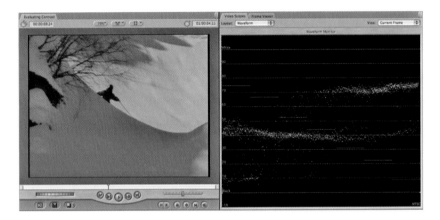

You may have noticed from looking at the image, but the waveform confirms that the whitest white in the image, even though it's snow, tops out around 80 percent, landing it firmly in the mids. Also, the darkest black, (the rocks at the left of the frame) don't really fall all the way to 0 percent.

The result is an image that looks somewhat murky, with washed-out shadows and lackluster highlights. This is the result of a narrow contrast ratio.

5 Press the Down Arrow key to navigate to the next cut, which is actually both clips superimposed with a split screen.

Once again, look carefully at the areas of light and shadow in the image, and try to imagine what it looks like without any color.

6 Select both clips, and choose Effects > Last - Desaturate.

Although you may have had difficulty seeing the difference between both images' contrast ratios when jumping between the two clips, the split screen makes it readily apparent.

As you can see, the blacks in the **Skier.mov** clip aren't nearly as deep as those in the **Dance_Club.mov** clip, nor are the whites as light. The graph in the Waveform Monitor shows this more dramatically.

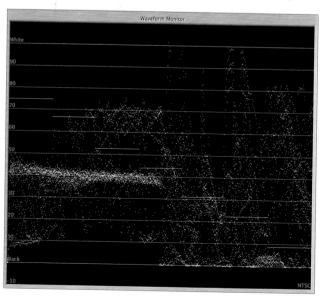

The graph in the Waveform Monitor is split just like the image in the Canvas, and you can see that the graph on the left side is not nearly as tall as the one on the right side.

Higher contrast ratios are not just more visually appealing—a low contrast ratio can limit your ability to manipulate color in an image later on.

Comparing Low- and High-Contrast Images

Another way to view contrast is to consider the balance of how much of an image is found within the mids, versus how much of the image is in the blacks and whites. The balance between midtones and blacks plus whites is probably the most conventional way to describe contrast.

Images with large regions in the mids are considered *low contrast*. This results in an image that is fairly neutral, but in extreme cases, may result in an image that looks somewhat washed out.

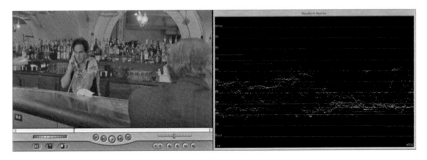

When the majority of the values in an image are found in the whites and blacks, with few pixels in the mids, the image is considered *high contrast*.

The borders between dark and light areas are usually perceived by viewers as edges, with the result that higher-contrast images may be perceived as being "sharper" than low-contrast images. On the other hand, extremes of black and white in very high-contrast images are typically harsher than we're used to seeing with the naked eye, so that high-contrast images can also lend a stylized look to a scene.

Whereas the *contrast ratio* of an image may be considered a simple qualitative issue (with higher contrast ratios able to bring out more detail in the image), whether or not the *perceived* contrast described in this section should be high or low is primarily a matter of preference and artistic license.

Comparing High- and Low-Key Images

Another way to describe contrast is in terms of the lighting strategy that was used to shoot the image. Terms such as *high-key* and *low-key* (originally used to describe methods of lighting on the set), have carried over to color correction to distinguish different methods of lighting a scene for dramatic effect.

High-key generally describes images that are well lit. The lighting tends to be softer, with fill lights eliminating harsh shadows from the subjects. High-key images also happen to be low contrast. There may well be black in the frame, but a look at the Waveform Monitor will reveal that most luminance values are spread throughout the mids and the whites.

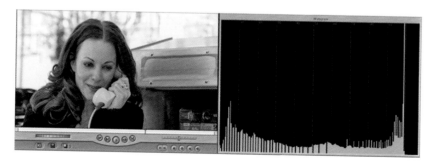

High-key images are often used to convey a light mood—the characters are happy, and all is well with the world.

Low-key images are the opposite. They are generally underlit, with deep shadows, and plenty of them. As you've probably guessed, low-key images are also high contrast. Highlights tend to be harsh and bright compared with the blackness of the image. A look at the histogram will reveal thin spikes in the whites, and large, wide swaths of values in the blacks, with few mids. Low-key lighting is often used to portray night, or a serious, dramatic moment. Think film noir.

Why all these different ways of describing contrast? It depends on who you're talking to, and what aspect of the image they're trying to describe. While the director of photography may try to impress upon you the importance of preserving a high-key look, the producer (who happens to be an amateur photographer) may counter that she thinks it should be low contrast—in reality, they're both describing a desire for the exact same look, they're just using different ways of describing it.

It's also worth pointing out that although an image may have a high contrast ratio, it doesn't automatically mean that it is a high-contrast, low-key image. Since the perceived contrast of an image is often dependent on the amount of brightness and visible detail in the midrange of an image, it's completely possible to have a relatively low-contrast image with a high contrast ratio.

Now that you understand the basics of contrast, it's time for you to manipulate it to achieve specific goals.

Controlling Contrast Using the Color Corrector 3-Way Filter

The Final Cut Pro Color Corrector 3-way filter is the workhorse for all of the following exercises. The Color Corrector 3-way filter is one of two filters (along with the more simply named Color Corrector filter) with a custom graphical interface that provides specific controls optimized for color-correcting images.

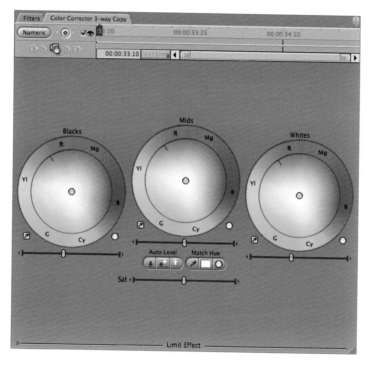

For now, you'll be ignoring the color wheels. The three sliders underneath let you push and pull the luminance values within an image with separate controls to target the image's black level, mids distribution, and white level.

In the following exercises, you'll learn how to use these three sliders to achieve complete control over the contrast in your images.

Adjusting the Black and White Points

Among its many virtues, the Color Corrector 3-way filter is able to play to an external monitor in real time, depending on your computer's configuration. Remember, you should *always* view the image you're manipulating on a broadcast monitor when preparing a program to be broadcast in NTSC or PAL formats.

1   Under the 11_Project_Start tab, press the Option key and double-click the Exercise 02 - Controlling Contrast bin.

2   Open the **Controlling Contrast - Basics** sequence.

The first clip in the sequence is a gradient generator. You'll notice that the default gradient is a ramp from 100 percent white to 0 percent black, with a direct correspondence to the diagonal graph shown in the Waveform Monitor.

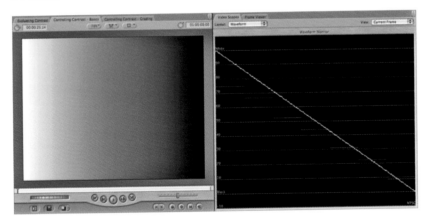

This is an ideal test image to see how changes you make with the Color Corrector 3-way filter manipulate the balance of luminance in an image.

3   Select the **Gradient** clip in the Timeline, then choose Effects > Video Filters > Color Correction > Color Corrector 3-way.

4   In the Timeline, double-click the **Gradient** clip to open it into the Viewer.

Even though you've added a filter, you'll notice an additional tab at the top of the Viewer.

This tab contains a custom interface for the Color Corrector 3-way filter that provides explicit control over the characteristics of your image.

5 Click the Filters tab.

As you can see, the Color Corrector 3-way filter is present.

6 Click the disclosure triangle to the left of the filter name to view the filter's parameters.

A tall stack of parameters appears. Don't worry if you don't initially understand their functions. Every one of these parameters is represented by a graphical control in the Color Corrector 3-way tab.

Later, when you know what each parameter affects, you can adjust the sliders and dials in the Filters tab if you feel you need to make more finely detailed changes to the image than the graphical interface allows.

Also, color correction filters, like the Color Corrector 3-way filter, cannot be removed or rearranged directly within the Color Corrector 3-way tab. Instead, these operations need to be performed in the Filters tab just like with any other video filters.

7 Click the disclosure triangle to close the parameters list, and click the Visual button to the right of the filter's name, or click the Color Corrector 3-way tab, to go to the Color Corrector 3-way graphic interface.

NOTE ▶ In the visual Color Corrector 3-way tab, you can click Numeric to go back to the Filters tab.

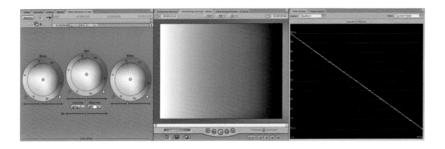

With the Color Corrector's controls in view, and the Viewer, Canvas, and video scopes open side-by-side in the Final Cut Pro default Color Correction layout, you have all the tools you need for analyzing, adjusting, and monitoring your images.

Even though the three color wheels may be the biggest, brightest things on the screen, and are simply screaming to be manipulated, ignore them for now. In this lesson, you are going to focus on the three slider controls located underneath the wheels. These are the controls you'll use to manipulate contrast.

Each slider corresponds to a color wheel in providing control over the blacks level, mids distribution, and whites level. These sliders adjust the luminance of the image independent of the chrominance level.

8   Drag the Whites slider to the left to lower the level of the whites.

Two things happen. The light part of the image darkens to a deeper gray, and the graph redraws itself so the diagonal line lowers.

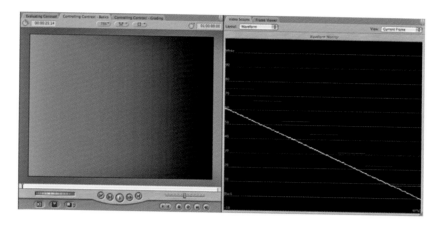

Notice, however, that the bottom of the graph didn't move. This is a vital characteristic of the three luminance controls in the Color Corrector 3-way filter. Changes to the whites leave the blacks untouched.

9   Drag the Blacks slider to the right, to raise the level of the blacks.

This time, you lightened the levels of the darkest parts of the image, which redraws the graph to reflect the new luminance distribution. Notice that, despite this second change, the whites level remains unchanged.

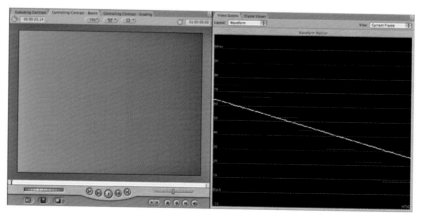

Incidentally, since you've just decreased the height from the blackest black to the whitest white, you've successfully lowered the *contrast ratio* of this image.

Changes you make to the blacks and whites levels are fairly easy to understand, since they essentially scale all of the luminance values in an image linearly, relative to the opposite end of the graph.

Adjusting the Mids

The Mids slider provides control over the distribution of all values falling between the black and white points of your image.

1   Shift-click any one of the Reset controls in the Color Corrector 3-way tab to reset all of the parameters to their default values.

Ordinarily, clicking a Reset control resets only the parameter associated with that control, but Shift-clicking any color-correction reset control in the top control group resets everything except for the Limit Effects controls (that appear in the collapsed section at the bottom of the Color Correction tab). As a result, the image and the graph in the Waveform Monitor will return to their previous states.

2   Drag the Mids slider to the left.

Immediately, you'll notice a far different effect. The whites and blacks remain largely where they are (although more extreme changes do move the white point), while the range of grays in the middle of the image appear to move towards the left as the image progressively darkens.

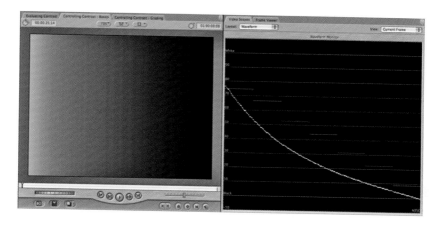

The result in the Waveform Monitor is even more dramatic. Changes to the blacks and whites resulted in a straight line in the graph, but lowering the mids had two effects: reshaping the graph into a downward curve, and moving the white point down.

3   Drag the Mids slider to the right.

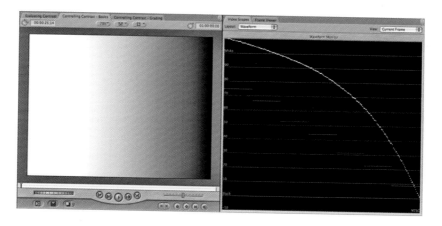

Predictably, this had the opposite effect, with the distribution of gray tones moving to the right as the image lightens, and the graph curving upward.

Basically, changes made to the mids redistribute the values falling between the white and black points of the image so the image can be lightened or darkened without muddying the blacks or whites. This change is nonlinear (as shown by the slope of the curve), which allows for subtle changes across the range of the image.

You can also see that the relationship between the mids and the whites is tricky. Changes made to one will require you to interact with the other.

Next, you'll see how adjusting the contrast in these three regions will enhance a real-world image. You'll also learn the proper sequence in which to approach these contrast corrections using the Color Corrector 3-way filter.

Stretching Contrast in a Video Clip

The contrast sliders give you total control over the contrast ratio of any image, by allowing you to adjust the distance from the brightest to the darkest value in the picture using the Blacks and Whites sliders. You can also control whether your image is high contrast or low contrast by redistributing the midtones that fall between with the Mids slider.

In the following exercise, you'll deal with one of the most common issues in video: murky-looking source footage with a low contrast ratio. You'll see how this is easily curable using the blacks, mids, and whites controls.

1   Press the Down Arrow key to move to the first frame of the
    Ski_Jump.mov clip.

    You've seen this image before. It's the one with the blacks that are too high, and the whites that are too low, resulting in murky shadows and lackluster whites. You've probably already guessed what needs to happen based on the last exercise, but methodically going through this process will help you to develop good habits for approaching the color correction process.

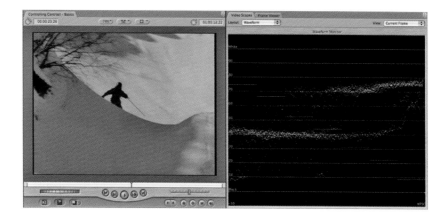

2 In the Timeline, select the **Ski_Jump.mov** clip, then choose Effects > Video Filters > Color Correction > Color Corrector 3-way.

3 In the Timeline, double-click the **Ski_Jump.mov** clip to open it into the Viewer, and click the Color Corrector 3-way tab to display the color correction controls.

> **NOTE** ▶ If the Color Corrector tab from another clip was already open in the Viewer, opening a new clip into the Viewer leaves the Color Corrector tab open, as long as the new clip has one color correction filter applied to it. This saves you from having to constantly click the Color Corrector tab in the Viewer as you adjust numerous filters.

The first step in any color correction is to set the black levels. As you saw in the preceding exercise, the black point is unaffected by changes made to the whites or mids, so it serves as the baseline for all changes you make to the image.

> **TIP** ▶ Although not disastrous, if you make a change to the mids or whites first, and adjust the blacks last, the change in the blacks will definitely affect the distribution of mids and whites, resulting in more fiddling around on your part. Get in the habit of setting the blacks first.

4   Examine the image in the Viewer.

You need to determine which parts of the image correspond to absolute black (0 percent) to make this adjustment. With few exceptions, most images should have at least a few pixels located at 0 percent. This results in deeper, richer blacks, which makes the lighter values pop out more by comparison.

One of the tricky things about this image is that the lighting is fairly diffuse, and the shadows of the trees aren't supposed to be that dark. However, there are some very dark shadows in the rocky outcropping at the left of the screen.

5   Look at the bottom left corner of the Waveform Monitor.

You can see a dip in the waveform graph that corresponds to the rocks. These levels seem low enough to qualify as the absolute black of the image, and, in fact, some of these pixels seem to be touching 0 percent black. Still, this image could benefit from a slightly deeper black level, although you don't want to make a big change.

6   To make a very slight reduction to the blacks, click the small arrow to the left of the Blacks slider five or six times.

TIP There are two good ways to use the mouse to make incremental adjustments with any effects slider: Click one of the little arrows at either end of the slider to nudge it in one-degree increments or, if you have a mouse with a standard scroll button, point the cursor at a slider and scroll upward to slide left or scroll downward to slide right. This is actually more accurate than dragging the slider itself.

You can also press the Command key while using the sliders, forcing it to move slower, allowing finer adjustments.

As slight as this change is, you can see the graph in the Waveform Monitor stretch downward.

Although it's difficult to see, the dots at the bottom of the graph begin to bunch up at the black line. As more and more of the graph hits the bottom, the result is typically referred to as *crushing the blacks*. Crushing the blacks increases the deepness of the shadows, which can be pleasing, but comes at the expense of losing detail.

7   To see the result of severely crushed blacks, drag the Blacks slider farther to the left.

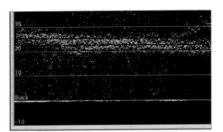

Notice that the dark areas of the image go completely black, and the bottom of the waveform graph bunches up. This is best way to tell if your blacks are crushed when it's difficult to determine in the Canvas.

Notice that the black levels never go below 0 percent. A value of 0 percent is the absolute bottom of the digital luminance scale. There is no way to create values that are "blacker than black". This is a very good thing when readying the video for broadcast because the broadcast formats like NTSC or PAL have regulations about black levels being lower than a certain amount. When working in Final Cut Pro, the values are simply digital percentages, so you don't have to worry about blacks being *unsafe*. This is true regardless of whether or not the source video was from a digital or analog format. Once digitized, all video is measured on a digital scale.

NOTE ▶ You need only be concerned with IRE black levels when outputting your program from digital to an analog format—and then it is simply a matter of properly setting up your video output hardware (and the software drivers that control it, if necessary) to the appropriate standard—0 or 7.5. There are no IRE settings internal to Final Cut Pro. The bottom line: when color correcting in Final Cut Pro, regardless of the system or format, always set blacks to 0 percent in the video scopes.

8   Press Command-Z to undo the last change.

Next, you'll address the biggest problem in this image—those dismal-looking whites in the snow. Adjusting the whites is generally the second step after adjusting the blacks, especially when the white level is so low.

9   Drag the Whites slider to the right to boost the whites until the top of the graph in the Waveform Monitor hits 100 percent.

The difference is huge, much more noticeable than the slight adjustment made to the blacks. The results of expanding the contrast ratio of this clip are immediately visible, almost as if you wiped a layer of dust off the monitor screen.

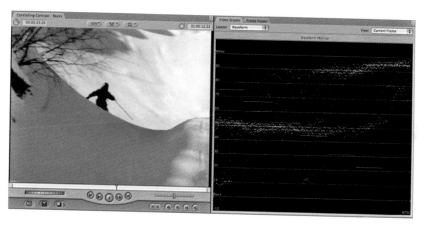

Incidentally, as you work it may be tempting to boost values into the super-white range, from 100 to 109 percent. Resist this urge. Although it may make your brights "whiter than white," you may also run into problems when you want to output your program to a broadcast format. Remember that when setting whites for NTSC, the levels should never rise above 100 percent.

Furthermore, even though the details are faint, there s still a lot of texture and detail in the bright regions of this image, and you want to avoid clipping them off and "flattening" the image.

Now that the blacks and whites points of the image are set, check to see if you need to make any changes to the mids.

10 Play the clip.

As you get a third of the way though the clip, you should notice an immediate problem. The whites are practically glowing, and they appear strangely flat. Stopping playback reveals that the whites in the frame you were balancing were far too dark, but other whites later on in the clip are much brighter. In fact, the later whites are being clipped off at the top of the Waveform Monitor. Unfortunately, the previous setting does not work throughout the entire clip.

This brings up an important point. When you pick an image to color correct, you must evaluate it over its entire duration to account for changes in lighting that might happen later on in the shot.

11 Drag the Whites slider to the left to bring the white levels back to 100 percent.

This very nearly brings the white level back to its original level, and the whites, while legal, lose their snap. Since you've now determined that this is the widest possible contrast ratio for this shot, it's time to adjust the Mids to make this a higher-contrast shot.

12 Drag the Mids slider to the right.

This gives the desired whiter-looking whites, by making the midtones brighten up.

As you saw in the previous exercise, however, the whites have been pushed up, which you'll need to fix.

13 Drag the Whites slider to the left to bring the top of the graph back to 100 percent.

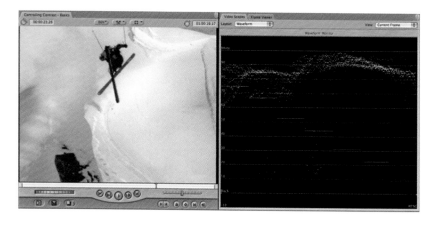

Ironically, this brings the Whites slider back to its default position. All of this effort illustrates that, oftentimes, adjusting the mids and whites is an interactive process of push and pull.

After all that, if you find yourself wondering whether this meddling has made any real improvement, there's a simple test you can perform to get a fast before-and-after look at the clip, to make sure you prefer the end result.

14 At the top of the Color Corrector 3-way tab, click the Enable Filter checkbox to toggle it off and on, comparing the two results.

As you've worked through this exercise, your eyes have gotten accustomed to the new contrast settings. Toggling the Color Corrector filter on and off is a good comparative tool you can use just to see how much you've changed the initial look of the video.

> **NOTE** ▸ You can also use the Frame Viewer controls to compare a corrected video image against itself with all filters turned off in a split screen, described in more detail in Lesson 14.

So that's it. Adjusting contrast is always the first step of color correction, and it comes before *any* changes you make to the clip's color. The process always begins by adjusting the blacks, then interactively making adjustments to the whites and mids until you've achieved the desired quality of contrast.

Setting Mood with the Mids

Adjusting the blacks and whites to establish the contrast ratio of an image is a fairly straightforward process. You want to provide the greatest contrast range for your image, and the only questions are which parts of the picture to map to absolute black, and which to absolute white.

Adjustments to the midtones, on the other hand, are much more subjective. Do you want a high-contrast look, or low-contrast? Is the picture supposed to be high-key, or low-key? There are no right or wrong answers, just what you and your client prefer.

The majority of the pixels in an image are generally found in the midtones. This is the luminance region with the most detail, and if the image is well-lit, it is also where faces are exposed. As a result, the distribution of midtones in an image goes a long way to defining the feeling of a shot.

For instance, by making simple adjustments to the midtones, you can influence the perceived time of day—is it midday, afternoon, or evening? Or, you can make sunlight look bright, or dark and overcast. These are all looks you can begin to define by adjusting the mids.

In this exercise, you'll make mids adjustments to a generally well-exposed image, in order to change the apparent time of day.

1   Open the **Controlling Contrast - Grading** sequence.

2   Scrub through the **Dance_Club.mov** clip and examine how the waveform changes over time.

> **NOTE ▶** The best way to see how the video scopes change over the course of the clip is to scrub through the image by dragging the playhead in the Canvas or Timeline. The video scopes don't update while a sequence or clip is either playing or shuttling.

As you can see, the contrast ratio of this clip is already as high as it can be, with many values at 0 percent, and several spikes at 100 percent.

3   Select the **Dance_Club.mov** clip, and choose Effects > Video Filters > Color Correction > Color Corrector 3-way.

4   In the Timeline, double-click the **Dance_Club.mov** clip to open the color correction filter into the Viewer. The Color Corrector 3-way tab updates to reflect the settings of the filter you just added.

As it is now, the quality of light in the image indicates afternoon, or an extremely well-lit evening. You'll first try to make this scene look more like an evening shot.

5   Drag the Mids slider to the left to lower the levels in the image.

This darkens the image, but now the highlights look dimmer. The Waveform Monitor confirms this observation by showing that the top of the graph has fallen to about 90 percent.

6 Drag the Whites slider to the right, to return the top of the waveform graph to 100 percent.

It's a small change, but it puts the snap back into the highlights of the image, while keeping the rest of the room darker.

7 To compare the before-and-after results, toggle the Enable Filter checkbox.

Next, you'll reset the color correction controls, and make the same clip look like it was shot closer to midday.

8 Shift-click any of the Reset controls in the Color Corrector 3-way tab to reset the default values.

9 Drag the Mids slider to the right, to boost the levels and create the illusion of more light coming into the room.

As you make this adjustment, pay particular attention to the quality of the light in the background—this is the darkest area you need to boost.

As you've seen before, boosting the mids also boosts the highlights, and in this case, boosting the mids as high as this is making the whites blow out well above 100 percent.

10 Drag the Whites slider to the left to bring the top of the waveform graph back down to 100 percent.

Now the image looks brighter, and the whites aren't blowing out any more.

It's not a bad range of options for using two simple sliders. Later on, you'll learn to combine contrast adjustments with color balance adjustments to create even more sophisticated looks, but the important thing to remember is that adjustments to the contrast are the first, and sometimes the only adjustments you need to make.

Creating Artificially High Contrast

So far, you've been adjusting the contrast to create a natural look. However, you can use these same controls to create extremely stylized, high-contrast images. You might do this for a number of creative purposes: to enhance the separation of different elements within the frame, to hide a flaw in the exposure, or simply to create a distinctive look.

Creating a High-Contrast Look

In this exercise, you will treat the image you've been working with as high contrast.

1   Under the 11_Project_Start tab, press the Option key and double-click the Exercise 03 - High Contrast bin to open it into its own tab in the Browser.

2   Open the **Higher Contrast - Finished** sequence.

In order to create high contrast, you need to push up the midtones of the image towards white and down toward black, and away from the center, as you see in this image.

3 Open the **Higher Contrast - Beginning** sequence.

4 Select the **Winner.mov** clip, and choose Effects > Video Filters > Color Correction > Color Corrector 3-way.

5 In the Timeline, double-click the **Winner.mov** clip to open the color correction filter you've just added into the currently open Color Corrector 3-way tab in the Viewer.

The original image is very well exposed, with a high contrast ratio and detail throughout the entire range of luminance.

The first step you'll take toward creating a high-contrast look is to crush the blacks.

6 Move the Blacks slider to the left.

The farther you drag left, the more values get crushed to the bottom of the waveform graph, and the darker your image gets.

It's not high contrast yet, it's just dark. For truly high contrast, you need to boost the highlights back up. However, since you're not going for a realistic look, you can take a shortcut and crank up the mids first, without regard for where the highlights fall.

7   Drag the Mids slider to the right to redistribute the midtones up towards the whites. Don't be shy.

The result is definitely high contrast, but with whites that are outrageously overblown. Stylized or not, you cannot allow whites to go above 100 percent.

8   Drag the Whites slider to the left, until the top of the waveform graph sits at 100 percent.

Now you have an extremely high-contrast image, with broadcast-legal luminance, and as an added bonus, you were able to retrieve some pleasing detail from the background.

Although this is not something you'd do to every image, it's good to know how to push the contrast to create more stylized effects.

However, suppose you didn't want to bring the whites back down in step 8. What if you wanted to blow out the whites, and leave them blown out? In the next exercise, you'll learn how to safely manage illegal values in an image—values that aren't broadcast safe—while getting the results you want.

Applying the Broadcast Safe Filter

Assume you want to deliberately clip the whites in the previous exercise. Leaving illegal levels in a clip is never good practice, because they can cause innumerable problems later. In these instances, you can use the Broadcast Safe filter.

The Broadcast Safe filter limits the maximum allowable luminance and saturation levels. In this case, it is the perfect tool to help you extend the contrast of the clip by compressing the highlights to a broadcast-legal level.

1 Drag the Whites slider to the default center position, so that the whites blow out once again.

An examination of the Waveform Monitor confirms that the white levels are completely illegal.

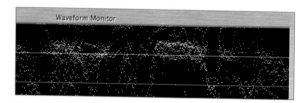

2 Select the **Winner.mov** clip in the Timeline, and choose Effects > Video Filters > Color Correction > Broadcast Safe to add the Broadcast Safe filter to the clip.

Instantly, you'll see that the illegal levels displayed in the Waveform Monitor have been compressed to a safe 100 percent, although the whites in the Viewer are still blown out.

If you look at the image in the Canvas, you can see that a bit of detail has crept back into the image. You can just make out the faint outline of the mountain in the background.

This is because the broadcast monitor is *compressing* the illegal levels, or squeezing them all together, rather than *clipping* them, or cutting them off. The end result is still quite bright, but the effect is a little more pleasing.

3   Click the Filters tab.

Notice that the default mode of the Broadcast Safe filter is Conservative. This setting is recommended for most situations.

4 Click the Color Corrector 3-way tab.

5 Drag the Whites slider to the right so you can see how the Broadcast Safe filter is limiting the increased values.

As you continue to drag to the right, the values in the graph climb to 100 percent and then compress and bunch up.

The Broadcast Safe filter is good to use whenever you want to make a range of light values brighter but don't want to worry about going into unsafe luminance ranges.

6 Click the Filters tab.

7 In the Broadcast Safe filter, click the Mode pop-up menu to see the available choices.

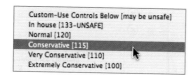

As a rule of thumb, you can use the default choice of Conservative, which limits values to 100 percent. The other choices, including the Custom option, set the top end of the luminance scale to better suit your needs.

NOTE ▶ When in Custom mode, these controls are all manual. In choices other than Custom, the sliders have no effect.

A Note about Contrast and Grain

What is the result of all this pushing and pulling of the contrast? Whenever you expand the contrast range of an image, you're stretching a limited amount of color information across a wider range. Depending on the image format, and the amount of data in the original image, you may be able to make your changes without creating any discernable artifacts in the image.

However, in cases where you need to make extreme corrections, such as with underexposed or overexposed images, making contrast adjustments can result in unsightly artifacts. This is especially true when using highly compressed video formats such as DV25 that also lack color information.

In these cases, the process of increasing contrast can also bring out certain elements of the image that you would rather conceal. One of the most common problems is that increased contrast can make the image appear more grainy, by highlighting its grain (with film) or noise (with video). In these cases, you'll have to strike a compromise between the level of correction you need to make versus the amount of image noise you're willing to tolerate.

Lesson Review

1. What does contrast ratio describe?
2. What do the mids describe?
3. What's better, a higher contrast ratio or a lower contrast ratio?
4. Does a high contrast ratio automatically create a high-contrast image?
5. How do you maximize the contrast ratio of a clip using the Color Corrector 3-way filter?
6. How would you adjust the Mids slider to make an image seem like it's shot in the late afternoon?
7. What are two ways you can eliminate illegal whites in an image?

Answers

1. The distance between the blackest and lightest values in an image.
2. The range of values that falls within the middle tones of the image, between shadows and highlights.
3. Higher contrast ratios are generally better.
4. No. Contrast ratios and perceived contrast are different.

5. Adjust the Blacks slider so that the blackest part of the image is around 0 percent, and then adjust the Whites slider so that any highlights in the image are around 100 percent.

6. Drag the Mids to the left, to lower the Mids distribution.

7. You could use the Color Corrector 3-way filter, and lower the whites, or you could apply the Broadcast Safe filter.

12

Lesson Files Lessons > Lesson_12 > 12_Project_Start

Media Media > Lesson_12_Media

Time This lesson takes approximately 60 minutes to complete.

Goals Identify color using a color wheel

Manipulate color with hue, saturation, and luminance controls

Incorporate color effects during grading

Use video scopes to identify and manipulate color

Use the Color Corrector 3-way filter

Use color balancing to enhance the final scene

Describe the color terms *hue*, *saturation*, *color wheel*, *color space*, *primary*, *secondary*, and *complementary*

Lesson 12
Controlling Color

So far, the focus has been on luminance and contrast. Once you've graded the contrast, the next step in the color correction process is to work on the color balance of the image.

Choosing the color balance is a creative, as well as corrective, endeavor. You may find yourself wanting to manipulate color to enhance an image, to alter the mood of a scene, or perhaps to create highly stylized color schemes for a title sequence or motion graphics segment.

Whatever your goals, you need to understand how to judge colors, and which controls to use to create the desired effect. This lesson focuses on how you evaluate and manipulate color in Final Cut Pro. You will learn how to read and understand the color balance of an image, and then use color correction to alter the color balance within that clip with total control.

Understanding Color Balance

Color balance refers to the relative amount of red, green, and blue in an image. As the name implies, by changing the balance of each color in relation to the others, you can change the hue and saturation of all the colors found within an image.

Final Cut Pro goes further by providing you with separate controls over the balance of the colors found in each of the three zones of luminance in an image, which allows you to make separate changes to the colors found in the blacks (such as shadows), those found in the mids (most of the image), and those in the whites (the bright areas and highlights). Each Color Balance control consists of a color wheel, at the center of which is a handle that allows you to make the necessary adjustments.

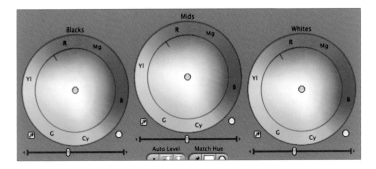

The contrast controls help you ensure that the video is broadcast legal, but the Color Balance controls help you ensure that the colors in the image *look right*. For example, by manipulating the color balance within an image, you can make video shot with too much orange tint look more natural by neutralizing the tint.

Using Primary Color Correction

Ideally, color correction is an extension of the original cinematography. As a colorist, you are a collaborator in one step of the artistic process, and your ideas and contributions help shape the final look and emotional impact of the program. You will probably work with the director of photography (though not always) to establish a starting point for the color correction process, and the two of you may continue to finesse the images into their final form. It's also likely that the director or producer will have a say about the look of the program, and this input will weave its way into the creative process.

At other times, color correction may take the form of damage control, as you attempt to rescue footage that was shot under less than ideal conditions, or footage that was shot using an aesthetic that is no longer compatible with the project goals. Furthermore, the client may be relying on color correction to implement ideas that are too difficult or costly to execute on location.

Whatever the issues you need to address, color correction (also called *grading*), is generally broken down into two stages: *primary correction* and *secondary correction*. This lesson focuses on primary color correction, which involves adjusting the contrast and color-balance of the overall image to achieve the desired look and feel.

In this lesson, you'll learn to evaluate an image to determine *color casts*, one of the most common color issues you'll have to address. For example, this image may seem, at first glance, to be fine, but a closer examination will reveal a subtle blue cast from the shadows through the highlights.

Once you learn to identify a color cast in a clip, you'll work towards being able to correct it to create a clean, neutral look, where whites are pure and blacks are solid.

Whatever the overall look, the first, and sometimes only, step you need to take is to apply a single primary color correction.

Secondary color correction, which involves adding color correction filters to fine-tune and manipulate specific colors within the frame, is covered in Lesson 15.

Understanding the Color Balance Controls

Before you start pushing and pulling the color balance in your shots, you'll be taking a few minutes to get a better understanding of the color wheel that's at the heart of the Color Balance controls. In doing so, you'll also learn how to better understand the Vectorscope, which presents a graph of the colors in your image against a backdrop of targets that are directly analogous to the color wheel.

In its various forms, the color wheel is an effective way to provide independent yet unified control over hue (color) and saturation (intensity of color). Once you understand how the color wheel represents the fundamental components of color, you can reliably predict and control the results of color adjustments.

Learning About the Color Wheel

The color wheel displays all of the possible hues around the outside of a circle. If you follow the edge of the color wheel, you can find the three *primary* colors: red, green, and blue.

The pure primaries are equally distant from one another, and divide the color wheel into thirds.

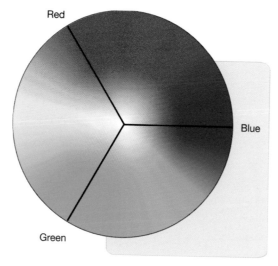

Video systems, regardless of the format, create color in an additive fashion, by mixing the three primaries together. The primary colors found on the color wheel correspond to the red, green, and blue components of a video signal; the red, green, and blue phosphors of a CRT display; and the red, green, and blue components of the pixels on a flat-screen monitor. (Incidentally, film also records color in three layers, or substrates, each of which is sensitive to red, green, and blue.)

By mixing these primary colors, any color of the rainbow can be displayed, and you can see this happening in the color wheel. As the primary colors blend together around the outer edge of the wheel, you can see other hues emerge.

An equal mixture of any two primaries creates the *secondary* colors on the color wheel. The three secondary colors are cyan, magenta, and yellow. For example, yellow (a secondary color) is a combination of green and red (both primaries).

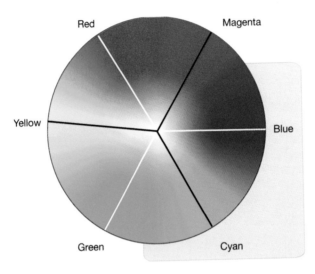

Notice that each secondary color falls directly opposite a primary color. Any two colors that are opposite one another—such as yellow and blue—on the color wheel are considered to be *complementary*.

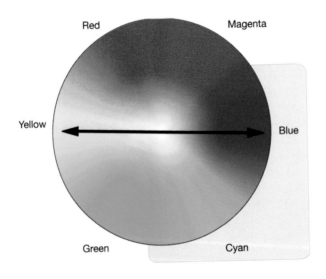

Combining any color with its complementary color on the wheel neutralizes it, effectively *desaturating* it. You can see this phenomenon represented in the color wheel—the outer edge of the wheel represents each hue at 100 percent saturation, and the center of the wheel has 0 percent saturation, which is represented by white.

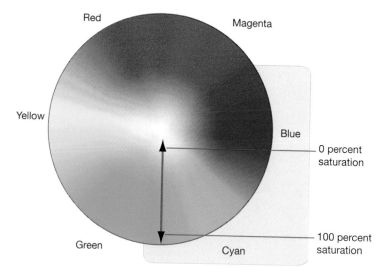

NOTE ▶ Even though 0 percent saturation is represented in the color wheel by white, it's important to remember that 0 percent saturation simply means an absence of color. Removing all saturation from an image does nothing to alter the luminance of the image, which may then consist of any shade of gray.

To effectively control colors with Final Cut Pro's color correction filters, you must understand the relationship between complementary colors, and the effect of blending them together.

Manipulating Color Channels with the Color Balance Control

This simple exercise will help you understand the color wheel's effect on an image and how those effects are displayed in the video scopes:

1   Open Lesson_12 > **12_Project_Start.**

If your workspace isn't already set up to include the video scopes in the Tool Bench window, do so now.

2   Choose Window > Arrange > Color Correction to open the Video Scopes tab.

3   From the Layout pop-up menu, choose All to switch the view of the window.

4   Press the Option key and double-click the Exercise 01 - Color Wheel Basics bin to open it into its own tab in the Browser.

5   Open the **Color Wheel Basics** sequence.

6   Double-click the first **Custom Gradient** clip in the sequence to open it into the Viewer. Then, at the top of the Viewer, click the Color Corrector tab.

The first clip in the sequence is a custom gradient generator that's been set to a low, neutral gray. A Color Corrector filter has been applied to the clip, but the filter is not currently set up to make any corrections.

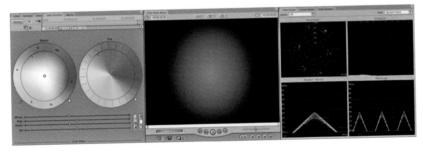

The first thing you should notice in the Vectorscope is the lack of any graph whatsoever. This means that the image is completely desaturated. The second thing you should notice in the Parade scope is that each color channel is equally strong. This latter graph shows the additive nature of the red, green, blue primary color system—adding equal amounts of each color results in a neutral gray.

7   Click anywhere in the Color Balance control and drag toward the R (red) target.

NOTE ▶ Although the Color Balance control appears to have a handle at its center, this is actually the balance control indicator, which shows you how the color channels are being redistributed.

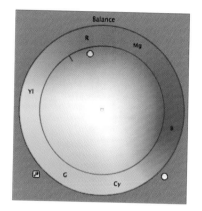

As you move the control, the image in the Canvas begins to turn red.

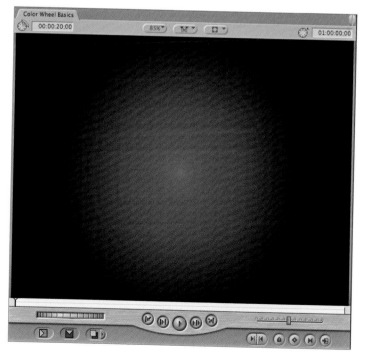

8   Control-click in the Vectorscope, and choose Magnify from the shortcut menu.

Since most adjustments you'll be making to an image happen close to the
center of the Vectorscope, the Magnify setting lets you see the results in
more detail.

As you adjusted the Color Balance control, the graph in the Vectorscope
stretched out in the same direction as the adjustment you made. The red
channel, represented by the red graph in the Parade scope, also increased
in intensity relative to the green and blue channels.

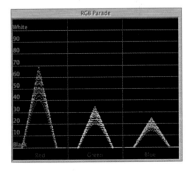

9   Click the Color Balance control and drag around the edge of the wheel towards the Cy (cyan) target. Watch the video scopes while you make the adjustment.

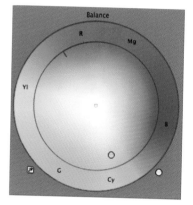

You can see the graph in the Vectorscope change to mirror the new direction of the balance control indicator. At the same time, you can see the three color channels in the Parade scope individually shift as you push and pull colors in each channel.

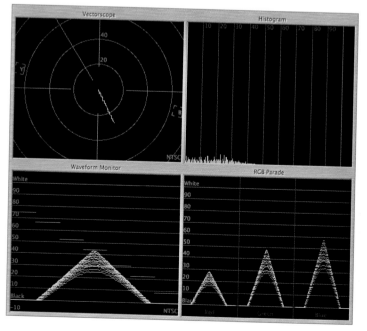

No matter what you do with the Color Balance control, and no matter how much the individual channel levels change in the Parade scope, the overall luminance of the image stays the same, as represented by the Waveform Monitor. This is an important concept. As its name implies, the Color Balance control lets you change the balance of colors in the red, green, and blue channels of an image, but the end result always has the same overall luminance.

More importantly, the Color Balance controls let you simultaneously rebalance the levels of all three color channels. This is an extremely powerful, and extremely fast, way to work.

10 Take a minute to make additional changes to the Color Balance controls, observing the changes in the picture and in the video scopes.

Adjusting Saturation and Neutralizing Colors with Their Complementary Colors

In the next exercise, you'll use the Color Balance control to control the saturation of a color, and to neutralize any single color by adding it to its complementary color.

1 Press the Down Arrow key to navigate to the second clip in the **Color Wheel Basics** sequence. Double-click the second **Custom Gradient** clip to open it into the Viewer.

This clip also has a Color Corrector filter applied, and the custom controls are automatically shown in the Viewer.

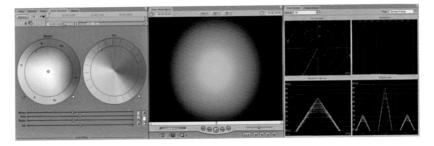

This clip is a circular gradient, just like the first clip. However, this clip already has a clear green cast, which you can see in both the Vectorscope and Parade scope.

2   Click in the Color Balance control, and drag towards a point somewhere between the Mg (magenta) and B (blue) targets, so that the spike in the green channel of the Parade scope diminishes, while the blue and red spikes remain roughly the same height relative to one another.

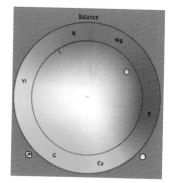

3   Stop dragging when the green has diminished, but not quite faded completely, and look at the video scopes.

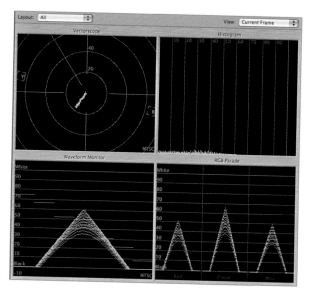

It's a little tricky to maintain the balance between the red and green graphs in the Parade scope, while pulling the green channel down, but keep at it until you have roughly the result shown in the preceding figure.

By moving color balance in the opposite direction of the original green color, you've begun to desaturate the image, as you can see by the shortening of the graph in the Vectorscope. Since the balance between the red and blue spikes in the Parade scope is roughly equal, you can be sure that you're moving in the direction of purely neutralizing the image, rather than tinting it another color.

4   Shift-click and drag the Color Balance control to the right, ever so slightly, until the three graphs in the Parade scope are the same height, and the graph in the Vectorscope is as close to the center as possible.

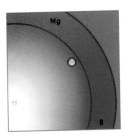

By Shift-clicking and dragging, you lock the angle of your adjustment. Since every hue is represented by an angle around the perimeter of the wheel, locking the angle lets you move the balance control indicator in and out from the center of the wheel to the edge, without changing its angle. This allows you to make saturation adjustments without also adjusting the hue of the image.

When you've made the adjustment, the gradient should not appear nearly completely gray.

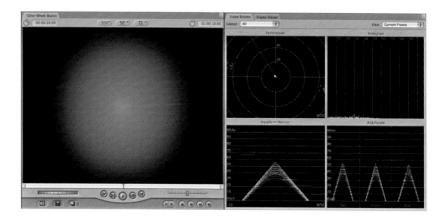

If the image is not gray, the channels as displayed in the Parade scope weren't balanced equally enough when you made the last change. Keep working at it until you've completely neutralized the color.

Feel free to continue experimenting with this last image until you get the hang of the technique. The most important thing to learn is that, by moving a Color Balance control, you can adjust each individual color channel of your image.

Even more important, the direction in which you rebalance colors with the color control is mirrored by the direction in which the graph moves in the Vectorscope. This direct relationship between the color control and the Vectorscope is a key element in your ability to predict necessary changes in color balancing.

Identifying and Correcting Color Casts

Have you ever taken a picture with a digital camera, or shot some video on vacation, only to get home and find that your footage is inexplicably orange, or blue, or green? What you're seeing is an incorrect white balance, often referred to as a *color cast*.

Every light source has a different *color temperature*. Each of the three types of light sources you'll typically encounter—incandescent (tungsten), fluorescent, and sunlight—produce light with spikes in different parts of the visible spectrum. Most of the time, you don't consciously notice these color temperatures, because the human eye is extremely adaptive and influenced by visual context. Generally, your perception of what is white and what is black is relative to the surrounding colors.

Film and video cameras are not usually so forgiving. Color casts are a result of the recording device not being correctly adjusted to interpret the color temperature of the dominant light source. With film, the film stock wasn't intended for the light source in use. With video, the white balance control was incorrectly set, or the automatic setting wasn't quite so automatic.

The results are sometimes obvious (The whites look orange!) and sometimes subtle (What's wrong with his face?); but, in any event, the colors in the image are not what was expected. No matter what your creative goals are for the color of an image, you generally want to begin with an image where the whites look white, the blacks look black, and faces look the way they're supposed to, instead of orange, or green, or blue.

For this reason, you must learn to spot a color cast, determine which color channel is creating a problem, and neutralize the cast using the Color Balance controls.

Identifying Color Casts

Colorists need to perceive nuances in color and color casts in an image, and know how to alter the colors to create a natural appearance. Although every colorist has subjective viewpoints on the use of color, finding a natural balance is often the first step to creating the final look of the video.

1   In the 12_Project_Start tab, Option-click the Exercise 02 - Auto Balance bin and open the **Auto Balance Exercise** sequence.

2   If you're not already set up with the Color Correction layout, choose Window > Arrange > Color Correction.

NOTE ▶ This lesson assumes that you are working on a calibrated external NTSC monitor. A computer monitor does not provide a true representation of the actual NTSC broadcast image. If your system is PAL, or you don't have an external monitor, you may complete this exercise using your computer's monitor, but be aware that it is not accurate for finishing purposes, and the resulting images will not look the same when output to broadcast video. If you have an SDI out from your video card and a DVI-D display, with the right adapter/converter, you can get a pretty reliable monitoring solution, although not 100 percent accurate.

3 In the Video Scopes tab, make sure that the Layout pop-up menu is set to All.

4 Before you do anything else, take a close look at the image in the Canvas.

Your first impression is extremely important. The longer you look at any image, the more your eyes adapt to the relative differences between the colors in the frame, and the less sensitive you'll be to a color cast in the picture.

You need to get into the habit of asking the following three questions: Do the shadows seem pure black, or are they slightly tinted? Do things that should be pure white seem properly desaturated? Do people's faces look healthy and natural, or do they look faded, tired, or motion-sick?

If the answer to these is a collective no, as it should be in this image, you need to quantify the problem. In this case, you may have noticed that the image has a slightly blue, cool quality to it. To confirm your suspicions, it's time to look at the video scopes to determine exactly what the problem is.

5   Look at the video scopes.

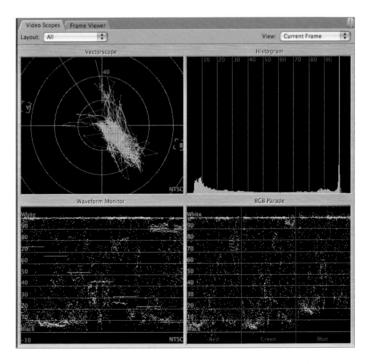

You'll notice that the image is well exposed, with a wide contrast ratio that stretches from 0 percent black all the way to 100 percent white. Furthermore, there is an enormous amount of detail throughout the mids. From the clustering at the top of the Waveform Monitor, however, you can surmise that there's a bit of overexposure, and the huge spike to the right of the Histogram at the 100 percent line confirms that there's a ton of white in the image.

As far as color casts go, however, the scopes reveal two telltale signs that the image is too blue. Before going on to the next step, see if you can guess what they are.

6   From the Layout pop-up menu, choose Parade.

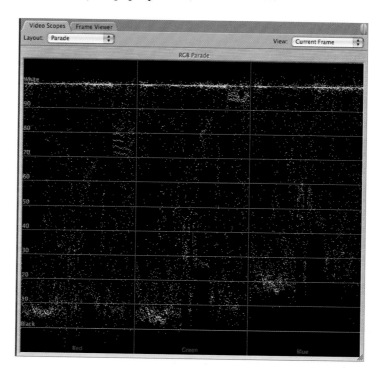

In many cases when there are abundant blacks and whites in the image, the three graphs that represent the red, green, and blue channels in the Parade scope look somewhat similar, in terms of their overall shape. Clearly, the mids will vary considerably, but because blacks represent an absence of all three colors, and whites represent the presence of all three colors, the tops and bottoms of each of the three graphs should fall roughly in the same places.

7   Carefully examine the top of the blue waveform.

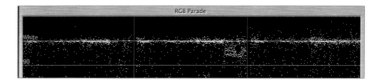

This confirms the problem. While the Waveform Monitor shows you the average luminance of all three color channels together, the Parade scope shows you that the blues in this image are considerably stronger than the reds and greens. The bottom of the Parade scope shows that the blue channel is lighter in the blacks, which explains why the blacks seem somewhat washed out, even though parts of the Waveform Monitor extend all the way to the bottom.

8   From the Layout pop-up menu, choose Vectorscope. Control-click the Vectorscope and deselect Magnify.

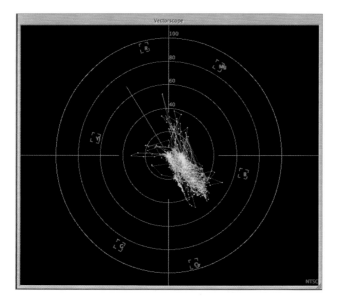

If you didn't have enough proof already, here's the smoking gun. In an image featuring three people, there are no traces clustered around the Flesh Tone line in the Vectorscope.

Furthermore, even though there is a lot of color within the image in the Canvas (the reds and yellows in the clown's outfit and on the phone signage) the entire graph within the Vectorscope seems oddly uncentered, and, in fact, is offset in the direction of blue and cyan.

Although you can oftentimes identify a color cast by sight, the Parade scope and the Vectorscope are your best tools for correctly identifying the type, and severity, of a color cast in any image. Even though you may develop the eye to accurately spot the hue of a color cast, the scopes are still useful for revealing just how much correction you need to make, based on the numbers.

Correcting Color Casts with the Auto Balance Eyedroppers

Now that you've identified an improper color cast, you'll want to eliminate it before taking any other steps. To expedite the process, Final Cut Pro provides three Select Auto-balance Color buttons that can automatically rebalance an image to make the blacks and whites neutral and rich.

1   Select the **Phone_Call.mov** clip in the Timeline, and choose Effects > Video Filters > Color Correction > Color Correction 3-way.

2   Open the **Phone_Call.mov** clip into the Viewer.

3   In the Video Scopes tab, choose All from the Layout pop-up menu.

You're now set to start correcting this clip. You'll notice a small eyedropper button at the bottom left of each Color Balance control in the Viewer. These are the Select Auto-balance Color buttons—one corresponds to each zone of luminance.

The most important of these buttons correspond to the blacks and whites. Whenever you use the automatic balancing controls in Final Cut Pro, you want to start where the color cast is most noticeable. In this case, it's in the blacks.

4   Click the Blacks Select Auto-balance Color button control so that it is highlighted.

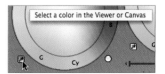

When you click the button, a tooltip appears with an instruction. What the instruction doesn't tell you is that you need to select an area that's supposed to be pure black.

This is an important decision, and it's not as easy as it may seem. You want to select an area that you think corresponds as closely to solid black as possible. In particular, since there's a color cast, you want to select an area that is *supposed* to be black, even if it doesn't appear to be so at first. In this image, there are several candidates: the woman's black dress, the shadow in the phone kiosk, or the color of the man's trousers. Each of these black areas is slightly different, however, and will yield different results.

NOTE ▶ After you've performed step 5, an optional step is to reset the Blacks Balance control and try selecting other black areas of the picture, to see how they're supposed to look.

5   Click in the shadows of the phone kiosk.

Immediately, three things happen. The most noticeable event is that the image immediately looks more natural.

If you look in the Color Corrector tab, you'll see that the balance control indicator in the Blacks Balance control has moved to the left, toward yellow. As you learned earlier, yellow is the complementary of blue, so this small adjustment neutralizes the cast in the blacks.

6   Look at the Parade scope.

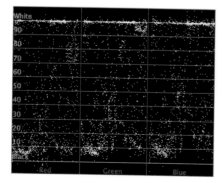

You should notice two things. First, the bottom of the blue graph now approximately matches the level of the red and green graphs. Second, the whites are still out of whack. Work remains to be done.

7   Click the Whites Select Auto-balance Color button so that it is highlighted.

Now, you want to click a region in the image that's supposed to be white. That seems easy enough, since there's plenty of white in the image.

8   In the Canvas, click the side of the white building.

Nothing happened! How can this be? The Parade scope clearly shows a blue cast in the whites. This situation illustrates an important rule you need to remember when you use the Whites Select Auto-balance Color button.

9   Press Control-Z to turn on Luminance Range Checking in the Canvas (or choose Viewer > Range Check > Excess Luma).

You now can clearly see that the area you tried to select is overexposed. When digital video is overexposed, the result is that all values over the maximum digital limit are clipped, and the resulting parts of the image are pure white. These areas will not have the color cast you're trying to correct because they're artificially white. Extreme whites that are likely to be overexposed—such as lens flares, glints, or hot highlights—are not good candidates for the Whites Select Auto-balance Color button.

You need to pick a new area of the picture. The shirt of the man standing next to the clown seems like a good choice. It's not overexposed, and it clearly looks like it has the blue cast you're trying to eliminate.

10 Press Control-Z to turn off Luminance Range Checking in the Canvas.

11 Click the Whites Select Auto-balance Color button, and then click the man's shirt.

Immediately, you should see another unexpected problem.

Instead of correcting all of the whites in the image, it turns them unexpectedly sepia. If you look at the Parade scope, the balance has been horribly skewed. Apparently the shirt is supposed to have a slightly higher blue level. You need to find something else that is supposed to be white.

12 Click the Whites Reset button next to the Whites Balance control.

Next, try the phone logo on the side of the phone kiosk. This looks like it's supposed to be a pure white, which is especially likely since it's a decal.

TIP Zoom in on the Canvas to make it easier to click smaller regions of white in an image. Press Z to select the Zoom tool, and click twice on the phone logo.

13 Click the Whites Select Auto-balance Color button, and then click the whitest group of pixels within the phone.

The result is a compromise. The building has become warmer, but this may be due to the quality of light at that time of day, or the fact that the paint on the building is a warmer shade of white. (In either case, a quick chat with the director of photography should clear that up).

The important thing is that the faces, which seemed anemic before, are now looking a little healthier, which is confirmed by the graph in the Vectorscope. Unfortunately, in this example, there is no absolute benchmark for the accuracy of this correction, and it becomes a matter of preference and experience.

NOTE ▸ In this case, if you wanted to set the building to pure white anyway, this would be a prime candidate for a secondary correction, but that will be covered in more detail in Lesson 15.

As you can see, the effectiveness of the Select Auto-balance Color buttons is highly dependent on selecting the right pixels in the image. This process may involve some detective work on your part. Remember that the Whites Select Auto-balance Color button can give you a quick head start, but it is not always a panacea.

Sampling from the Mids

When correcting color casts, you typically only need to adjust two color balance wheels to balance the image. Why? Because the Whites Balance control primarily affects the top 75 percent of the image. (The influence of this control falls off at this point, fading out around 10 percent luminance.) Everything from dark-gray shades of color up to white is affected.

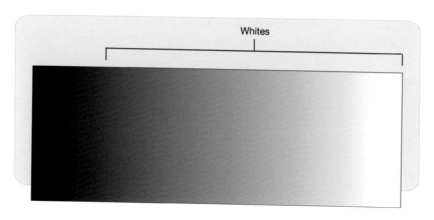

You probably noticed, however, that there are three eyedroppers, and so far you've ignored the one for mids.

In general, you should begin to color balance a scene by working in the whites or the mids to make the scene natural and realistic. Then, depending on the scene, additional adjustments may or may not be necessary.

If there is nothing white in the frame, your next best bet is to sample something that is as close to 50 percent gray as possible using the Mids Select Autobalance Color button. The mids typically make up a large percentage of an image, and a balance wheel for the mids has influence over the colors falling between 10 percent and 90 percent luminance, with the maximum area of influence being the center 75 percent.

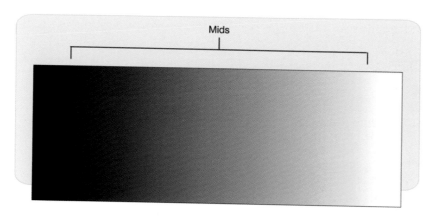

If the entire image is lit with light of the same color temperature, you may get away with balancing just the mids. The advantage of doing the primary color balancing with the mids is that you can avoid overly tinting the bright whites or deep blacks, if these regions are relatively free from color casts. This is, of course, highly dependent on the distribution of color throughout the three luminance zones of the image. Every image is different and requires a unique approach.

TIP ▶ When dealing with strong, saturated colors, the Whites Balance control has the strongest influence on yellow, cyan, and green. The Blacks Balance control has the strongest influence on red, blue, and magenta.

Manipulating Color Directly in the Blacks, Mids, and Whites

As you've seen, the Final Cut Pro color correction filters let you separately manipulate the colors in the blacks, midtones, and whites zones of an image.

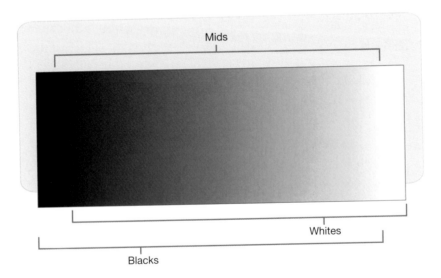

Any control that targets the blacks will only affect colors found in the shadows of the image, from full black up into the mid-gray tones.

Any control that targets the whites will only affect colors found in the highlights, from the mid-gray tones up to white.

Any control that targets the mids affects all the colors found in the midrange of the image, which constitutes the largest percentage of the viewing area.

These three zones have a great deal of overlap. For example, the controls that affect the mids extend their influence into the blacks and whites, but the effect tapers off before reaching the extreme blacks and whites, in order to preserve the ultimate black and white points you want to define.

Learning Each Color Wheel's Zone of Influence

Before moving to a practical example of color balancing, you'll do one last grayscale exercise. (It's the last one, we promise!) This time you'll explore the amount of overlap exerted by each color control.

1   In the 12_Project_Start tab, press the Option key and double-click the Exercise 03 - Blacks, Mids, Whites bin.

2   Open the **Blacks, Mids, Whites** sequence.

3   Double-click the **Gradient** clip in the sequence to open it into the Viewer, then click the Color Corrector 3-way tab at the top of the Viewer. (A Color Corrector 3-way filter has already been applied.)

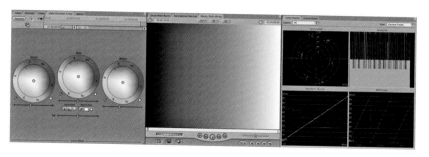

The clip you'll be working on first is another linear gradient generator, this time with the black on the left and the white on the right. It's an ideal way to see the effect each color control has on an image, stretching from absolute black to absolute white.

4   Click in the Blacks Balance control, and drag the balance control indicator in any direction to tint the blacks within the image. It's not necessary to drag all the way to the edge, just drag until the blacks are well tinted.

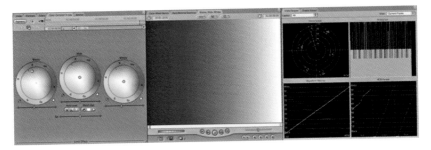

As you can see, the Blacks Balance control actually influences color well into mids. It's important to see, however, that this influence tapers off gently towards the end, so that by 80 percent luminance the control is barely having an effect, and this control has absolutely no effect on the upper 10 percent of whites.

5   Click the Blacks Reset button.

6   Drag the Mids balance control indicator in any direction.

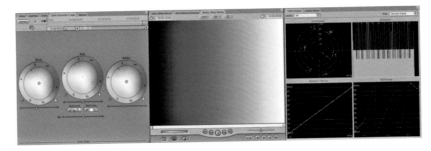

Predictably, you can see that the mids area of influence is strongest in the center region of luminance, tapering off at the blacks and whites, leaving them unaffected.

7   Click the Mids Reset button.

8   Drag the Whites balance control indicator in any direction.

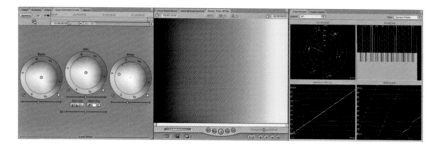

The effect of the whites adjustment is pretty much the inverse of the blacks, such that the lower 10 percent of the luminance range remains unaffected.

9   Take a minute to play around with all of the Color Balance controls at once, and observe how the colors mix together.

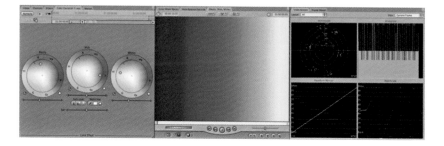

You can see that the blacks and whites both have a profound effect on the mids, yet a strong mids adjustment still manages to create a unique tint at the center of the gradient. Furthermore, you should also observe that the extreme blacks and whites remain unaffected by changes to either of the opposing controls.

You should now have a complete understanding of how the three Color Balance controls allow you to influence the color balance in each of the three zones of luminance. It's time for you to put this knowledge to a real-world test.

Color Balancing Zones of Luminance in an Image

Now you're going to use everything you've learned to color correct a shot manually, without using any automatic controls. In the process, you'll see that, with practice (and the help of the video scopes), it is often easier and faster to manually address color casts and other issues within an image.

1   Open the **Color Balancing Zones** sequence.

2   Double-click the **Phone_Call_CU.mov** clip in the sequence to open it into the Viewer, then at the top of the Viewer click the Color Corrector tab. (A Color Corrector 3-way filter has already been applied.)

Ordinarily, you would first adjust the contrast with the Blacks, Whites, and Mids sliders. In this case, you're lucky, the shot has exactly the contrast the client wants, so you can skip this step.

3   Look at the Parade scope.

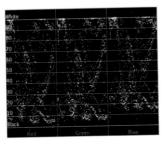

The Parade scope reveals that the blacks have abnormally high blue levels, so this is the first thing you'll need to address.

4   Look at the Vectorscope.

The scope reveals an offset into the blues. This provides you with a valuable clue about how to resolve the color cast issue.

5   Look at the Blacks Balance control, and find the direction of the complementary color to the biggest spike in the Vectorscope.

This tells you the direction in which you want to drag the Blacks Balance control in order to neutralize the color cast.

6   Drag the balance control indicator in the direction of the complementary color, in this case, somewhere between yellow and red.

Keep dragging, with one eye on your image, another eye on the Vectorscope (to keep track of the overall shift in hue), and a third eye on the bottoms of the three graphs in the Parade scope to make sure they become relatively balanced.

Don't worry if you don't drag the control very far. In real-world images, you'll typically find that very small changes in the Color Balance controls have a very big impact.

TIP ▶ At first, you may not notice any movement while dragging on a balance control indicator. By default, the balance control indicators in the color correction filters move in very small increments, which is appropriate for most corrections. If necessary, you can Command-drag to make adjustments in larger increments.

When you're happy with the quality of the blacks, it's time to work on the whites.

7   Since the color cast in the whites is also in the blues, also move the balance control indicator towards a point between yellow and red.

This time, as you drag, keep your eye on the woman's skin color. Because of the large degree of overlap between the whites and mids, this is an opportunity to warm up some of the highlights on her face.

As you make this adjustment, you'll run into the same problem you saw earlier, when the building you thought was white began to turn sepia. It can be helpful to spot something else in the picture that is being affected by the whites color cast. This image has few whites, but there are some highlights on the ring on her finger that can serve as a rough guide.

Again, don't be surprised if you find yourself making a small adjustment to avoid severely tinting the background. In color correction, a little goes a long way. In any event, keep your change minimal, because there's one more step you can take.

8   In the Video Scopes tab, choose Vectorscope from the Layout pop-up menu.

For the last step in this procedure, you're going to boost the red channel in the mids to make the woman pop out a little more from the background. As you do this, keep a close eye on the Vectorscope, so you can keep track of how closely her adjusted skin tones come to the Flesh Tone line.

9   Drag the Mids Balance control in the direction of the complementary color, in this case, somewhere between yellow and red.

This will be your most subtle adjustment of all. You want to drag the balance control indicator out far enough to add more color to her face and some luster to her hair, but you don't want to move it out so far that the image turns brown.

NOTE ▶ If at any point you feel that you're doing more harm than good, don't get frustrated. It's easy for your eyes to get tired after looking at the same color shifts for a long time. Just click the Mids Reset button, and start over.

As you drag the balance control indicator, keep your eye on the Vectorscope. You'll see her flesh tones near the Flesh Tone line, but they don't have to lie directly on the line. Indeed, if they did, she might look a little sallow. In this case, having the traces of the Vectorscope fall just above the Flesh Tone line seem to produce the most pleasing results, but this is a matter of interpretation.

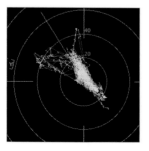

With this last adjustment, you're finished!

10 To see the before and after for this exercise (which is quite dramatic), toggle the Enable Filter checkbox on and off.

In this lesson, you've learned how to perform the most common color-correction task there is—identifying color casts in images and adjusting them. You've learned some of the most common ways of spotting problems in your images using the video scopes, and you've learned precise methods of adjusting the different regions of an image, based on the luminance zone that a particular set of colors happens to fall into.

Lesson Review

1. What is primary color correction?
2. What is a color cast?
3. Which color channels does the Mids Balance control affect?
4. What happens when you mix a color with its complementary color?

5. If the graph in the Vectorscope extends all the way out to the 80 percent ring, what does that mean?

6. If the bottoms of the three graphs in the parade scope are all around 0 percent, but they aren't lining up, which color balance control should you adjust to correct the apparent color cast?

7. Which two Select Auto-balance Color controls should you use first?

8. Do the areas affected by the Color Balance controls overlap?

Answers

1. The first adjustment of the contrast and color-balance of the overall image.

2. An unwanted color that appears to tint the image.

3. Trick question. Each Color Balance control affects all color channels together.

4. They neutralize each other.

5. The image is very highly saturated.

6. The Black Balance control.

7. The Blacks and Whites.

8. Yes.

13

Correcting and Coloring Images

In previous lessons, you learned how to analyze and control the contrast and color quality of an image. In this lesson, you'll apply these skills in a variety of real-world situations.

You'll learn the best way to simultaneously correct contrast and color. You'll also realistically change the look of scenes, correcting skin tones under different lighting conditions and simulating different times of day in exterior shots. Last, you'll use the Color Corrector 3-way filter to create highly stylized color effects.

Color Balancing a Master Shot

Color correction always begins by finding a single shot that's representative of the entire scene. In many cases, it may be a master shot, if it's wide enough to include the environment and all the characters that appear in it. In some cases, it may be a medium shot, if the scene contains several close angles.

Once you've corrected the first shot, you can work on applying that look to the other shots in the scene, so that the entire scene blends seamlessly together (a process you'll explore in Lesson 14).

No matter what the scene, you always begin with a single shot to figure out what corrections and improvements you need to make.

Getting Started

1   Open the Lesson_13 > **13_Project_Start** project.

    If your workspace isn't already set up to include the video scopes in the Tool Bench window, set it up now.

2   If necessary, choose Window > Arrange > Color Correction to arrange your layout to accommodate the Video Scopes tab.

3   From the Layout pop-up menu, choose All.

4   Press the Option key and double-click the Exercise 01 – Balancing Master Shots bin to open it into its own Browser window.

5   Open the **Balancing Master Shots – Finished** sequence.

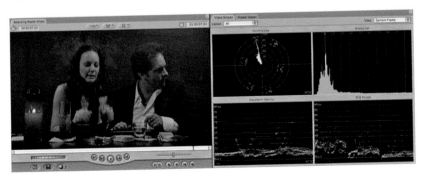

This sequence shows you what you'll be aiming for in the next two exercises. The first clip in the sequence is the original, uncorrected shot.

6   Play to the end of the sequence.

As you can see, the other three clips are duplicates of the first, and each one takes a different approach to the lighting. The second clip is a neutral correction, with solid blacks and clean whites. The third clip has some magenta added in throughout the midtones, for a warmer look. The fourth clip has the lighting skewed towards the greens, simulating the very unpleasant effect of uncorrected fluorescent lighting.

In the next two exercises, you'll learn to create all of these effects.

Adjusting Contrast and Color for a Neutral Balance

First, you'll create a neutral version of this shot. When you're first starting out, go through the process of expanding the contrast ratio and correcting any color casts in the image before you start making creative choices. In doing so, you maximize the image quality *and* create a baseline neutral image that is simpler to manipulate creatively.

1   Open the **Balancing Master Shots** sequence.

This sequence consists of four duplicate clips for you to work on. You'll start with the first one.

When you inspect the shot in the Canvas, you immediately can see that this is an extremely *warm* shot, with reds showing through the blacks. Furthermore, there's an additional color cast that's not quite so readily identifiable in the skin tones and whites of the image.

When most people sit in a post-production suite and discuss color, it's generally in terms of the image being warm (more red) or cool (more blue). Although these terms are generally descriptive, you'll need to perform a more detailed analysis to understand what you need to do to this image to clean it up.

2   Look carefully at the Waveform Monitor. Note the black and white levels.

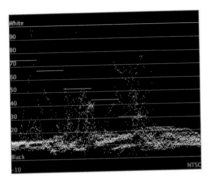

3   Look at the Histogram. Note the distribution of values.

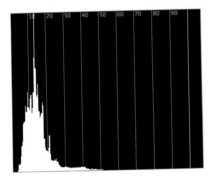

Notice how few values are at 0 percent black and 100 percent white. Although it's not imperative that these extremes contain lots of pixels, your image will have a little more snap if there are at least a few highlights and shadows at either extreme.

NOTE ▶ If you have trouble discerning the narrow percentages being discussed in these scopes, choose Waveform or Histogram from the Layout pop-up menu in the Video Scopes tab to make each graph larger.

4 In the Timeline, select the first **Bar_2Shot.mov** clip, and choose Effects > Video Filters > Color Correction > Color Corrector 3-way to add a color correction filter to the clip.

5 Double-click this clip to open it into the Viewer, and click the Color Corrector 3-way tab to view the filter's custom controls.

When correcting a clip, the proper workflow is to adjust the contrast of the clip to the desired levels *before* you manipulate the Color Balance controls. This is because the zones into which each part of the image fall will change depending on how you adjust the Blacks, Whites, and Mids sliders. This, in turn, changes the effect the Color Balance controls will have.

Furthermore, increasing the distance between the darkest and lightest areas in a clip gives you more control over the colors that fall into these zones. Remember, there's a lot of overlap among the areas affected by the three Color Balance controls. If you don't have blacks and whites that are far enough away from the midrange of the image, you'll find everything in the shot being affected by any changes you make with the Mids Balance control, which means you won't be able to make separate adjustments with the three controls.

6 Move the Blacks slider about six points to the left to lower the black point, until three or four points at the bottom of the Waveform Monitor graph just touch the 0 percent line.

You don't always have to make a drastic change to see significant improvement. In this case, adjusting even a few points serves to visibly enhance the richness of the blacks, without losing valuable detail.

NOTE ► The luminance sliders snap at the midpoint, the default position at which there is no change. Press the Command key while you drag any of the color correction sliders to move them at a slower rate, and disable the snapping at the center, in order to make small changes. Or, you can click the tiny arrows to the left and right of each slider to lower or raise the value by one point per click.

7   Move the Whites slider a few points to the right, until the points at the top of the left most spike in the graph just touch the 100 percent white line.

Again, it's not necessary, or desirable, for this change to be drastic. In this case, you're setting the flame of the candle in the foreground of the image to become the brightest highlight.

NOTE ► Because the candle is flickering, which changes its brightness level, it's a good idea to scrub through the clip and make sure that this boost doesn't go above 100 percent at any point.

In this particular image, the only thing bright enough to plausibly belong at 100 percent is the candle's flame, which can just barely be made out at the upper left corner of the Waveform Monitor.

In this image, you want to leave the mids alone, since it's supposed to read as a dimly lit interior. As you've already seen, the general distribution of tones you can see in the Histogram shows an abundance of dark values that already gives that impression.

8   Look at the Parade scope.

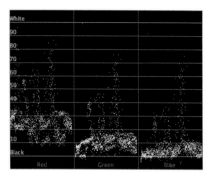

Notice how strong the red channel is and, by comparison, how weak the
blue channel is. Clearly, the spikes on the left and right of the red channel
graph correspond to the wallpaper in the scene, which should be red. In
the Viewer, this is visible as a soft red "haze" that suffuses the image. This
clearly tells you that the desire on the set was for a rich, red lighting scheme,
but the image as it stands is a little muddy. Note that the bottom of the
red channel graph is still well above 0 percent, and the blue channel is well
below 0 percent. According to the Parade scope, you need to boost the balance of the blues in the image.

9   Look at the Vectorscope.

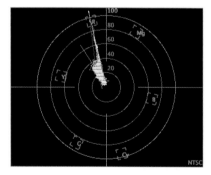

The red wallpaper and overall color cast of the image is clearly visible as a
sharp spike into the red angle of the Vectorscope. This angle shows you the
direction you need to adjust the Blacks Balance control to neutralize the
red color cast with its complementary color.

10 Drag down the Blacks Balance control, in the direction of the Cy (cyan) target, which is the complementary color to red.

As you drag, watch the bottom of the three graphs in the Parade scope—when they line up, you've probably succeeded in correcting the cast.

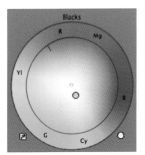

Another glance at the Parade scope shows that the tops of the graphs are somewhat uneven. Although you'd expect the red channel to be stronger because the wallpaper and candle dominate the image, the green channel appears to be a bit stronger than it was in the shadows.

Furthermore, a glance at the Vectorscope shows that the section of the graph most likely to represent the skin tones (which are visibly anemic) is clearly off target, falling just below the Flesh Tone line.

These indicators tell you that the Parade scope is truly showing you a color cast. They also suggest that, to correct those anemic flesh tones, the whites will require more blue than the cyan adjustment you just made to the Blacks.

11 Drag the Whites Balance control toward the B (blue) target, watching the top of the green and blue graphs in the Parade scope as you boost the blues to neutralize the reds and greens in the highlights.

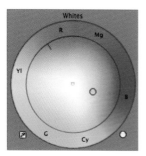

When you've successfully neutralized the cast in the highlights, the white shirt should seem very clean, and the flesh tones should appear natural and pleasing.

Simple adjustments to the Blacks and Whites Balance controls were sufficient to eliminate the excessive red cast and to bring out the natural colors within the image. This is especially convenient because it leaves the Mids Balance control at a neutral position from which to make more stylistic changes to the image.

Adjusting Color for Emotional Impact

From an early age, people develop cultural responses to color. Red can mean stop, connote danger, or elicit appeal as a color for cars, candy, or lipstick. Meanwhile, green means go, gives the impression of safety, or represents envy, depending on the context. Blues, for their part, can indicate cold, darkness, or even emotional detachment. The list is endless, and there are many reference works dedicated to the exploration of color and its meaning.

As a colorist, you can use these cultural responses to reinforce a scene's emotional intent. For example, deep reds in the lighting can make a restaurant scene more intimate. Conversely, pale green lighting might make an unpleasant office scene even drearier.

In the next two exercises, you'll adjust the previous clip to create two different color scenarios. In the process, you'll learn how to make adjustments look as if they come from specific parts of the original lighting scheme.

1   With the custom controls of the first clip visible in the Viewer, copy the filter from the first shot to the second by dragging the copy filter icon to the second clip in the Timeline.

2   Move the playhead to the beginning of the second clip, then double-click it to open it into the Viewer.

There are two ways you can change the color temperature of the dominant light source. You can add color to the whites, or you can add color to the mids. Each method has slightly different results. To see the difference, you'll try both.

3   Adjust the Whites Balance control, dragging it from its initial position towards the Mg (magenta) target.

Before   After

Remember, the goal is to add a bit of color to the lighting while maintaining a realistic feel in the shot. This adjustment should be subtle.

When you adjusted the Whites Balance control, you added color to the entire upper range of the image. If you look at the man's shirtsleeve, you'll see that you've just eliminated the pure whites in the picture. The highlights are clearly colored. This is a good choice if you want to infer a strong, colored *key light*.

NOTE ▸ In lighting, the key light is the brightest lighting instrument that is directed at the scene, which creates the dominant light source and highlights in the picture. The lighting that falls on the right side of the actors' faces is from the key light.

4   Copy the filter from the first clip to the third clip.

5   Move the playhead to the beginning of the third clip, and double-click it to open it into the Viewer.

Next, you're going to make a similar change by adjusting the mids, while leaving the whites alone.

6   Drag the Mids Balance control from its default center position, toward the Mg (magenta) target.

Again, this should be a fairly subtle adjustment.

By making an adjustment to the mids, you only add color to the midrange of the image, retaining some pure whites in the highlights. You can see the difference by examining the man's shirtsleeves. Although the shadowed areas have some color, the highlights are still pretty clean.

7   Use the Up and Down Arrow keys to move the playhead back and forth between the second and third clips, so you can compare the difference.

Depending on your needs, the second adjustment can give you a more sophisticated look, and one less likely to appear to be a simple tint. This is a good choice if you want to infer colored *fill light* bouncing in from the rest of the scene.

NOTE ▶ In lighting, the fill light is a softer, more diffuse light source used to minimize shadows cast by the key light. The fact that the left sides of the actors' faces don't fall off into hard black shadows shows you that some fill light was used.

Next, you'll make a different adjustment to the Mids Balance control to give the same clip a completely different mood.

8   Copy the filter from the third clip to the fourth clip.

9 Move the playhead to the beginning of the fourth clip, and double-click it to open it into the Viewer.

10 Click the Mids Reset button.

11 Drag the Mids Balance control towards the G (green) target, leaving the blacks and whites alone.

This adjustment attempts to simulate the unpleasant color cast that uncorrected fluorescent lighting would add to the scene.

This renders the bar a truly dismal place to be, indeed.

The ability to manipulate color in the three luminance zones of an image gives you an enormous amount of control over the different light sources that illuminate the shot.

Rendering Faces Naturally

Most of the time, human faces are the primary focus of a scene. Regardless of what you're doing to the other colors in a clip, audiences generally expect actor's complexions to be recognizably flesh-toned. When trying to create a natural color balance, the human face is one of your key reference points for determining the correct hue of an image.

As you learned in an earlier lesson, the Final Cut Pro Vectorscope is the fastest way to spot the hues in an image. A special target, the Flesh Tone line, helps you make sure your subjects' skin hues are accurately represented.

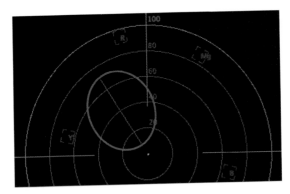

Regardless of the lightness or darkness of a person's complexion, the facial hues of all people fall close to this target. Variations will move the distribution of skin tones to the right or left of the Flesh Tone line, but all skin tones should fall close to it.

1   In the 13_Project_Start tab, Option-double-click the Exercise 02 - Rendering Faces bin.

2   Open the **Rendering Faces** sequence.

3   In the Video Scopes tab, make sure that the Layout pop-up menu is set to All.

4   Control-click within the Vectorscope, and choose Magnify from the contextual menu to enlarge the center of the Vectorscope so you can better see the distribution of values.

5   With the playhead at the beginning of the clip, compare the image to the Vectorscope.

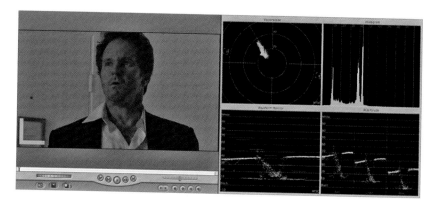

Clearly, there is a color cast throughout the room, and it's resulting in the actor's face looking a little yellow, the direction into which the Vectorscope graph is skewed.

Furthermore, it should be clear that this is a low-contrast image, with a distinct lack of highlights, and no absolute black. Before you try to correct the skin tone, you need to adjust the contrast.

6   Add the Color Corrector 3-way filter to this clip, open it into the Viewer, and click the Color Corrector 3-way tab.

7   Drag the Blacks slider so that the bottom of the Waveform Monitor graph hits the 0 percent line, then drag the Whites slider so that the top of the graph hits just under the 100 percent line.

The image springs to life, but now the clip looks like it was shot at noon, and the client wants it to be evening. As you learned in Lesson 11, the best way to achieve this is to bring down the mids.

8 Drag down the Mids slider, so that in the Waveform Monitor graph, the centermost group of values moves to the 50 percent line.

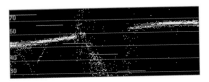

This provides the overall brightness the shot needs.

Next, it's time to balance the colors of the shot. First, you should correct the clear color cast that's visible in the blacks. A glance at the bottom of the graphs in the Parade scope shows that the blue level is far too low, and the reds are too high.

9 Drag the Blacks Balance control towards the center of the Cy (cyan) and B (blue) targets. Watch the bottoms of the graphs in the Parade scope, and stop dragging when the bottoms of the graphs line up.

In addition to creating deep blacks, this adjustment results in a clear improvement in the skin tones. However, there's still a bit of a cast at the high end, and the Vectorscope graph is still falling a little below the skin tone target.

You could try to use the Whites Select Auto-balance Color control on the wall or shirt, but what if neither is pure white? This time, you'll make this correction manually, by watching the color of the man's skin.

10 Drag the Whites Balance control towards the Mg (magenta) target while watching the Vectorscope. Focus on pulling the Vectorscope graph up, so that it falls just above the Flesh Tone line.

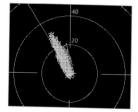

The result is a significant warming in the man's skin tone.

The wall and shirt still seem a little warm, though, and his face seems a bit oversaturated.

11 Pull the Whites Balance control a bit towards the B (blue) target, to neutralize some of the red. This time, your goal is to keep the general distribution of the graph above the Flesh Tone line, but pull the graph back towards the center of the Vectorscope, which will reduce the saturation of the reds in the image.

When the man's face loses its red cast, you'll find that the wall and shirt have been made more neutrally white, also.

To see how far you've come, toggle the Enable Filter checkbox at the top of the Color Corrector tab to get a before-and-after view of the clip.

Don't worry too much if you initially find it difficult to discern an oversaturated skin tone from a desaturated skin tone. The Flesh Tone line is more of a general guide than an absolute rule. If you examine an image containing a row of several people in the Vectorscope, chances are that their skin tones would fall across a range. However, the range should be clustered somewhere around the flesh tone indicator.

The best skin tone depends on many factors, including the makeup (is the actor made up to be sunburned?); the character's health (should the character appear pale or jaundiced?); and the person's individual complexion (it'd be a shame to neutralize such a nice tan). The more color correction you do, the easier it will be to make these judgments.

Changing Time of Day in Exteriors

One of the biggest challenges when shooting with available light on location is getting the time of day right. The sun waits for no cinematographer, and the logistics of filmmaking often dictate that a shoot needs to happen at exactly the wrong time of day.

Fortunately, the Final Cut Pro color correction tools give you options when you need to change a shot's time of day. In this exercise, you'll adjust contrast and color to create two distinctly different qualities of light using the same shot.

Creating a Morning Look

1   In the 13_Project_Start tab, Option-double-click the Exercise 03 - Exteriors bin to open it into the Browser.

2   Open the **Changing Time of Day - Finished** sequence.

3   Play the sequence.

    The first clip is the original, uncorrected clip. The second clip has been corrected to create an early morning look, and the third clip has been corrected to create an evening look.

4   Open the **Changing Time of Day** sequence.

5 In the Video Scopes tab, make sure that the Layout pop-up menu is set to All.

In the video scopes, notice that the contrast ratio shown in the Waveform Monitor is already stretched across the entire range of luminance, from 0 to 100 percent. Second, the distribution of hues in the Vectorscope seems to be skewed towards cyan, which makes sense since the red graph of the Parade scope is the lowest one. Finally, you'll notice two distinct spikes in the Histogram—one near the whites, to the right, and one at around 35 percent, near the majority of the luminance values.

You'll use this information to make your corrections.

6 Add a Color Corrector 3-way filter to the first clip, open it into the Viewer, and click the Color Corrector 3-way tab to show its controls.

The first look you'll be creating will suggest a morning shoot. The best way to do this is open to interpretation, but for this correction you'll implement bright, golden morning light. Begin by adjusting the contrast of the image.

7 Command-drag down the Blacks slider a very small distance, to crush the blacks a little bit. Not too much, just a little. Keep your eye on the bottom of the Waveform Monitor to make sure you're not overdoing it.

Even though there are some absolute black areas of the image, for purposes of making the brights seem brighter and the shadows deeper, you can sacrifice a bit of detail in the shadows to increase the contrast of the image.

Because the whites are already at 100 percent, you can't make the image any brighter by boosting this part of the image, so the next step is to boost the mids.

8   Drag the Mids slider to the right, until the parking lot and trees lighten up. In this example, the densest distribution at the left of the Waveform Monitor graph should rise from 40 percent to around 50 to 60 percent.

This definitely brightens the light, but the result sends the whites well over 100 percent.

9   Drag the Whites slider to the left, lowering the whites until the top of the Waveform Monitor graph goes back to 100 percent.

The next step is to create that golden look. The color of natural light is extremely dependent on the sun's position in the sky. The lower the sun is, the denser the atmosphere between you and the sun, and the warmer the sunlight becomes. This is why light is "whitest" around noon, turns golden in the late afternoon, and then becomes the vivid red of sunset just before disappearing behind the horizon.

On the other hand, the physics of light must be tempered by the emotional quality you want to lend to the scene. In this case, evoking the golden sunlight tones from later in the morning, rather than the magenta tones of early morning, may lend an optimistic, relaxing feeling to the scene.

10 Drag the Whites Balance control to add some orange to the highlights.

In exteriors, the sun is usually the brightest thing in the picture. As a result, adjustments made to the whites generally change the perceived color temperature of the sunlight. As a result, nearly the entire scene acquires an orange tint.

This isn't quite what you had in mind, however. All the midtones in the image have acquired the same cast as the sky. It would be a little more pleasing if the sky and highlights had a little more color than the midtones.

11 Drag the Mids Balance control in the direction of the complementary color of the orange you added to the highlights, which in this case is a hue almost halfway between blue and cyan.

Add enough of this complementary color to neutralize the pavement and trees, while retaining the color in the sky and highlights of the building and window.

As a result, you get more of a color spread in the image, which looks much more natural. In particular, you get a lot of the green back in the forest.

Finally, you'll adjust one last slider. The colors in the image are where you want them, but they're a little weak after all this pushing and pulling. Increasing the saturation would give everything a little more punch, but you don't want to overdo it.

12 Choose View > Range Check > Excess Chroma to turn on range checking for chroma.

13 Drag the Sat (saturation) slider at the bottom of the Color Corrector to the left, watching the range-checking icon at the top of the image in the Canvas, until the green checkmark becomes a warning icon. Then drag the slider back to the left until the colors are richly saturated, but not overpowering. (Clearly, this is extremely subjective.)

This last change has added color intensity to the sky and the trees, creating a more vivid image. You'll explore more uses for the saturation slider in Lesson 14.

Creating an Evening Look

Next, you'll quickly readjust these controls to create an evening look. This time, the goal is a post-sunset twilight.

1   Copy the current filter to the second clip in the Timeline. Press the Down Arrow key to move to the next clip, and open it into the Viewer to show its color correction controls.

2   Before doing anything else, drag the Sat slider to its default center position.

    This time, you start by darkening the image. Instead of achieving the brightness you associated with morning, you want to darken the midtones to indicate twilight.

3   Drag the Mids slider to the left to darken the image, redistributing the mids down to about 20 to 30 percent in the Waveform Monitor.

As a result, the whites dip down well below 100 percent. Although you want the image to be darker overall, you still want the highlights to fall at 100 percent, because this preserves color and lends visual appeal to the image.

4   Drag the Whites slider to the left until the top of the Waveform Monitor graph falls just under 100 percent.

Interestingly, this ends up being the default center position of the Whites slider.

Next, you want to intensify the colors in the sky. Whereas the previous goal was a golden-orange light, this time you want the vivid reds of sunset.

5   Drag the Whites Balance control farther towards the reds, to add more red to the highlights.

This adjustment, while successfully adding a sunset color, has more of an effect on the midrange of the image. You'll want to neutralize this to return more variety of color to the image.

6   Drag the Mids Balance control towards the Cy (cyan) marker, to offset the red adjustment.

At this point, things are looking good, but there are two more things you can do to this correction that indicate twilight. Audiences, conditioned by countless movies, have come to associate the color blue with nighttime. You can use this to further influence perception of this scene.

7   Drag the Blacks Balance control toward the blue target to add a touch of blue to the shadows of the image.

It's important not to add too much, since you've adjusted the image so heavily towards the blacks.

Lastly, it's been shown that the human eye is less sensitive to color in low light conditions. This is another fact you can use to make the shot more like evening.

8   Drag down the Sat slider to desaturate the colors, but not so much as to make the image grayscale.

And now you have your evening look.

As you've learned here, a colorist can combine a knowledge of lighting, psychology, human vision, and Hollywood film history to create corrections that reinforce the original lighting, and enhance the creative intent of the program.

Creating Stylized Looks

So far, you've concentrated on correcting images to achieve naturalistic looks, with a focus on manipulating colors to mimic plausible lighting situations.

Another approach, however, is to take these color correction tools to greater extremes. By altering color and its intensity, you can alter the mood of the scene more overtly.

In the remainder of this lesson, you will learn ways to use color to achieve a more stylized and sophisticated look for a scene.

Creating a Faded Magenta Photo Look

In this exercise, you'll manipulate an image to have the desaturated magenta cast that typical of faded color photographs.

1   In the 13_Project_Start tab, Option-double-click the Exercise 04 – Stylized Looks bin to open it into its own window in the Browser.

2   Open the Stylized Look 1 sequence.

3   In the Video Scopes tab, make sure that the Layout pop-up menu is set to All. Control-click the Vectorscope and turn off Magnify in the contextual menu.

4   Because you'll be making significant color adjustments, make sure that Excess Chroma range checking is turned on (View > Range Check > Excess Chroma).

5   Add a Color Corrector 3-way filter to the clip, open it into the Viewer, and click the Color Corrector 3-way tab to show its controls.

This clip is a very well-exposed clip, with a wide contrast ratio, and healthy saturation. It's a bit dark in the mids, but that's to be expected since it looks like it was shot to be an evening scene.

6   Drag up the Mids slider to brighten the midtones.

This is the first step in creating a faded look—reducing the contrast of the image.

7   Drag down the Whites slider to bring the whites back down to 100 percent in the Waveform Monitor.

The last contrast adjustment will fly in the face of every other exercise you've done. You're going to raise the black level above 0 percent. Remember, however, that this time you want to deliberately wash out the image, which requires aggressively reducing the contrast of the image. Even so, you don't want to overdo it.

8   Drag the Blacks slider to the right, so the bottom of the Waveform Monitor graph falls around 8 percent.

The resulting image is now brighter and, as a result, the chroma in the lamps is spiking out of the legal range. Ignore this for now. You'll correct it later. Next, it's time to add the color cast to this image.

9 Drag the Mids Balance control towards the Mg (magenta) target, to tint the midrange of the image.

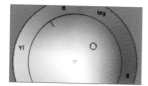

If the chroma was illegal before, now it's *really* illegal. Now that you've made the biggest color shift in this process, you need to bring back the levels to broadcast legal and, in the process, realize that faded look.

10 Drag the Sat slider to the left. The chroma warning icon in the Viewer disappears almost immediately, but keep dragging the slider left until the colors in the image look suitably faded.

The resulting image looks good—definitely tinted and definitely faded.

For extra credit, there are two more adjustments you can make to enhance this look. At this point, the colors towards the blacks and whites are resisting the tint, which is understandable since you adjusted only the mids. You can expand the effect by creating slight tint variations in these areas.

11 Drag the Blacks Balance control a little towards a blue/magenta hue, then drag the Whites Balance control more aggressively towards a blue/cyan hue.

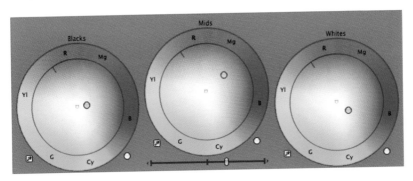

The result is a severely faded color cast that varies across the luminance range of the clip and adds more visual interest than a more monochromatic color cast. Notice that despite the extremity of the correction you've applied, there are still other colors in the frame that are clearly discernable.

Creating a Cool Desaturated Look

In this exercise, you'll create a high-contrast appearance that also uses a low-saturation color cast to achieve a cool blue look.

1   Open the **Stylized Look 2** sequence.

2   Add a Color Corrector 3-way filter to the clip, open it into the Viewer, and click the Color Corrector 3-way tab to show its controls.

Begin by boosting the contrast, thereby washing out the midtones and crushing the blacks.

3   Drag the Mids slider far to the right, so that the main cluster of midtones appears around 80 percent to the right of the Waveform Monitor graph.

4   Drag the Whites slider to the left, to bring the top of the Waveform Monitor graph back to 100 percent.

5   Command-drag the Blacks slider to the left just a bit. As you make this adjustment, you'll see the bottom of the Waveform Monitor graph bunch up at the 0 percent line.

The image already had plenty of blacks, but you'll crush them even further, sacrificing some shadow detail to stylize the image. Again, making such an adjustment in moderation is the key to stylizing the image, rather than butchering it.

Now that you've created the high contrast, it's time to add in the cool blue.

6   Drag the Mids Balance control towards a hue between the B (blue) and Cy (cyan) targets to create a steel-blue wash of color across the midtones.

You want to make sure not to make such an extreme adjustment that you can no longer discern the skin tone of the actors.

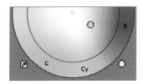

This is the only color shift you need to make, because the abundance of blacks and whites in the image preserves enough tonal variation to make the image interesting.

7   Drag the Sat slider to the left to reduce the saturation of the image so that the graph extends just around 25 percent in the Vectorscope.

This reduces the color uniformly across the entire image. You retain the cool blue of the image relative to the other hues throughout the picture, but it's no longer overpowering.

Tinting Images with the Color Corrector 3-Way Filter

In this last exercise, you'll use extreme settings in the Color Corrector 3-way filter to create monochromatic color tints. Unlike using the Sepia or Tint filters (found in Effects > Video Filters > Image Control), tinting the image by using the Color Corrector 3-way filter allows you to constrain the tint to specific areas of the picture.

1 Open the **Stylized Look 3** sequence.

2 Add a Color Corrector 3-way filter to the clip, open it into the Viewer, and click the Color Corrector 3-way tab to show its controls.

3 Drag the Blacks slider to the left, until the bottom of the Waveform Monitor graph hits the 0 percent line.

This expansion of contrast is important because it will preserve some dark tones that will later give the tint some depth.

4 Drag both the Blacks and Mids Balance controls towards the Cy (cyan) target, all the way down to the edge of the wheel.

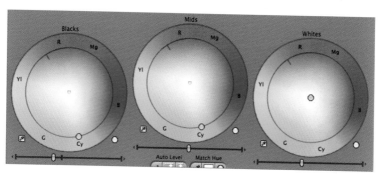

As a result, the blacks through mids are tinted, while the sky remains untouched. This, of course, completely blows the chroma out of the legal range, which you'll need to correct.

5   Drag the Sat slider to the left until the warning icon in the Canvas turns into a green checkmark.

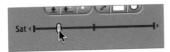

The advantage of this technique is that the whites are still relatively neutral, so if you wanted to create a duotone, you could tint the sky differently than the buildings. Furthermore, making additional adjustments to the contrast would allow you to expand or contract the range of the image affected by each tint. The variations are endless.

Lesson Review

1. When balancing a shot, what's the first thing you do?

2. If you want to adjust the overall color of the scene without tinting the shadows and highlights, which Color balance control should you adjust?

3. How can you quickly tell if skin tones are accurate?

4. What color cast does fluorescent lighting give?

5. How can you give the brightest highlights a color cast, but prevent this from overly affecting the midtones?

6. How can you uniformly reduce the saturation of the entire image?

Answers

1. Adjust the contrast using the Blacks and Whites sliders.

2. The Mids.

3. Check how close they fall next to the Flesh Tone line.

4. Green.

5. Adjust the Whites Balance control to give the color cast, then adjust the Mids Balance control to compensate for this as much or little as necessary.

6. Using the Sat slider.

14

Lesson Files Lessons > Lesson_14 > 14_Project_Start

Media Media > Lesson_14_Media

Time This lesson takes approximately 90 minutes to complete.

Goals Use comparison to aid in color matching

Color correct a scene from beginning to end

Learn a workflow for color matching

Use Frame Viewer, Copy Filter controls, and playhead sync during color correction

Color Correcting for Scene Continuity

Now that you've learned the many methods of evaluating and correcting individual images, it's time to move on to the bigger picture—correcting an entire scene from beginning to end.

You will begin, as always, by correcting a single shot using the methods covered in the previous lessons. Then, to create a sense of visual consistency among each coverage shot, you'll use the same tools, with some new techniques, to match the look of the initially corrected shot to every clip in the scene.

Achieving Visual Harmony

In a dramatic program, most scenes portray an event that takes place at a single time, in a single place. As such, the general intensity and color of the lighting should be the same from shot to shot.

This is often at odds with the logistics of filmmaking, where the light may be quite different from one angle of coverage to another. This is especially true for projects shot outdoors using available light. If the scene took several hours to shoot, the quality of light in Actor 1's close-up may be very different from the quality of light filmed two hours later in Actor 2's reverse close-up.

When the lighting is different in two consecutive shots in a scene, the cut between those clips becomes noticeable. The audience may not understand why, but they'll notice the difference, and this will defeat the editor and film-maker's goal of achieving seamless continuity. Any discontinuity in the look of consecutive images can be jarring, and may take the viewer out of the moment as surely as a poorly timed edit.

Visual harmony is important for many types of programs. Reality TV, documentaries, and interview shows all aim to integrate footage shot in different lighting conditions into a coherent whole. Even though there may be no real need to fool anyone into thinking that the shots happened at the same time and place, any unjustified change in lighting or color from one shot to the next can distract viewers from the flow of the program and the point you're trying to make.

Regardless of the lighting variances or the color of the source media, the color correction tools you use to make corrections to a single clip can also balance the colors of multiple clips in a scene. In this way, you can impose a seamless continuity lacking in the original edit, so that every angle appears to be in exactly the same time and place, and every clip fits together.

Getting Started

1   Open the Lesson_14 > **14_Project_Start** project.

If your workspace isn't already set up to include the video scopes in the Tool Bench window, set this up now.

2   Choose Window > Arrange > Color Correction to arrange your layout to accommodate the Video Scopes tab.

Customizing Window Layouts for Color Correction

There are a number of available window layouts specifically for color correction. If necessary, you can customize the interface and save additional window layouts to best suit your style of working.

The selection of built-in layouts available in the Window > Arrange submenu is dependent on the number of monitors you have, and on their resolutions. Some window layouts require a specific minimum resolution to ensure room for the arrangement of windows used by that layout.

Configuring the Resolution of your Monitor

If your monitor is set to a horizontal resolution of 1024 pixels or less, you may want to increase it, if possible, to enable additional window layouts in the Window > Arrange submenu.

1   Quit Final Cut Pro if it is running.

2   In the Apple menu, choose System Preferences.

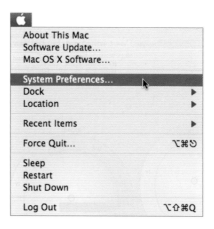

3 In the System Preferences window, click the Displays icon.

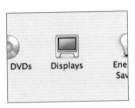

4 Choose a horizontal resolution of 1280 or higher. The horizontal resolution is the first number (the number on the left) when reading from the available resolutions.

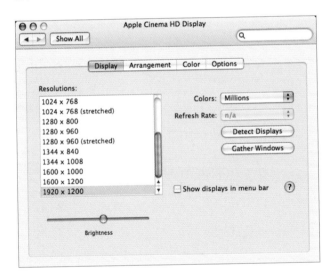

NOTE ▶ If you are using a PowerBook or other small screen, you may not be able to set your resolution this high. Don't worry, you can still complete all of the exercises, but your screen may seem a bit cramped.

Select the "Show displays in menu bar" option so you can change your monitor resolution on-the-fly, without having to go through the System Preferences window.

5 Press Command-Q to quit System Preferences.

Choosing a Window Layout for Color Correction

For most of the following exercises, you'll use the same Color Correction layout you've been using in the previous four lessons. If you're using a two-monitor system, however, use the Dual-Screen Color Correction layout, which moves the Browser onto the second monitor and provides room for a wider Timeline. When you begin copying color correction filters from one clip in a sequence to others, you'll appreciate being able to see more of your program.

1 Open the Scene 1 sequence, and move the playhead to the second clip.

2 Choose Window > Arrange > Color Correction (or Dual-Screen Color Correction if you have two monitors).

There's also a second color-correction-oriented window layout that comes in handy when you want to compare a clip to those on either side of it: the Multiple Edits layout.

3   Choose Window > Arrange > Multiple Edits (or Dual-Screen Multiple Edits).

This layout takes advantage of an additional window tab available in the Tools menu: the Frame Viewer. Frame Viewers are tabs added to any Tool Bench window that can display any one of a range of frames adjacent to the playhead.

This layout sandwiches the Canvas between two Frame Viewers (which you'll learn to use later in this lesson) to display three consecutive shots from the current scene: the previous shot, the current shot at the position of the playhead, and the next shot. With this presentation, you quickly can make approximate judgments about how the visuals are fitting together.

Creating and Saving Customized Window Layouts

If you have two or more computer monitors (oh, the luxury!), or a large single monitor such as a Cinema Display HD, you can set Final Cut Pro to display additional video scopes and/or Frame Viewers with which to analyze adjacent shots in a scene.

For example, you can create a custom layout that displays two Waveform Monitors, one showing the waveform of the current clip, and one showing the waveform of the first frame of the next clip. In this layout, you can directly compare the black point, white point, and mids distribution of both clips while you work.

1   Choose Window > Arrange > Color Correction.

This is the basic window layout for your new layout.

2   Choose Tools > Video Scopes to create a second Video Scopes tab.

The additional video scopes open as a tab (named Video Scopes 2) in the open Tool Bench window.

3   Drag the Video Scopes 2 tab out of the its current window. When you release the mouse button, it appears in a new Tool Bench window.

4   Resize the original Tool Bench window so that it's half as wide as it was, and move it to the right half of the area in which it appears.

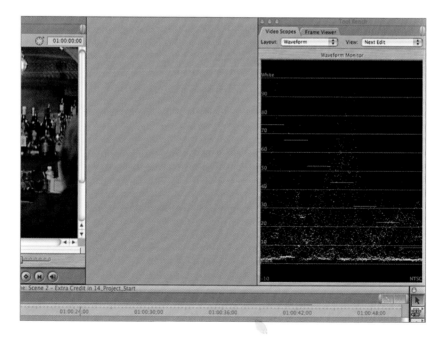

5 Drag the new Tool Bench window into the resulting empty space, and resize it so that it fits neatly to the left of the original Tool Bench window.

6 From the View pop-up menu of the Video Scopes tab, choose Current Frame. From the View pop-up menu of the Video Scopes 2 tab, choose Next Edit.

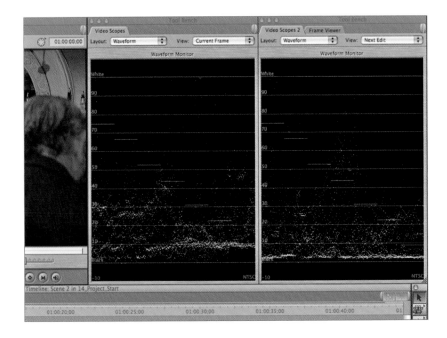

The View pop-up menu in the video scopes contains many options for identifying which frame to analyze.

By default, the pop-up menu displays the frame at the current position of the playhead, but you can also set it to analyze frames from previous or subsequent shots in the Timeline (relative to the clip at the position of the playhead), or even the current frame displayed in the Viewer.

7 Choose Window > Arrange > Save Window Layout and name the layout *Dual Video Scopes.*

In the future, you can restore this saved custom layout by choosing it from the list of all custom layouts that appears at the bottom of the Window > Arrange submenu.

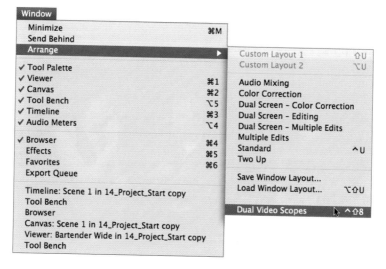

You can create as many special-purpose screen layouts as you need, and switch among them as your current task requires.

Saving a custom window arrangement saves more than just the position of the main Final Cut Pro windows; it also saves the following Tool Bench parameters:

▶ Number of Tool Bench windows open.

▶ Specific combination of Video Scopes and Frame Viewer tabs.

▶ In the Video Scopes tab, the layout, frame, and contextual options, such as the brightness of the overlays and whether targets are displayed. (For instance, you could save the following array of options: Vectorscope window, magnified, targets off, viewing the previous edit.)

▶ In the Frame Viewer, the green- and blue-labeled pop-up choices, as well as the split-screen border. This saves all the custom options of the Frame Viewer.

To take a customized window layout with you to another computer, you'll find custom layouts saved in */UserName/*Library/Preferences/Final Cut Pro User Data/Window Layouts.

If you find yourself using a layout over and over, Final Cut Pro provides two custom layout slots available at the top of the Window > Arrange menu for quick access.

To store your quick access custom layout, hold the Option key and choose Window > Arrange. You'll notice the options Custom Layout 1 and 2 are now accessible. Choose the one you'd like, and your custom layout will be stored.

To retrieve these layouts, simply use the shortcuts Shift-U or Option-U, respectively. (Or, you can also access them via the Window > Arrange menu, of course.) These options let you quickly set up and restore the layouts you'll be using the most.

Comparing Two Clips

It may sound obvious, but before you can correct one clip to match another, you must be able to compare both images in such a way as to quickly and accurately identify their differences. Before getting started with color correcting a scene, you'll spend a little time familiarizing yourself with Final Cut Pro techniques for comparing two clips.

Toggling Between Images in the Canvas

The process of comparing two images is deceptively simple. It's always critical to judge the quality of an image using a calibrated broadcast-quality monitor, and not your computer's display; but it's even more critical when you start balancing the color of an entire scene.

For this reason, the most reliable and accurate method for comparing two images is also the lowest-tech solution, and that is to simply flip back and forth between two clips while watching the images change on your broadcast monitor.

The Show Edit commands allow you to temporarily jump to other edit points in the Timeline and then return to the frame at the initial position of the playhead:

▶ *Show Previous Edit* (Control-Up Arrow) toggles the last frame of the clip located immediately to the left in the Timeline.

▶ *Show 2nd Prior Edit* (Shift-Control-Up Arrow) toggles to the last frame of the second clip to the left in the Timeline.

▶ *Show Next Edit* (Control-Down Arrow) toggles to the first frame of the clip immediately to the right.

▶ *Show 2nd Next Edit* (Shift-Control-Down Arrow) toggles to the first frame of the second clip to the right.

▶ *Show In Point* (Control-Left Arrow) works only if you have defined an In point in the Timeline or Canvas to toggle it.

▶ *Show Out Point* (Control-Right Arrow) works only if you have defined an Out point in the Timeline or Canvas to toggle it.

In the following exercise, you'll practice using these keyboard shortcuts to compare shots in an edited sequence.

1   If you have an external broadcast monitor connected to your computer, make sure that it's set up properly, and that External Video is set to All Frames.

2   With the **Scene 1** sequence open, move the playhead to the third clip of the sequence, **Side Wide Angle (02)**.

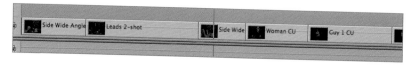

Its image appears simultaneously in the Canvas and in the broadcast monitor.

3 Press and hold Control-Up Arrow.

The playhead immediately jumps to the last frame of the previous clip, showing you how the last image from the previous clip will segue into the current clip.

NOTE ▸ If the Show Edit keyboard commands don't respond, move the playhead off the first frame of the clip and repeat the command.

4 Release the keys you've been pressing.

The playhead goes back to its initial position.

NOTE ▸ As you do this exercise, make sure you don't inadvertently make the Viewer the active window. When the Viewer is active, the Show Edit commands still work, but when you release the keys the playhead doesn't return to its original position. To enable the proper key behavior, make sure the Timeline is the active window.

5 Press and release Control-Up Arrow a few times, and notice how you can flip back and forth between each image, getting an instant sense of the differences between color and brightness.

When you quickly jump back and forth between images, your eyes don't have time to adjust to each image, which makes it easier to spot the variations.

As you flip between images, glance at the video scopes, and notice how they update with the image. You can use the Show Edit commands to compare images numerically, as well as visually, by flipping between their graphs on the scopes. This is an important technique that you'll be using a lot.

6   Press and hold Shift-Control-Up Arrow.

This time, the playhead jumps to the last frame of the second clip to the left. When correcting a scene with many angles of coverage, using Control-Up Arrow and Shift-Control-Up Arrow lets you quickly compare many different clips to get a sense of the colors throughout the scene.

7   Release the keys you've been pressing, and press Control-Down Arrow and then Shift-Control-Down Arrow, to jump to the clips to the right of the current playhead position.

These commands are very useful when you're balancing shots that appear next to one another in a sequence; but if you want to balance clips that appear in entirely different parts of your program, you'll need to use the Show In Point and Show Out Point commands.

8   Set an In point at the current playhead position.

9   Move the playhead to the last clip in the sequence.

10   Press and hold Control-Left Arrow.

The playhead jumps to the exact frame defined by the In point. This shortcut is useful for comparing two clips that are separated from one another in a sequence. It's also good for comparing the current frame with a specific frame in an adjacent clip, and not just In or Out points.

Making Side-by-Side Comparisons with the Frame Viewer

Another useful tool for comparing two images is the split-screen function found in the Final Cut Pro Frame Viewer.

As you have learned, the Frame Viewer lets you display other edit points relative to the current position of the playhead. The Frame Viewer also lets you compare two images *within the same frame* using a split-screen mode.

1   Move the playhead to the first clip in the sequence.

2   In the Tool Bench window, click the Frame Viewer tab.

By default, the Frame Viewer is set to a vertical split-screen mode, showing the current frame with filters on the left side of the frame, and the current frame without filters on the right. Since there are no filters applied to the current clip, there's no visible split in the image.

Like the View options in the video scopes, the Frame Viewer is flexible enough to compare a range of images in split-screen mode. The two pop-up menus underneath the image frame itself let you assign images to each part of the split-screen mode.

3   From the pop-up menu at the lower right of the Frame Viewer (next to the blue square), choose Next Edit.

The left side of the Frame Viewer screen now displays the current frame, and the right side displays the first frame of the next clip to the right. As you saw in the menu, there are numerous options for comparing clips in your sequence, most of which correspond to the Show Edit commands you used previously.

If you look carefully at the corners that define the left half of the split screen, you'll see four square, color-coded handles. Each control and menu in the Frame Viewer is color-coded green or blue. These colors correspond to each of the two pop-up menus at the bottom of the Frame Viewer. The pop-up menus define which clips in the Timeline appear in each half of the frame, and relate to the timecode values (at the top of the Frame Viewer) that show you which frames are being viewed.

In the current split-screen view, you can see that there is a color discontinuity between the two shots, but it may be difficult to make an "apples to apples" comparison because there is no single visual element shared by both images. Fortunately, you can customize the split between the two images.

4   At the bottom of the Frame Viewer window, click the H-Split button.

Now, instead of the vertical split screen, there is a horizontal split screen.

If you're ever confused about which clip is in which part of the screen, you can rely upon the color-coded handles that appear within the frame. In the current horizontal split, the four green handles at the corners of the bottom half of the screen correspond to the green icon next to the lower-left pop-up menu that's set to Current Frame. The blue half-handles, then, correspond to the icon next to the lower-right pop-up menu set to the Next Edit relative to the current frame.

At this point, you can compare the woman's shoulder in one shot to her arm in another, but it's still difficult to make an accurate comparison.

5   Click the Swap button.

The images are reversed on either side of the split, but it's still difficult to compare the lighting on her arm in each picture.

TIP You can also swap the two sides of a split screen by clicking the H-Split or V-Split buttons repeatedly, as long as you haven't customized the split rectangle.

6   Move the pointer to the lower-left edge of the split screen. When the pointer turns into a resize arrow, drag the left edge to the right until you can see the woman's arm in each clip.

The Frame Viewer split screen is incredibly flexible because the split between both images is defined by a user-customizable rectangle. You can drag each of the four corner handles, and each side, of the split around the frame independently, so you can selectively compare any two areas of an image, regardless of their position. Having made the adjustment, you can now compare the woman's arm in each clip, and the difference between each image is obvious.

There are several ways you can manipulate the split between two images.

7   Drag up the lower-right corner handle of the split screen so that the split area is a small square.

8 Move the pointer into the center of the split, and when the pointer becomes a hand, drag the split around in the frame.

It's easy to move the split rectangle, comparing different parts of both images.

9 Click the V-Split button to reset the Frame Viewer to a vertical split screen.

10 In the Timeline, move the playhead to the second clip.

The clips displayed in the Frame Viewer are always relative to the current playhead position. As you move the playhead around in your sequence, the Frame Viewer updates to display the appropriate images.

As you move around the sequence, however, you should notice one crucial thing. The only image that is displayed on your external broadcast monitor is *the current frame at the position of the playhead*. The split screen displayed by the Frame Viewer cannot be output to video, and cannot be relied upon for making crucial comparisons.

The best time to use the Frame Viewer is after you make the first few corrections, flipping between clips and viewing the external monitor. Later, if you're having difficulty determining the difference between an uncorrected clip and another clip that has been corrected relative to the broadcast monitor, the split screen might give you more clues (particularly if flipping between both pictures and examining the video scopes graphs isn't revealing enough).

Split screen is also a good way to view your results as you begin learning how to correct a second shot to match a first, but you should always, always flip between both images on your calibrated broadcast monitor to finish the job.

Setting Up for Scene-by-Scene Color Correction

Several interface options make it easier to color correct a scene. In this section, you'll set up Final Cut Pro to take advantage of these options. Bear in mind that these settings are a matter of personal preference—what's good for one colorist may not work for another. Be aware that some Final Cut Pro features that have nothing directly to do with color correction can still provide numerous benefits to the colorist.

Setting Playhead Sync to Open

As you've seen, all color correction in Final Cut Pro is done with filters, and the color correction filters have custom controls in the Color Corrector 3-way tab of the Viewer. Opening another color-corrected sequence clip into the Viewer automatically reveals its Color Corrector parameters within the same tab, as long as the Color Corrector 3-way tab was already open.

You can take advantage of this behavior to automate the process of opening clips into the Viewer by using the Open setting in the Playhead Sync pop-up menu in the Viewer or Canvas. As its name implies, the Open playhead sync setting automatically opens into the Viewer any clip that becomes visible in the Canvas.

If all of your clips have color correction filters applied, simply moving the playhead to another clip automatically opens its color correction controls into the Viewer. Not only does this save you a few mouse clicks, but it also ensures that you are always adjusting the color correction controls of the clip you happen to be looking at.

> **NOTE ▶** Although this is a useful way to work, you are advised to leave playhead sync set to Off while doing the exercises in this lesson, unless otherwise instructed.

1   Open the **Scene 1 - Finished** sequence.

2   In the Timeline, double-click the first clip to open it into the Viewer.

All of the clips in this sequence have already been corrected, so they all have Color Corrector 3-way filters applied.

3   In the Viewer, click the Color Corrector 3-way tab to expose the first clip's color correction controls.

4   From the Playhead Sync pop-up menu in the Canvas, choose Open.

TIP ▶ You can also choose the playhead sync option from the Playhead Sync pop-up menu in the Video tab of the Viewer.

5   Drag the playhead from left to right through the Timeline, pausing briefly at each clip.

As you scrub from clip to clip, you'll see how the Viewer window automatically displays the same image as the Canvas.

6   Move the playhead to the third clip in the sequence.

The Open playhead sync mode even works with the Show Edit commands.

7   Select the Timeline, press Control-Up Arrow, then press Control-Down Arrow.

Notice how the Color Corrector controls update every time the playhead moves. It might take a moment or two, but the Viewer always updates.

Although this style of working is convenient, there are many times you'll want to disable this behavior. For example, you'll probably want to turn playhead sync off if you want to keep the Color Corrector 3-way tab from one particular clip open in order to scrub over to another section of the Timeline and drag it onto another clip, or when using the Match Hue controls.

If you routinely use the Open playhead sync mode, periodically check that Open is selected in the Playhead Sync pop-up menu, because it's fairly easy to accidentally deselect this mode.

Also note that Final Cut Pro always opens the clip on the highest track that has Auto Select enabled. If you have clips on multiple tracks, Option-click the Auto Select icon to select just that track you want to color correct.

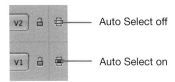

Choosing Timeline Options

There are also several Timeline options you can set that make it easier to navigate and manage filters in a sequence. In this exercise, you'll set up the Timeline to take advantage of these options.

1   Open the **Scene 1** sequence in the Browser.

2   In the Browser, Control-click the **Scene 1** sequence, and choose Settings from the shortcut menu.

3 In the Sequence Settings window, click the Timeline Options tab.

Sequence Settings

Name: Scene 1

General | Video Processing | Timeline Options | Render Control | Audio Outputs

Starting Timecode: 01:00:00;00 ☑ Drop Frame
Track Size: Small
Thumbnail Display: Name Plus Thumbnail
Audio Track Labels: Sequential (A1, A2, A3, A4)

Track Display
☐ Show Keyframe Overlays
☐ Show Audio Waveforms
☐ Show Through Edits
☐ Show Duplicate Frames
☐ Show Audio Controls

☐ Clip Keyframes
Video:
☑ Motion Bar
☑ Filters Bar
☑ Keyframe Editor
☑ Speed Indicators

Audio:
☑ Filters Bar
☑ Keyframe Editor
☑ Speed Indicators

Load Sequence Preset...   Cancel   OK

4 If it's not already set, choose Name Plus Thumbnail from the Thumbnail Display pop-up menu.

Since you're not changing the edit points while you color correct a sequence, you don't have to worry too much about the computing overhead of redrawing the thumbnail images. In any event, thumbnails are incredibly useful for quickly spotting which clips come from the same angle of coverage, which facilitates copying filters among similar clips.

5 Turn on Clip Keyframes, and turn off everything within the Clip Keyframes section except for the Video: Filters Bar option.

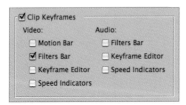

The Filters Bar option places a thin, gray area underneath each clip in the Timeline. Green stripes (filter bars) appear underneath every clip that has a filter applied, which enables you to determine, at a glance, which clips have color correction filters applied.

Filter applied   No filter applied

6   Click OK to close the Sequence Settings window.

7   Move the pointer to the top of track V1 in the Timeline.

8   When the pointer turns into the resize arrow, drag up the top of the track to make it taller.

As useful as the Timeline's clip thumbnails are, they don't do you any good if you can't see them.

If you're working on a sequence with a lot of video tracks, you might consider dragging down the border between the video and audio tracks, obscuring the audio tracks to make room for more video tracks.

TIP ▶ It's pretty typical for colorists to begin work on a program after the picture has been locked, so accidentally moving a clip when you only meant to double-click it, even a few frames, is a bad thing. If you lock all of the audio tracks of a sequence you're correcting, but not the video tracks, and keep linked selection turned on, you can minimize your risk of inadvertently nudging clips around as you work.

Color Correcting a Complete Scene

Now that you've set up your window layout, learned how to compare images, and customized your Timeline, it's time to start working on an actual scene.

Choosing a Reference Shot

The first thing you need to do is determine which clip to use as the starting point for color correcting the scene. In general, you want to choose a reference shot that contains most of the characters that appear in that scene. If your scene features two characters, look for a two-shot that clearly shows both actors. If it's a group scene, find the widest shot that's representative, with as many people as possible clearly visible, which makes it easier to balance the skin tones in each individual's close-up with their skin tone in the corrected reference clip.

In any event, it's important to work on a reference clip that is an average shot from that scene, because after you've made your corrections and stylistic adjustments to that clip, you'll be comparing every other clip in the scene to that reference. If you pick a shot that's anomalous in any way, (the only shot in which someone's in a spotlight, or standing in a huge shadow), you run the risk of incorrectly balancing all the other clips in that scene.

> **TIP** It's always a good idea to communicate with the director and cinematographer to see if they have an opinion about which shot most represents the intended look of the scene.

1 Open the **Scene 1** sequence, and choose Window > Arrange > Color Correction to reset the window layout.

2 Scrub through the first four clips in the Timeline, and see if you can pick the best one to use as a reference shot.

The fourth clip is the easiest to rule out. As a close-up, it shows the least amount of background, and it excludes all the other actors in the shot.

The first and third clips (both from the same angle of coverage), appear at first glance to fit the bill. They're wide shots, and they show every character in that scene. The only problem is that the two most important characters (according to the director) are shown in profile, and we see only the back of the woman's head. On second thought, this is not an ideal starting point.

This leaves us with the second clip in the sequence, **Leads 2-shot**. It's the best shot of both lead actors, and it's wide enough to show a lot of the foreground, as well as the wall behind the actors. Correcting this shot will give you an excellent starting point for balancing this scene.

Developing the Scene's "Look"

One of the interesting things about being a colorist is that your job is one-third technician and two-thirds artist. On the one hand, you have an obligation to provide a reasonably strong video signal, pleasingly visible detail, and minimal noise, and to keep your adjustments within the accepted broadcast limits.

On the other hand, you have an obligation to achieve your client's creative goals, to make shots darker or lighter, warmer or cooler, more saturated or less, depending on the aesthetic needs of the program.

Assuming you have well-exposed footage, it's usually easy to strike a balance between both parts of the job. In this exercise, you'll correct the shot you selected in the last exercise and choose a look for it.

If this shot looks familiar, it should. It appeared in one of the exercises in Lesson 13. After you've gone through the exercises in this section, feel free to remove the filters from the sequence and see if you can regrade the scene using different looks.

Remember, as you correct this first shot, it's critical to view the output on a properly calibrated broadcast monitor.

> **TIP** This exercise provides only suggested changes. Feel free to veer off at any time and create your own look. To see a complete, color corrected sequence, open **Scene 1 - Finished** from the Browser.

1 Locate the second clip in the sequence, the one you've chosen as the reference shot for the scene, and apply a Color Corrector 3-way filter.

   If you turned on Clip Keyframes in the previous exercise, a green filter bar appears underneath the second clip to show you that a filter is applied.

2   Open the second clip into the Viewer, and click the Color Corrector 3-way tab.

3   Press Control-Z to turn on Range Check > Luma.

It's always a good idea to have range checking on while you make adjustments, to give you an instant warning if you push anything too far.

4   Adjust the Blacks, Mids, and Whites sliders to set the black point of the graph in the Waveform Monitor at 0 percent, and the white point for highlights at 100 percent. Watch the range checking icon at the top of the Viewer, as well as the Waveform Monitor, while you make this adjustment. Afterwards, lower the Mids slider just a few points to deepen the shadows.

NOTE ▶ If an image doesn't have any bright whites, or highlights, or any section that would plausibly go all the way up to 100 percent, it's neither necessary nor desirable to automatically boost the level of the brightest area in the image to 100 percent. In these cases, adjust the white point relative to how bright the lightest area in the picture would realistically be in order to keep the contrast from becoming artificially high. In other words, don't set someone's face to 100 percent white just because it happens to be the brightest element in a very dark picture.

5   Make any necessary adjustments to the Blacks and Whites Balance controls, using the Vectorscope and the RGB Parade scope as your guide

Do this to neutralize the yellowish cast, and warm up the skin tones. In this exercise, that involves adding some cyan to the blacks to create true blacks, and some blue to the whites to clean them up.

6   Add some red to the mids, to give some kick to the skin tones and give the impression of warmer lighting in the room.

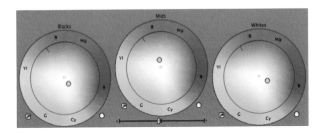

Next, you'll correct the other clips in this sequence so they match the tone and color you've achieved in your reference shot.

Matching Contrast Between Two Shots

The two clips that are adjacent to the **Leads 2-shot** reference clip are from the same angle of coverage, **Side Wide Angle**. You'll begin balancing the rest of the scene to the corrected reference clip by working on the first **Side Wide Angle** clip. As always, you'll begin this correction by adjusting the clip's contrast—in this case, to match that of the reference shot.

It's useful to note that the human eye is more sensitive to changes in brightness than in color, so you want to take particular care to make the contrast of all shots in a scene match as closely as possible.

1   Move the playhead to the beginning of the first clip in the sequence, **Side Wide Angle (01)**.

2   With the Timeline active, press Control-Down Arrow a few times, flipping back and forth between this clip and the previously corrected reference clip to the right of it. Start examining the two clips for differences in contrast.

As you flip back and forth, make sure you check both the visual image and the graphs in the video scopes. When you're examining differences in contrast, the Waveform Monitor is a good guide.

TIP ▶ If you want to do a direct comparison of the waveforms of both clips, you can use the Dual Video Scopes layout you created earlier, placing the playhead on the first clip in the sequence to compare it to the reference clip at the right. When you've finished adjusting the contrast, return to the Color Correction window layout.

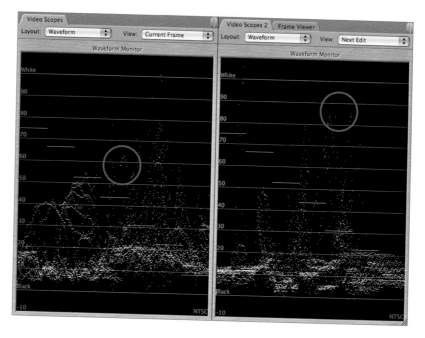

In comparing the two waveform graphs, you should notice that the black point in the uncorrected clip to the left is not as low as in the corrected clip to the right.

You should also notice that some of the distributions within the midtones are a little high, and the white point of the first clip's graph seems to match that in the second clip. In other words, the densest clump in the middle of the graph on the left (which is probably the cocktail bar surface) is about three percent higher then the densest clump in the graph on the right. This makes the **Side Wide Angle (01)** clip seem slightly brighter. This also tells you that you'll later be making an adjustment to the Mids slider.

There's a good way to measure these differences. Once you've spotted an identical feature in each graph, move the pointer within the Waveform Monitor, and an indicator appears. By dragging the indicator to line up with different features in the graph, you'll get a tooltip at the top of the Waveform Monitor that displays the digital percentage. The tooltip can help you determine how much correction you need to make.

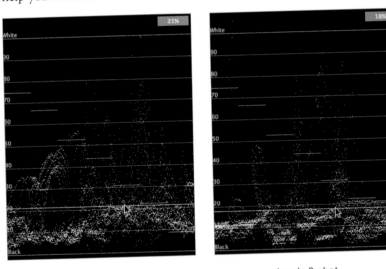

Side Wide Angle (01)   Leads 2-shot

In this example, the first clip to the left measures the top of this feature at about 21 percent; the reference clip at the right measures the same feature at about 18 percent—a 3 percent difference, but enough to be noticeable.

Learning which parts of the graph correspond to which areas of each shot takes practice. Remember that the Waveform Monitor scans the entire image from left to right, drawing a graph based on the brightness of each vertical slice of the picture. Bright parts of the picture, such as the woman's arm, cause upward curves in the midtones at the middle of the graph. Highlights, such as the candles, cause spikes into the whites at the top of the graph. Dark areas, like the man's jacket sleeve and the bar surface, will cluster near the bottom of the graph.

TIP ▶ Sometimes it's easier to see how the graph corresponds to the image when the clip is moving. Ordinarily, the video scopes don't update while the video is playing, but if you choose Mark > Play > Every Frame, the playhead will step through each frame, updating the Canvas and the Video Scopes as it goes, giving you a not-real-time animated view of the graph.

3   Add a Color Corrector 3-way filter to the **Side Wide Angle(01)** clip, and open it into the Viewer.

4   Adjust the Blacks slider so that the average distribution at the bottom of the Waveform Monitor graph for **Side Wide Angle(01)** approximately matches that of **Leads 2-shot**. This will be a very slight adjustment, so you may want to Command-drag the Blacks slider so it doesn't snap to the center position.

If necessary, make the Timeline active and press Command-Down Arrow a few times to flip back and forth, comparing your results before making further adjustments.

NOTE ▶ Remember that if you use the Show Edit commands while the Viewer is active, the playhead won't go back to the original position when you release the keys. For this reason, make sure the Timeline is selected each time you use the Show Edit commands.

5   Drag the Mids slider a few points to the left, lowering the mids so that the overall level of brightness in both clips appears to be the same and the relative distributions start to line up in the middle of the Waveform Monitor graphs.

This will also be a slight adjustment—one that requires you to look at the image, in addition to watching the scopes.

It's important to realize that although the top and bottom of the waveforms are important, the distribution of values between them is even more important to the overall brightness of the clip. Even if the tops and the bottoms of the two graphs line up, the clips won't match if the inner distribution of values is significantly different.

6   To check the adjustment you've just made, make the Timeline active, and press Control-Down Arrow a few times, flipping back and forth between this clip and the reference clip, to make sure your correction matches. If it doesn't, keep making adjustments, checking the video scopes and flipping between images until you're satisfied that the shots match.

Matching Color Between Two Shots

Now that the contrast of the second clip has been set to match the reference shot, it's time to adjust the color.

1   In the Video Scopes window, choose Parade from the Layout pop-up menu, and make sure that View is set to Current Frame.

TIP You could also choose the Dual Video Scopes window layout and set both Video Scopes tabs to display the Parade scope, but it's a good idea to get used to using the Show Edit commands to toggle back and forth. Once you get used to the back and forth method of comparison, it will become second nature.

2   Make the Timeline active, and press Control-Down Arrow a few times, flipping back and forth between the **Side Wide Angle (01)** clip and the **Leads 2-shot** clip, comparing the images on the monitor and the graphs in the Parade scope.

The Parade scope shows you the balance of red, green, and blue in an image. When you're comparing two images, the Parade scope is a powerful tool for identifying exactly which color channels need balancing, and in which luminance zones.

As you toggle back and forth, look at the bottom of each graph. You should notice that, compared to the reference clip, the blues are too low, and the reds are too high. This tells you what kind of adjustment you need to make to the Blacks Balance control.

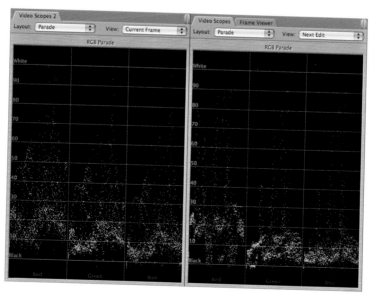

3   Drag the Blacks Balance control somewhere between the Cy (cyan) and B (blue) targets, until the bottoms of the red, green, and blue graphs match those of the reference clip.

To check your work, make the Timeline active and press Control-Down Arrow a few times to compare the images and the graphs. Keep making adjustments until you're satisfied. When you're finished, the bottoms of the graphs should approximately line up.

4   When you're finished, toggle between the images again, this time examining the tops of the graphs.

You should see that the first clip has much more yellow in the highlights of the skin tones than the reference shot. The tops of graphs in the Parade scope reveals this as green and blue channels that are too strong (remember that red + green = yellow).

5   Drag the Whites Balance control towards the B (blue) target to neutralize the yellowish cast in the highlights, but not so far as to overcompensate and tint the highlights blue.

For this last adjustment, it's a bit difficult to accurately spot the tops of the red, green, and blue graphs, because there are so few values there. So, you have to rely upon your judgment of the image itself.

Now that the blacks are black, and the highlights are equally neutral to those in the reference image, it's time to adjust the mids to complete the match. For this last adjustment, you'll be relying on the Vectorscope.

6 In the Video Scopes window, choose Vectorscope from the Layout pop-up menu.

Once you've matched the colors in the blacks and the whites, it often becomes difficult to see how the colors in the mids line up in the Parade scope. In these cases, the Vectorscope can give you a clearer picture of the differences between the overall color temperatures in two images.

TIP ▶ If you're using the Dual Video Scopes window layout, set both Video Scopes tabs to display Vectorscope.

7 Once again, make the Timeline active and press Control-Down Arrow a few times to compare the images and their graphs.

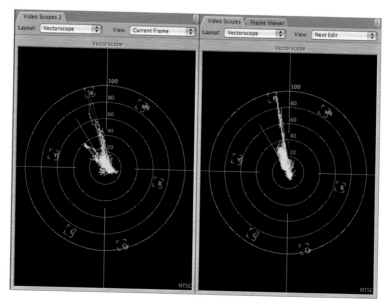

You should immediately see that the first clip doesn't have as much saturation towards the reds as the reference image. In particular, the cluster
of values that fall just above the Flesh Tone line in the reference image's
Vectorscope (to the right) extends all the way up to about 33 percent,
and the same cluster of values in the Vectorscope to the left is down
around 18 percent—a large difference.

8   For **Side Wide Angle (01)**, drag up the Mids Balance control towards the
Flesh Tone line until the cluster of values at the center of the Vectorscope
matches those displayed by the reference clip. If necessary, make the
Timeline active and flip back and forth, adjusting and comparing until
you're satisfied you have a match.

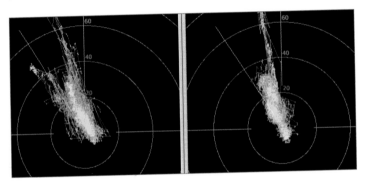

When you're finished, the shots should match just about perfectly. Play
through both clips to make sure.

Copying Filters Forward to Other Clips from the Same Angle

Before you make any more manual adjustments to clips in this scene, it's time
to ask yourself if there are any more clips from the same angles of coverage
and with the same lighting as the clip you've just corrected. If so, you can copy
the color correction filters, along with their settings, from the previously corrected clip to others from the same angle.

It's very common for scenes to be constructed by repeating sequences of clips
drawn from a few angles of coverage. For example, if there are three angles of

coverage—shot A (a master shot of the room), shot B (a two-shot), and shot C (a close-up of actor 2)—the scene might be edited:

A–B–A–C

That's the situation in this scene. A quick look at the Timeline should reveal that the third clip is from the same angle as the first clip you corrected (**Side Wide Angle (02)**), so you might as well copy the color correction filter forward to save yourself some work and guarantee consistency.

To facilitate this, each Color Corrector 3-way filter has a group of Copy Filter buttons that let you copy the currently open filter, along with its settings, to other clips that follow it in the sequence.

Interestingly enough, the Copy Filter commands work similarly to the Show Edit commands. There is one command to copy the current filter forward to the next clip in the sequence, and a second command to copy it to the second clip forward. In the hypothetical edited sequence (A–B–A–C), you'll note that shots from the same angle rarely fall next to one another in narrative filmmaking, so these commands allow you to skip adjacent cutaway or insert shots and apply the correction to the next instance of a shot from the same angle.

1   Make sure the color correction filter from the first clip in the sequence is open in the Viewer, and click the Copy to 2nd Clip Forward button.

If you turned on Clip Keyframes in the previous exercise, a green filter bar appears underneath the third clip to show you that the filter has indeed been applied.

Playing through the sequence will show that all three clips are properly balanced. The ease with which color correction filters can be propagated through a sequence brings up an interesting issue—if you make a change to any of the filters that are applied to these clips, you'll need to copy that change to any other clips that have an identical correction.

This is because once you copy a filter to another clip, its settings are completely independent of the original filter. However, the Copy Forward commands have an additional function to help you in this situation. If you use those commands to copy a color correction filter to another clip that already has a color correction filter applied, the settings of the filter in the second clip are overwritten to match those in the current filter.

2   Make sure the color correction filter from the first clip is open in the Viewer, and drag the Sat (saturation) slider to the left to noticeably desaturate the image.

3   Play through the sequence to verify that the first and third clips don't match.

4   Move the playhead back to the first clip and open the Color Corrector filter into the Viewer.

5   Click the Copy to 2nd Clip Forward button.

6   Play through the first three clips again and verify that the third clip has changed to match the first.

7   Press Command-Z twice to undo this change.

As you can see, the Copy Filter buttons are extremely handy for propagating corrections to other clips in an edited sequence. You should know, however, that the manner in which color correction filters and their settings are copied forward depends on how many color correction filters have been applied to a clip, and on which of potentially several stacked color correction filters you're copying forward.

Here are some simple rules for using these commands:

▶ If you're copying forward a Color Corrector 3-way filter to a clip that has no filter, the filter and all of its settings will be copied.

▶ If you're copying forward the first Color Corrector 3-way filter in a clip to a clip that already has a filter, the settings of the existing filter in the second clip will be overwritten with the settings of the currently open filter.

▶ If you're copying forward the second Color Corrector 3-way filter in a clip to a clip that only has one filter, that filter will be copied forward as a second filter.

▶ When copying forward a Color Corrector 3-way filter from a clip with multiple filters to a clip that also has multiple Color Corrector 3-way filters, settings will be copied to the target Color Corrector 3-way filter in the same position of the filter stack as the current filter. In other words, settings from the second filter from the top will be applied to the second filter from the top in the second clip.

You'll notice that there are also buttons for copying color correction filter settings from color correction filters that are applied to the first and second clips behind the current clip (in the Timeline). For more detailed information on using the Copy Filter controls, see the Final Cut Pro 5 documentation.

Matching Color with the Match Hue Controls

So far, you've learned how to manually adjust contrast and color to match shots. When you develop a facility with the tools, this is often the fastest way to proceed, and they certainly afford you the greatest amount of control in any possible color correction.

The color correction filters have another feature to make your life a bit easier, however—the Match Hue controls, found in the middle of the Color Corrector 3-way filter's custom controls, underneath the Mids controls.

The Match Hue controls are designed to automate the process of balancing a color within one zone of luminance to match a designated color in a different clip. It does nothing to adjust contrast; you must first adjust that manually. However, it does provide a way to quickly and automatically adjust Color Balance controls to match a specific hue that you select, similar to the way Select Auto-balance Color eyedroppers in the Color Balance controls work.

Match Hue works well with clips that are from the same location, matching the color of a subject in one clip to the color of the identical subject in another clip. In the scene you're currently balancing, for example, the woman appears in every shot that's been corrected, and the location and situation is identical, even though the lighting varies from shot to shot. This is an ideal situation in which to use the Match Hue controls.

You can use the Match Hue controls in other situations, but your success will be completely dependent on your ability to accurately select analogous colors in each shot. For example, it's a mistake to assume that you can match the skin tone of any two people with similar skin color. Subtle differences in hue, even by a few percentage points, may result in significant deviations in the end result. Still, in even less then ideal situations, the Match Hue controls may provide you with a starting point if you're unsure how to proceed.

1   Move the playhead to the fourth clip in the sequence, **Woman CU**.

2   Apply a Color Corrector 3-way filter to the **Woman CU** clip, open it into the Viewer, and click the Color Corrector 3-way tab to expose its controls.

This clip has a yellow/red combination cast similar to that found in other clips in this scene, but a closer examination reveals that it's different enough not to benefit from automatic application of any of the filters from the clips you've color corrected so far. Since it's the same actor as in the reference shot, however, and because the clip is an insert shot (a close-up taken from the same angle as the wider two-shot), this is a perfect candidate for using Match Hue.

Before you do anything else, you need to adjust the contrast of this clip to match the reference clip. Otherwise, the Match Hue controls won't work as you expect.

3   Press Control-Shift-Up Arrow a few times to flip back and forth between the reference shot and the current shot, comparing the Waveform Monitor graphs.

4   Adjust the Blacks, Whites, and Mids sliders until the contrast ratio is identical, and the overall brightness in the midtones matches.

The adjustments will be fairly subtle, and you may see the value of relying on a comparison of the Waveform Monitor graphs. The yellow cast becomes a bit more pronounced when you brighten the image, and you might find that making this adjustment visually might boost the brightness too high, because the color cast gives the illusion that the image is darker than it really is. The Waveform Monitor, however, provides a more objective reference.

Now with the contrast matched, you can move on to using the Match Hue controls.

5   Click the Select Auto-balance Color button (the Match Hue eyedropper).

A tooltip appears with the only instruction you'll ever need, an exhortation to choose a color to which you want to match the current clip—neglecting to mention that it should be from a second reference clip.

It's important to understand that the Match Hue controls only make an adjustment to one of the three Color Balance controls, in an attempt to match a hue you select in a second reference image. The saturation and luminance of the selection are ignored. You can indirectly control which Color Balance control is adjusted—the blacks, mids, or whites—by the area of the reference image you choose with the eyedropper.

The first thing you need to do is to identify a frame in the reference image containing clear highlights, midtones, and shadows in the subject you want to match.

6   Move the playhead back to the already-corrected **Leads 2-shot** clip that you've been using as the reference image, and scrub through the clip until you find a frame of the woman in profile, with a clear highlight visible on her forehead. The first frame of the image is good.

7   Since the entire image needs to be matched to the reference clip, and the location is identical, begin by clicking a highlight in the woman's forehead with the eyedropper.

Immediately, two things happen. First, the Match Hue color swatch is populated with the hue you just selected.

Second, the Whites Select Auto-balance Color button turned green.

NOTE ▶ If the Whites Select Auto-balance Color button didn't turn green, and the Mids or Blacks Select Auto-balance Color button turned green instead, you didn't successfully pick a highlight. Click the Match Hue eyedropper and try clicking the highlight in the reference image again.

At this point, the Match Hue controls are set up for you to make the match.

8 In the Color Corrector 3-way tab of the Viewer, click the now-green Whites Select Auto-balance Color button.

9 Move the playhead back to the **Woman CU** clip, and scrub forward until you find a similar frame with the woman in profile that shows a clear highlight on her forehead matching the highlight you picked in the reference shot. (There's a suitable frame midway through the clip).

10 Click the highlight with the eyedropper.

Immediately, the Whites Balance control is adjusted, and the highlights are rebalanced.

The success you have with the Match Hue controls is completely dependent on which pixels you click with the eyedropper. If the result is significantly off, you probably mismatched a value in the whites with a value in the mids, or vice versa. For this reason, the Match Hue control may sometimes appear to be more idiosyncratic than it really is. The bottom line is that you have to be very careful when choosing reference and match colors. If necessary, zoom in to the Canvas to better see which pixels you're selecting.

Next, you're going to match the hue of the blacks.

11 Reset the Match Hue controls by clicking the Reset button (next to the color swatch).

12 Click the Match Hue eyedropper, move the playhead back to the first frame of the reference clip, and click in the shadow of her cheek.

If you chose the right part of the image, the Blacks Select Auto-balance Color button turns green.

13 Move the playhead back to the clip you've been correcting, scrub back to the frame range showing the woman in profile, then click the green Blacks Select Auto-balance Color button in the Color Corrector 3-way tab in the Viewer.

14 Click a shadow in her cheek that's similar to the first shadow you picked.

Again, you'll know you picked well if the image assumes a closer match. If it doesn't, you can click the Blacks Reset button and repeat steps 11 through 14, picking different areas of the image.

It still seems that there's a bit of a yellow cast to her face. The even distribution of the cast would indicate that it's time to use the Match Hue controls on the mids.

15 Reset the Match Hue controls, then click the Match Hue eyedropper. Move the playhead back to the first frame of the reference clip, and click a midtone color somewhere between the highlight and shadow.

If you've chosen well, the Mids Select Auto-balance Color button should turn green.

16 Return the playhead to the clip you've been correcting, scrub back to the frame range showing the woman in profile, then click the green Mids Select Auto-balance Color button in the Color Corrector 3-way tab in the Viewer.

Click a midtone on her forehead similar to the midtone you picked on the reference image.

Assuming you chose good colors, the Mids Balance control is adjusted, and the image should now be a good match to the reference image.

As you can see, the Match Hue control packs a lot of functionality into a minimal interface. To use Match Hue well, you need to have a solid understanding of how the colors of an image fall into the blacks, mids, and whites. The same criteria you would use to decide whether to adjust the Blacks, Mids, or Whites Balance controls manually also apply to the use of the Match Hue controls. In fact, you can elect to use Match Hue for only one or two of the Color Balance controls, adjusting the others manually.

There's one other thing you should know. Once the Match Hue color swatch and Blacks, Mids, or Whites Select Auto-balance Color button is set, these controls are available from every color correction filter in your sequence. This allows you to make the same adjustment in several different clips. To return to using the Select Auto-balance Color buttons for making regular blacks, mids, and whites balances, you must click the Match Hue Reset button.

Choosing and Balancing a Second Group of Images with Different Contrast

The second half of this scene focuses on two people on the other side of the room. Since it's in the same scene, you'll want to match the color in these clips to the color in the clips you've just corrected. The lighting in the **Guys_2-shot** seems to closely match the lighting in the insert close-up shots that accompany it. If you focus on matching **Guys_2-shot** to the original reference shot for this scene, there's a chance you might be able to apply that single correction to the insert shots as well, saving yourself more time and effort.

In any event, it's always good to start with a shot that has as many of the people in the scene as possible. Since the skin tones of people in any scene will vary slightly, finding the ideal look for the wide shot will provide you with a reference for each close-up insert shot.

1   In the Timeline, move the playhead to the first frame of the **Leads 2-shot** clip you've been using as a reference shot, and set an In point in preparation for flipping back and forth between this clip and the next one you'll be correcting.

2   Move the playhead to the **Guys_2-shot**, and scrub through to find a representative image.

3   Add a Color Corrector 3-way filter to the **Guys_2-shot**. Open the shot into the Viewer, and click the Color Corrector 3-way tab.

4   Press Control-Left Arrow a few times to flip back and forth between the reference clip and the current clip, getting a sense of the contrast corrections you'll need to make.

In this clip, the black level matches the reference clip, and the mids and whites also seem to be in the ballpark, but there's a noticeable difference in brightness between the two images. The **Guys_2-shot** appears darker on average than the reference. A closer examination of the bottoms of the scopes reveals that the dense clump of values representing the shadows in the current clip is much narrower then the same cluster of values in the graph of the reference clip.

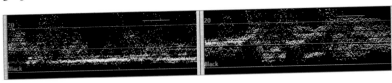

This indicates that the shadows are being compressed without being crushed at 0 percent. The result is to darken the shadows to the point where you cannot make out detail, although the detail is still there waiting for you to extract it. You can do this with a peculiar combination of settings.

NOTE ▶ It's also worth noticing that the highlights are considerably shinier in this shot than in the reference clip. This will be addressed by the same correction.

5   Drag the Mids slider to the right, stretching up the blacks so that the detail in the shadows approximately matches the reference image, while leaving the blacks pegged to the bottom.

Don't worry if the highlights seem excessive, you will address them in a second step. For now, it's important to pull some detail out of the shadows.

6   Drag the Whites slider to the left, compressing the whites and bringing down the top of the waveform graph back to match the highlights in the reference clip.

The end result of this somewhat unconventional correction is that you've brought some detail out of the shadows, and minimized the shine on the actor's faces, by selectively reducing the contrast in the clip—while boosting the overall brightness.

7   Toggle the Enable Filter checkbox on and off a few times to see a before-and-after comparison.

8   Use whatever techniques you prefer to match the color balance in the blacks, whites, and mids in the **Guys_2-shot** clip to the reference clip.

You can do this manually by dragging the Color Balance controls, or you can try to use the Match Hue controls, even though there is no clearly analogous character in this shot. As you work, see if you can determine which of the two men has the pinker skin tone.

When you're finished, the resulting adjustments in the Color Balance controls should look something like this:

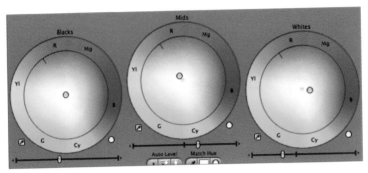

Dragging Filters onto Other Shots

In the preceding section, the reason you corrected the two-shot was so you could apply the same correction to the two identically lit close-ups. One of the nice things about insert shots is that they're often lit with the same lighting setup. (Often, but not always, so don't count on it.)

If the lighting matches, your job is easy. If not, it's no big deal—you can try modifying the filters from the first clip, using them as a starting point, or simply correct the other shots from scratch.

1   Make sure the color correction filter that's applied to the **Guys_2-shot** is open in the Viewer, and deselect the Enable Filter checkbox.

2   Or, press Control-Up Arrow and Control-Shift-Up Arrow a few times to compare the uncorrected waveforms of all three clips.

In this case, you've gotten lucky. The black point, white point, and mids distributions in the Waveform Monitor, and the color balance in the Parade scope seem to match for all three shots.

This means you can copy the correction you've made to the **Guys_2-shot** clip to the other close-up shots. However, the distribution of clips is a little too awkward to use the Copy Filters commands, and besides, you want to apply this filter and its settings to three clips all at once. This is a good time to drag a filter from one clip to copy it to a selected group of other clips.

3 Click the **Guy_1_CU**, then Command-click the **Guy_2_CU_(01)** and **Guy_2_CU_(02)** clips.

4 With these clips selected in the Timeline, click the Drag Filter control, and drag the filter onto one of the selected clips in the Timeline.

5 When the clips highlight, release the mouse button to apply the filter.

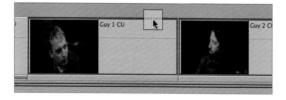

You're finished!

Extra Credit

For extra credit, try removing the filters from Scene 1 with the Remove Attributes command, and then rebalancing the entire scene with a different look.

Once you've exhausted the possibilities of the first scene, open **Scene 2-Extra Credit**, and see how fast you can balance the entire scene by copying filters among shots from identical angles of coverage.

1 Identify a reference shot to use as your starting point, and make your master correction.

2 Identify how many angles of coverage there are. In other words, mentally group all of the shots in the scene that have the same angle and lighting. Chances are, you can apply the same correction to all of them.

3 Work your way through the scene until it's finished.

Lesson Review

1. What are your principal goals when color-correcting a scene?
2. What do you want to look for when choosing a reference shot to begin correcting?
3. When matching two shots, what's the first thing you do?
4. What are the Copy Filter buttons for?
5. What is the Parade scope best at showing?
6. What are the Show Edit commands for?
7. What kind of clips can you usually use the same color correction filter settings for?

Answers

1. Maintain consistency in shots that appear in the same scene, that occur at the same time, and in the same location.
2. A shot that's representative of the scene, perhaps a wide angle that shows the actors and the environmenat, and ideally a clip that has most of the actors that appear within that scene onscreen at one time.
3. Match their contrast.

4. They copy a filter and its settings forward to other clips in the sequence.

5. Color balance in the blacks and whites.

6. Flipping back and forth between clips to compare them.

7. Clips with identical lighting, from the same angle of coverage.

15

Lesson Files Lessons > Lesson_15 > 15_Project_Start

Media Media > Lesson_15_Media

Time This lesson takes approximately 60 minutes to complete.

Goals Perform secondary color correction for color enhancement on specific colors

Use the Limit Effect controls

Create special-effects looks using secondary color correction

Lesson 15

Secondary Color Correction

The process of enhancing targeted regions of an image is referred to as *secondary color correction,* and is typically performed after the overall image has been color balanced.

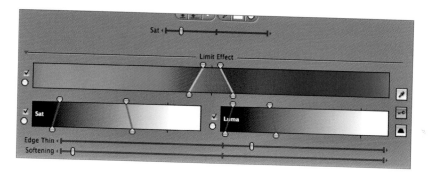

You won't always use secondary correction. Oftentimes, a single well-adjusted Color Corrector 3-way filter can do the job with individual adjustments in the three overlapping luminance zones of an image. On the other hand, there are many instances when you'll want to make an adjustment to a very specific portion of the image—such as desaturating someone's fire engine–red shirt—and the Blacks, Whites, and Mids controls affect the image too broadly. This is when you'll use secondary correction.

In this lesson, you will isolate adjustments to specific parts of an image using the Limit Effect controls, located within a collapsible section at the bottom of the Color Corrector and Color Corrector 3-way filters.

Choosing to Use Secondary Color Correction

The Final Cut Pro Limit Effect controls let you make color enhancements that are limited to a specific range of chrominance and luminance. For example, in this first exercise, you'll isolate the sky in an image and replace the color entirely.

Before

After

First, you will adjust the contrast and color of the image using the methods you've learned in earlier lessons. Then, you will attempt to put some blue into the sky to make the scene appear earlier in the day. In the primary correction, you'll find that the basic controls cannot make such a limited change.

1   Open Lesson_15 > **15_Project_Start**.

2   Choose Window > Arrange > Color Correction.

3   Open the Exercise 01 - Sky Correction bin, and open the **Sky Correction** sequence.

4   Scrub through the **SF_Skyline.mov** clip, and examine the graphs in the video scopes.

You should immediately notice that the image has washed-out blacks, and the contrast is generally low, confirmed by the Waveform Monitor. The image also has a very low saturation, with a graph in the Vectorscope that barely extends past 20 percent. As always, you'll continue by adjusting the contrast.

5   Apply a Color Corrector 3-way filter to the **SF_Skyline.mov** clip, open it into the Viewer, and click the Color Corrector 3-way tab to reveal its controls.

6   Drag the Blacks slider to the left until the bottom of the graph touches 0 percent—maximizing the contrast ratio in the image—then drag the Mids slider to the right to increase its general brightness.

7   After the mids adjustment, you'll need to readjust the Blacks and Whites sliders so the Waveform Monitor's graph sits comfortably between 0 and 100 percent.

Next, you want to add some blue to the sky. Clearly, the sky is up in the whites, so perhaps you can use the Whites Balance control to add some blue.

8   Drag the Whites Balance control towards blue, the complementary color to yellow, until the sky appears blue.

Unfortunately, the adjustment that affects the sky also tints the entire image.

9   Click the Whites Reset button to remove this extreme tint.

Clearly, this task requires a different approach—it requires a secondary correction.

NOTE ▶ The term *secondary color correction* should not be confused with secondary colors in the color wheels. Secondary color correction refers to altering a single color or a unique range of colors, regardless of whether those colors are primary or secondary on the wheel.

Using the Limit Effect Controls

The solution is to use the Limit Effect controls to perform one of the most common corrections for exterior shots—adjusting the color of the sky without affecting the rest of the image. You select a region of the picture to correct, preview the selected region, and fine-tune the selected region to achieve a seamless result.

Applying a Secondary Correction

Since you've already performed your primary correction with the filter you previously applied, you want to leave that filter as it is. As the name implies, secondary corrections are often applied using a second filter.

1   Apply a second Color Corrector 3-way filter to the **SF_Skyline.mov** clip.

A second Color Corrector tab appears at the top of the Viewer.

You can add as many Color Corrector and Color Corrector 3-way filters to your clip as you wish. Each color correction filter adds another custom interface tab to the top of the Viewer whenever that clip is open, and each tab is numbered in the order in which its corresponding filter is applied.

2   Click the Color Corrector 3-way - 2 tab.

3   Click the disclosure triangle at the lower left of the Color Corrector tab to expose the Limit Effect controls.

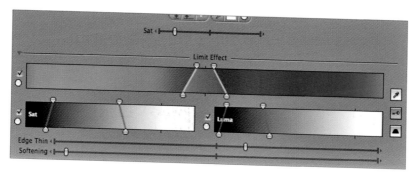

TIP ▶ On smaller computer monitors, opening the Limit Effect controls makes the color wheels fairly small. To compensate, drag the lower-right corner of the Viewer window to enlarge it and to automatically scale up the color wheels and other controls. Using larger controls increases the spacing in the controls, helping you make more subtle adjustments in any of the controls. Using a relatively large Viewer window is useful in any situation in which you want subtle control in a color correction filter.

If you went through the keying exercises in Lesson 9, these controls should look suspiciously similar to those of the Chroma Keyer filter. In fact, they are virtually identical. It turns out that limiting the effect of a color correction filter simply involves keying part of the image, and limiting the color correction filter's contrast, color balance, and saturation controls to the keyed region of the picture.

Here's a basic recap of the Limit Effect controls:

▶ The Select Color button (the eyedropper) lets you make an initial selection of a region in the image.

▶ The View Final/Matte/Source button (the key) lets you toggle between the final image, a preview of the key, and the original.

▶ The Invert Selection button lets you reverse the effect of the key.

▶ Three bars that occupy the majority of the Limit Effect area let you define the key by fine-tuning the hue (the top colored bar), saturation (the leftmost grayscale bar) and luminance (the rightmost grayscale bar).

▶ Two sliders at the bottom let you adjust the edges of the key that's limiting the effect.

Making an Initial Selection

To activate the Limit Effect controls, you must make an initial color selection. You'll begin by using the eyedropper to select the majority of the sky.

1 In the Color Corrector 3-way tab of the Viewer, click to select the Select Color button (the eyedropper).

          — Eyedropper

NOTE ▶ Be careful to select the Select Color eyedropper, not the Hue Match eyedropper above it.

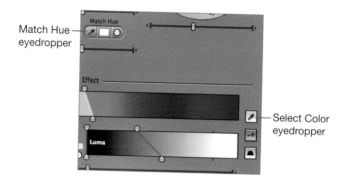

Match Hue eyedropper

Select Color eyedropper

2 Move the pointer to the Canvas.

The pointer changes to the eyedropper icon. When making an initial selection with the eyedropper, you want to plan ahead. The regions you want to select seldom represent a single, monochromatic value. Typically, you'll find yourself attempting to key out a range of related color and brightness values.

It's usually best to start by choosing a value near the border that divides what you're selecting from the area you don't want to affect, and then expand the selection away from the unaffected area.

In this case, since the sky is a subtle gradient that is brightest at the bottom and darkest at the top, start by choosing the brightest sky color that appears lowest on the skyline.

3 Click the lowest area of sky appearing between the buildings. (Don't click directly on the edge of a building itself—you don't need to get that close.)

Although clicking with the eyedropper has no visible effect in the Canvas, you can see that the Limit Effect controls of the clip are now all selected, and the ranges within each control have been modified to reflect the color value you clicked with the eyedropper.

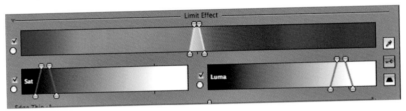

Whenever one of the Limit Effect range controls is selected, you'll know which portion of the image is being selected by which of the controls is selected. For example, if you clicked the eyedropper on a portion of the image that's completely desaturated, the Luma control may be the only range control that's selected. In this case, there's enough golden color in the sky that you can do a full chroma key.

4 Drag the Whites Balance control towards blue, to add color to the area you selected in step 3.

Whenever any of the Limit Effect controls are turned on and you adjust the controls of a color correction filter, the corrections you make are limited to the keyed area you've defined. Since the sky is a gradient of lighter to darker color values, your initial selection is limited to the lighter bottom area. You need to expand the selection.

5   Click the Whites Reset button.

Note that when you reset any of the Color Balance controls (or Shift-click to reset all of them), the Limit Effect controls remain unchanged. Likewise, resetting any of the Limit Effect controls leaves the Color Balance controls unchanged. (You can also Shift-select the Limit Effect controls to reset all of them.) The adjustments you make to the Color Balance controls are independent of adjustments to the Limit Effect controls.

TIP   To quickly and simultaneously reset both the Limit Effect and the color and contrast controls at the top of the filter, click the Filters tab and then click the Reset button (the red X) for the entire filter.

6   Click the Select Color eyedropper, then Shift-click another spot in the Canvas, this time about one-half inch below the top of the sky. (When you Shift-click, the eyedropper icon appears with a small + above it.)

Notice that the ranges defined by the Limit Effect controls have expanded to include the additional Hue, Sat, and Luma values.

Shift-clicking with the eyedropper lets you expand the current selection. Each time you Shift-click the image, the hue, saturation, and luminance values of the pixel you click are added to the range that has already been selected.

If you *don't* press the Shift key before clicking with the eyedropper, you replace the previously defined ranges with completely new values.

In this case, since the sky you're trying to select is a fairly simple gradient, choosing the darkest and lightest colors in the sky expands the selection to encompass most of the sky area.

TIP Instead of Shift-clicking to add to a selection, you can also Shift-drag to quickly sample values throughout a region: Select the eyedropper, press Shift, then click and drag over the desired region until you've selected all of it. This method works best when you're trying to isolate a region that has widely varying color values.

7   Drag the Whites Balance control towards blue again, and see how much of the sky is affected.

Depending on how close to the top of the sky you Shift-clicked, the correction should now be affecting most of the sky, with only a small, uncorrected strip at the very top of the frame, and some fringing around the outside of the buildings. You'll take care of these unselected areas next.

NOTE ▸ Don't worry if your results look slightly different. The area of the Limit Effect selection is highly dependent on the exact color values of the pixels you selected. Some degree of variance is to be expected due to grain, noise, and the random color distribution of the image.

Toggling Between Viewing the Final, Matte, and Source

Your selection is close to being finished, and it's time to refine it. Before continuing, however, you'll turn on an additional control in the Limit Effects section that makes it easier to identify which parts of an image are being selected: the View Final/Matte/Source button. By default, the key is red with a gray background. This represents the Final view, in which the Canvas shows the video image with the final color effect.

1   Click the View button once.

     The key becomes black on a white background.

This is Matte view. The Canvas now shows a grayscale image that represents the area being selected with the Limit Effect controls.

Solid white represents the selected areas, and all the gray areas represent regions that will be partially affected (less and less the darker the area). Solid black areas represent unselected parts of the image. You're probably thinking that this view looks an awful lot like an alpha channel, and you're correct—the general idea is the same.

The best thing about this view is that it gives you a clear idea of how much of the image is selected, even if you've made no adjustment to the main color correction controls. This view is especially useful for spotting translucent areas that might be difficult to identify in a still image—even when looking at the Final view—but which can be a source of unwanted image noise in the final result.

TIP ▶ If you have an external broadcast monitor connected to your computer, and you set External Video to All Frames, you view the output image on your broadcast display at the same time the Canvas is displaying the Matte view.

2   Click the View button once again.

The button changes to a red key against a blue background, which indicates the Source view.

Regardless of the settings in the color correction filter, you should now see the original, unfiltered video image in the Canvas.

This view is important, not simply as a "before" image, but as a way to sample additional pixels using a version of the image that's unaffected by your correction. If you sample from the Final image with the eyedropper, you'll be selecting color values that are being altered by the correction you're making, which will produce unexpected results.

3   Click the View button again to return to the Final view. The button changes back to its original appearance.

This is the view you started with. Anything you do to the video image with this filter is seen when using Final view.

As you've seen, the View Final/Matte/Source button is a three-way toggle. Unless you're making an obvious color correction, it can be easy to confuse the Source and Final views. If you click only once on the View button after viewing the matte, you are looking at the image without any effects.

Whenever you're using the color correction filter and you don't see the results of an adjustment, first make sure that the Enable Filter option is selected, and then make sure the View button is set to *Final*. (The key is red on a gray background.)

Expanding the Limit Effect Range

The selections you made with the Select Color eyedropper resulted in automatic adjustments to the range controls on the three bars in the Limit Effects controls: hue (which is untitled), saturation (Sat), and luminance (Luma).

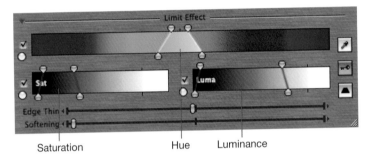

Saturation   Hue   Luminance

Each time you Shift-click in an image with the Select Color eyedropper, any or all of these three ranges is expanded to include the new values you select. After you've used the eyedropper to get close to the selection you want, though, it's a good idea to turn to the manual adjustments for these controls. Often, this is the best way to make the subtle adjustments necessary to create a smooth and complete selection.

The areas of the chroma, saturation, and luminance gradients that fall within the pairs of white handles indicate the range of the selection within that color component.

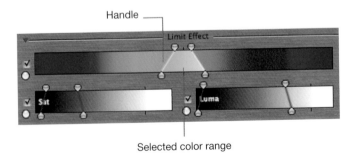

Selected color range

The top handles affect the width of the values included in the most solid parts of the selection—represented by the solid white areas of the matte. They create the inner area of the selection.

Top handle

Bottom handle

The bottom handles define the *tolerance* of the selection—represented by the progressively darker gray areas of the matte. They create the soft edges of the selection and enable you to manipulate the falloff at the edges of your correction.

In general, avoid over-selecting with the top handles. (Over-selecting can also be the result of relying too heavily on Shift-clicking with the eyedropper.) Instead, use the top handles to ensure that the inner selection is solid, and use the bottom handles to fine-tune the outer areas of the selection, areas where the region you want to manipulate mixes with the areas of the picture you want to leave unaffected.

In this exercise, you'll use these handles to refine the initial selection you made with the eyedropper.

1   In the Canvas, click the View button once to display the Matte view.

The Limit Effect controls, by default, perform a Chroma key operation. The color gradient at the top of the Limit Effect controls let you increase or decrease a specific range of hues that define the selection.

2   Drag out the topmost Chroma handles a little bit to select a wider range of colors.

You immediately can see the results at the top of the Canvas. First, the fringe at the top of the frame is gone. This is good.

Second, and more insidious, is the introduction of some "holes" in the building at the bottom of the image. This is bad, because it will cause your buildings to turn blue like the sky.

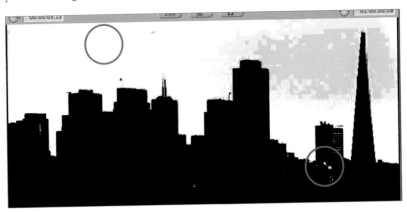

3 Undo the last change you made, and drag the bottom handles a little bit outward.

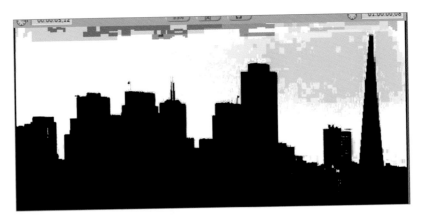

This time, the fringing at the top doesn't turn white; instead it turns varying degrees of gray. Also, the holes in the building at the bottom are also a shade of gray. This is fine—gray areas can usually be manipulated using other controls, and it's generally better to have a soft edge than a hard one at an awkward transition between the inside and outside of a selection.

4   Drag the top-right handle of the Luma control to the right, to extend into the superwhite area.

After the initial hue adjustment, the luminance is a good second adjustment to make. The grayscale gradient of the Luma control tells you what range of luminance you're including, with black representing 0 percent, and the white at the two marks above and below the gradient representing 100 percent. The uniform white area at the right side of the control represents the superwhite area.

With this adjustment, you can see that the large gray area to the right (above the three buildings) has turned white, thereby filling in the hole in the sky, and preventing any noisy "buzzing" in the sky during playback.

NOTE ▸ Be careful when including large translucent areas in a Limit Effect selection. Although these regions may look fine in the still frame, changes in brightness and color while the image is in motion can result in unsightly image noise.

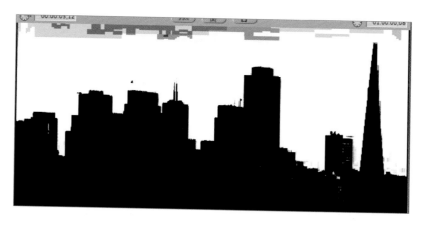

Unfortunately, there's no other adjustment you can make to the Luma control that will do anything other than include more of the buildings in the selection, which is what you're trying very hard to avoid.

5   Drag the top-left handle of the Sat controls all the way to the left.

This is a very subtle adjustment, but if you look closely at the building to the right, you'll see that some of the fringing around its edge is gone. As with the Luma adjustment, the black end of the gradient represents 0 percent saturation (completely unsaturated), and the white end of the gradient represents maximum saturation.

Unfortunately, the fringe at the top of the image is still there. It looks like you'll have to make a more extreme adjustment to the Hue control.

6   Drag the topmost Chroma handles farther outward, until the gaps at the top of the sky are filled in.

This eliminates the fringing at the top of the sky, but it once again creates holes in the building at the lower right.

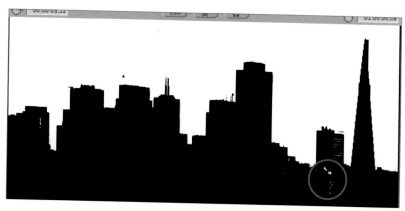

7   Move the pointer to the middle of the Hue gradient. When the pointer turns into a hand, drag the gradient itself to the right to include more green in the selection.

This way, you can change which hues are included in the current selection, without changing the width or tolerance of the hue range.

In this case, this adjustment partially eliminates the holes in the building, but introduces more gray, this time around the buildings.

This is okay, as long as none of this fringing is solid black. Sometimes, the adjustments necessary to strike a balance between including necessary areas and creating unwanted holes results in gray fringe; however, you can partially address this with the Edge Thin slider.

8   Drag the Edge Thin slider to the right until you strike the best possible balance between thin fringe on the inside of the selection and holes outside of the selection.

The Edge Thin slider lets you weaken or strengthen the translucent areas in a Limit Effect selection. Dragging the Edge Thin slider to the left eats away at the selection, eliminating translucent areas and eroding solid areas. Dragging the Edge Thin slider to the right strengthens translucent areas and expands solid areas.

Whenever you have a problematic transition area, such as the one in this example, one possible strategy is to allow some gray within the selection and hope that judicious use of the Edge Thin slider will allow you to eliminate it. In this case, you can get rid of almost all of the fringing, without causing more holes in the building—but not quite.

9   Add two or three points of Softening by clicking the right arrow on the Edge Thin slider two or three times.

This last change ever so slightly blurs the edges of the selection. Too much blur in this image would mix the color correction over the area you're trying to exclude from the effect. However, a little bit can anti-alias the edges of the selection and minimize any remaining fringe by blurring it out.

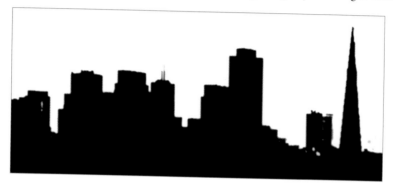

The example shown here represents one version of a good compromise for this image. Your results will vary.

10 Click the View button two times to look at the Final result, and you can see that the sky is now completely corrected.

As this exercise shows, you don't have to do everything with a single filter. You can always add additional secondary color correction as needed, isolating additional regions until you've corrected everything that needs adjustment.

This example also highlights an important point: making perfect selections with the Limit Effect controls can sometimes be difficult. Because you're usually trying to isolate colors in footage that's rarely shot with isolation in mind, you'll often find that the hue, saturation, and luminance values you're trying to select overlap with those you're trying to exclude, resulting in a push and pull of adjustments.

Another limitation you'll confront when making secondary color correction selections is in clips that were captured using a highly compressed format, such as DV. Since you're basically keying, you have all the same problems that you do when trying to key compressed footage: blocky artifacts and minimal color information. In general, the less compressed your media is, the better results you'll have when making secondary selections.

In general, a deft touch is required in all of these situations, but bear in mind that imperfect selections are often fine when you're doing a secondary color correction, especially when you're making a subtle adjustment. Depending on the type of image and the amount of edge softening you can get away with before it becomes noticeable, you may be surprised at what you can get away with.

Emphasizing a Single Color

As you've seen, the Limit Effect controls let you isolate and manipulate specific ranges of color values in an image. In the next exercise, you'll use the Limit Effect controls to select a single color for *enhancement*, rather than wholesale change.

1   Open the Exercise 02 - Clock Face Correction bin, and open the **Clock Face Correction** sequence.

2   Scrub through the `Clockface_CU.mov` clip. and examine the graphs in the video scopes.

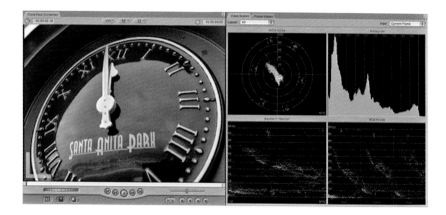

You can see that the contrast ratio in this image is already as high as possible, with strong blacks and healthy highlights. The color balance is also fine, since you want the elegant dark green to predominate. The only problem is that the key design colors for the program are green and gold, and the gold in this image is a little washed out. The goal, then, is to intensify the gold color without affecting the rest of the image.

3   Apply a Color Corrector 3-way filter to the `Clockface_CU.mov` clip, open it into the Viewer, and click the Color Corrector 3-way tab to reveal its controls.

4   Click the disclosure triangle at the bottom of the Color Corrector tab to expose the Limit Effect controls, and click to select the Select Color eyedropper.

5   Move the pointer to the Canvas. When it changes to the eyedropper icon, click on the *P* of *Park*, within the clock face.

6   Click the View button to view the matte in the Canvas.

As you can see, this gives you only the barest start, but it's enough.

7   While viewing the matte, scrub through the clip.

Notice how noisy the selection is. As you learn to refine your selections using the Limit Effect controls, this is exactly the kind of matte noise you want to avoid. As you make adjustments, occasionally scrub through the matte and see how it holds up in motion.

In this example, since you're trying to isolate only a single color, you'll use manual adjustments to the Limit Effect controls. In situations like this, manual adjustment can often be the fastest technique. The eyedropper selection gave you your start, identifying the central hue, saturation, and luminance values for the color selection you're trying to make.

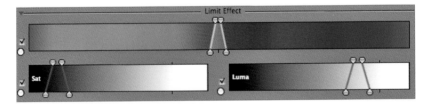

The hue range picked by the eyedropper demonstrates the value of beginning this process by clicking a pixel in the image. Although you might have been tempted to begin selecting values in the yellows, an objective analysis of the color you're trying to select reveals that it has a lot of orange in it. Now that you know this, all you need to do is expand the Limit Effect parameters to include the many variations of this color.

8   Drag the upper Hue range controls outward. Do this in small steps, dragging and releasing to check the result on the matte image in the Canvas. Continue until you've reached the point when dragging the control no longer has an effect on the selection.

The result, in this case, should be a selection that just barely touches all the areas you're trying to isolate.

9   Drag the upper Luma range controls to include more of the image. This time, don't keep dragging until the control no longer has an effect. Instead, stop when you've added some definition, but while the newly included region still seems sharp.

The result is a strengthening of the selection, without spilling over the fine details you're trying to isolate.

It's important to understand that the three Limit Effect range controls interact with each other. Increasing or decreasing the range of one color component usually results in adjustments to the other two. In this case, even though you're adjusting Luma, you always want to see how a Sat adjustment will affect the result before you finish.

10 Drag the upper Sat range controls outward until they no longer expand the selection.

The result should significantly strengthen the selection.

11 As a result, you might want to shrink the left (darker) part of the Luma range selection to return some detail into the text. At this point, push and pull the handles in small increments until you're happy with the selection. The selection should be sharp and well-defined, but not bleed beyond the text.

12 Toggle between the Matte and Final views to get a sense of how the mask is corresponding to the dial.

13 Drag right the Soften slider to blur the selection a little bit.

This helps prevent jagged edges in the selection and also prevents noise in the gray areas by blurring the key created by the limit effect controls.

14 Toggle the View back to Final, and drag the Whites Balance control towards a point somewhere between the Yl (yellow) and R (red) targets to boost the golden color the client wants in the clock dial.

Targeting Highlights with the Limit Effect Controls

It's not always necessary to use all three range selection controls when you're trying to limit an effect. A common example of this is when you're isolating image highlights. Since highlights are defined by luminance values at the top end of the scale (and are generally within a much smaller range than that of the Whites controls), it's easy to isolate these values using only the Luma control.

> **TIP** This is also one of the highest-quality methods of limiting an effect when you're color-correcting DV media. Since the Y (Luma and green) channel of DV clips has the most information, it yields the sharpest selections.

1   Open the Exercise 03 - Targeting Highlights bin, and open the **Targeting Highlights** sequence.

2   Scrub through the **Motel_Walkway.mov** clip.

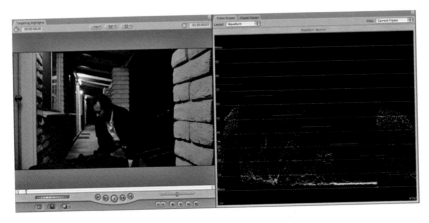

Although generally well-exposed, the highlights are a cold blue. In this case, you might want to make them a more tungsten-orange color

3   Apply a Color Corrector 3-way filter to the **Motel_Walkway.mov** clip, open it into the Viewer, and click the Color Corrector 3-way tab to reveal its controls.

4   Drag the Whites Balance control towards an orange hue.

Unfortunately, this adjustment adds an orange tint to the majority of the image, which you don't want. An examination of the Waveform Monitor reveals that the highlights of this image are falling between 70 and 100 percent, an easy segment of the image to isolate using the Limit Effect Luma range controls.

5   Click the disclosure triangle at the bottom of the Color Corrector tab to expose the Limit Effect controls, and select the checkbox next to the Luma control. Leave the other controls deselected.

The immediate result is a little odd, because the default setting for the Luma range controls isolates the bottom 30 percent of the image's luminance.

6   Drag the top-right Luma range handle all the way to the right, then drag the top-left Luma range handle approximately two-thirds of the distance to the right.

You immediately can see the result in the Canvas. The brightest parts of the lights should now be tinted orange, and the rest of the picture retains a slightly blue cast.

7   If you'd like, drag the bottom-left handle farther to the left to expand the range of luminance to include the highlights on the brick pillar to the right of the screen.

It was a little odd to have such a narrow portion of the highlights affected by this change. Expanding the tolerance let you increase the range of highlights that were selected, but with a very subtle falloff.

Replacing a Specific Color

Now you'll climb the Mount Everest of effect limiting—replacing the color in an article of clothing. In the process, you'll learn how to deal with one of the biggest problems you'll run into when using the Limit Effects controls: color spill.

Changing the Color of Clothing

Your goal in this exercise is to change the color of a woman's red dress to blue.

1   Open the Exercise 04 - Changing Dress Color bin, and open the **Changing Dress Color** sequence.

In this clip, the contrast and color are fine, you simply need to change the color of the red dress to address a change of heart on the part of the director.

2   Apply a Color Corrector 3-way filter to the **Spectators_MS.mov** clip, open it into the Viewer, and click the Color Corrector 3-way tab to reveal its controls.

3   Click the disclosure triangle at the bottom of the Color Corrector tab to expose the Limit Effect controls, and select the Select Color eyedropper.

4   Move the pointer to the Canvas. When it changes to the eyedropper icon, click a highlight within the woman's red dress.

The Limit Effect controls automatically are adjusted to match the color value you selected. Next, you're going to Shift-drag the eyedropper control to quickly expand the selection throughout the highlights and shadows of the dress.

5   Choose the Select Color eyedropper, then Shift-drag the eyedropper on the woman's dress moving from the highlight all the way to the darkest shadow.

NOTE ▶ You cannot hold the Shift key down and drag until after you've made the initial selection with the eyedropper in step 4. Shift-dragging only expands an existing selection, it doesn't create a selection from scratch.

6   Click the View button to see the matte of the selection in the Canvas.

You should immediately notice two things. First, you have a fairly complete selection of the dress, with only some minor edge details to resolve. Second, the selection includes some unwanted details elsewhere in the image.

These unwanted parts of the selection appear in people's faces, and they highlight one of the problems in trying to use the Limit Effect controls with red colors. Namely, there's a lot of red in skin tones. Invariably, you run into this issue whenever you're trying to isolate red objects in a frame that includes people.

Since this is an extremely thorny problem, you'll ignore it for now, focusing on creating as good a selection as possible for the dress. You'll resolve the problem areas in the next exercise.

7   Make *small adjustments* as you expand the Hue, Luma, and Sat range controls to select as much of the dress as possible, while excluding as much of the rest of the picture as possible. Remember, it's not going to be perfect, you just need a fairly solid dress color.

As you make your adjustments, scrub through the clip and see how the selection looks when it's in motion. Ideally, there should be as little animated noise in the selection as you can achieve. It won't be entirely smooth, because the lighting and shadows change with the woman's movements, but you don't want it to be excessive, either.

When you're finished, your settings may look something like this:

8   Drag the Edge Thin and Softening a bit to the right to fill in some of the holes and blur the edges of the selection.

9   Now that you've made the selection, click the View button twice to see the Final image in the Canvas, and adjust the Blacks, Mids, and Whites Balance controls until the dress appears a vivid blue.

This illustrates another important point. Often, the Limit Effect controls will create a selection that includes color values in all three luminance zones of your image. In this example, the dress you've isolated includes both shadows and highlights. As a result, you must make adjustments to all three Color Balance controls to successfully change its color.

Unfortunately, the end result is so saturated it's practically glowing.

10   Drag the Mids and Sat sliders to the left until the dress is a less saturated, darker blue.

This shows another important point: you can make contrast adjustments, as well as color adjustments, within a Limit Effect selection.

The end result no doubt looks a little odd, as there's plenty of blue in people's faces in addition to the blue of the dress. It's time to do something about that.

Cropping to Omit Unwanted Spillover

Sometimes in a Limit Effect selection, you have to include color values that overlap with other areas of the picture, simply to achieve the necessary results. In this exercise, you'll resolve this situation by cropping the unwanted color spill from the clip being corrected, and superimposing it over an uncorrected duplicate of itself.

1 Duplicate **Spectators_MS.mov** in the Timeline by selecting it and Shift-Option-dragging upward to V2.

2 Open the clip from track V1 into the Viewer and click the Filters tab.

3 Delete the color correction filter.

4 In the Canvas, choose Image+Wireframe from the View pop-up menu.

5 Select the clip on track V2.

6 Select the Crop tool from the Tool palette, and drag the four edges of the selected clip in the canvas to crop out everything but the woman's dress.

You'll see that all the unwanted spill disappears, changing only the portion of the picture that you wanted. Now, you have to make sure that the crop settings you've selected account for any camera movement that might move part of the dress out of the cropped area.

7   Scrub through the clip, and adjust the cropping as necessary on either side of the woman's dress to include the dress and exclude any color spill.

The problem is solved. You've succeeded in credibly changing the color of the woman's dress. As mentioned previously, the example clips you're working with are pretty highly compressed. The fairly extreme adjustments you find yourself making to account for the jagged edges of a Limit Effect selection diminish as you use media with less and less compression.

NOTE ▶ If you're prepared (or lucky) enough to be able to influence your video's look before production, try to choose colors in the frame that are unique from other colors, rich in saturation, and evenly lit. This makes them easier to select in post-production. This is just as crucial as the use of green screens or blue screens when color keying.

Inverting a Limit Effect

In this last exercise, you'll invert a Limit Effect selection to exclude part of an image from the your correction. This is an extremely powerful technique, yet it is no more difficult than making any other Limit Effect selection. You can use it to create extreme effects, such as coloring a subject against a black-and-white background (used to excellent effect in the film "Pleasantville"), or you can use it to create more subtle variances between a subject and the rest of the image.

In this example, you'll isolate an object in the frame to protect it from a slight desaturated treatment you'll apply to the rest of the image.

1   Open the Exercise 05 - Excluding Glasses bin, and open the **Excluding Glasses** sequence.

In this exercise, you'll begin by isolating the woman's opera glasses.

2   Apply a Color Corrector 3-way filter to the **Spectator_CU.mov** clip, open
    it into the Viewer, and click the Color Corrector 3-way tab to reveal its
    controls.

3   Click the disclosure triangle at the bottom of the Color Corrector tab to
    expose the Limit Effect controls, and select the Select Color eyedropper.

4   Move the pointer to the Canvas. When it changes to the eyedropper icon,
    click a midtone within the brass-colored opera glass.

5   Use whatever techniques you'd like to expand the selection to include as
    much of the opera glasses as possible, while excluding as much of the face
    as possible. In this image, because there are so many overlapping color val-
    ues between the woman's face and the glasses, and because the finish of
    the glasses is worn, the result won't be 100 percent inclusive.

This image will benefit from leaving some translucent areas on the woman's face, and a subsequent aggressive adjustment of the Edge Thin parameter to the left, with more than a little use of Softening.

NOTE ▶ As you expand the selection, bear in mind that not every part of the opera glasses is colored brass. The center focus knob, for example, is supposed to be silver, and in this image there are shadows and highlights in worn parts of the finish that aren't actually colored.

6   When you've finished, click the View button to display the Matte view in the Canvas, if you haven't already.

The result should look approximately like this:

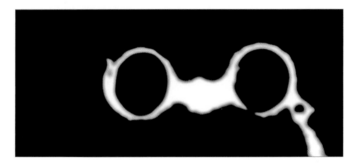

The mask may look a little raggedy, but it'll do the job for the task at hand.

At this point, you know what will happen if you make any color adjustments. They'll be limited to the parts of the glasses that fall within the selection.

7   Click the Invert Selection button.

When Invert Selection is selected, the button becomes a white icon against a black background. When viewing the selection's matte in the Canvas, the result is immediate.

The selection is now inverted.

8   Click the View button twice to return to the Final view in the Canvas, and
drag the Sat (saturation) slider to the right until the color of the woman's
face is muted.

As a result of the inverted selection, the glasses now pop out relative to the
woman's face, because they're excluded from the desaturation you just
applied.

These are just a few of the powerful corrections you can make with a skillful application of the Limit Effect controls. Whenever you find yourself grappling with a portion of an image that just won't cooperate with whatever color-correction you're trying to apply, stop to consider if perhaps handling that part of the image in a second step might not be a better way to proceed.

Lesson Review

1. What's the first step you typically take when using the Limit Effect controls?

2. What are two ways to expand an initial selection?

3. How can you use just one of the Limit Effect range controls to create a selection?

4. What does the Edge Thin slider do?

5. How can you eliminate unwanted corrections in parts of an image that fall outside of a Limit Effect selection without making adjustments to the selection itself?

6. How can you apply a color correction effect to every part of the image except for the currently selected region?

Answers

1. Use the Select Color eyedropper to select a starting color for the selection.

2. Shift-click with the eyedropper, or manually adjust the Limit Effect range controls.

3. Click the checkbox next to the range control you want to manipulate, and make sure the other two are deselected.

4. The Edge Thin slider either eats away at the selection or grows the selection.

5. Composite the corrected clip over an uncorrected duplicate of the same clip, and crop out the parts of the image from the corrected clip that have the unwanted corrections.

6. Click the Invert Selection button.

Titling with LiveType

Using LiveType with Final Cut Pro

LiveType was created with the goal of giving artists, editors, and producers the ability to create exciting motion graphics sequences with a minimum of effort. What's more, LiveType uses a completely different approach to creating animated effects than Final Cut Pro.

In this lesson, you'll learn how to use LiveType to create motion graphics sequences and how to share content between Final Cut Pro and LiveType. The lesson (in PDF format) and all the project and media files you need are located in the Lessons > Lesson_16 folder and the Media > Lesson_16_Media folder.

Using LiveType to Create a Motion Menu

In this lesson, you'll use some of LiveType's more powerful features to create a much more sophisticated sequence using superimposed textures and mattes. You'll also be shown techniques for copying and pasting, and retiming effects. The lesson (in PDF format) and all the project and media files you need are located in the Lessons > Lesson_17 folder and the Media > Lesson_17_Media folder.

Animating Type with LiveType

In many ways, LiveType is the perfect DVD authoring companion because of how quickly you can obtain professional-looking results. And since both iDVD and DVD Studio Pro allow you to import your own custom-designed motion menus, it makes perfect sense to use LiveType as an integral part of your DVD production pipeline.

In this lesson, you will use LiveType to create a motion menu for use in a DVD. The lesson (in PDF format) and all the project and media files you need are located in the Lessons > Lesson_18 folder and the Media > Lesson_18_Media folder.

Final Cut Studio Workflows

Apple's professional audio and video applications are designed to work together seamlessly, even in the most demanding postproduction workflows. The Final Cut Studio product line—a comprehensive and integrated postproduction package—comprises Final Cut Pro 5, Soundtrack Pro, Motion 2, DVD Studio Pro 4, Compressor 2, LiveType 2, Cinema Tools 3, Shake 4, and Logic Pro.

The appendix on the DVD accompanying this book details the roles of each application in the Final Cut Pro movie production process. You will also find a sample Final Cut Studio workflow and information on "roundtripping," the ability to embed and open project files while working in another application. See **Appendix-Final Cut Studio Workflows.pdf**.

Glossary

A comprehensive glossary of terms is included in PDF format on the DVD. See **Lessons > x_Glossary**.

Index

The Apple Pro Training Series

The official curriculum of the Apple Pro Training and Certification Program, the Apple Pro Training books are a comprehensive, self-paced courses written by acknowledged experts in the field.

- Focused lessons take you step-by-step through the process of creating real-world digital video or audio projects.
- All media and project files are included on the companion DVD.
- Ample illustrations help you master techniques fast.
- Lesson goals and time estimates help you plan your time.
- Chapter review questions summarize what you've learned.

Apple Pro Training Series: Final Cut Pro 5
0-321-33481-7

In this best-selling guide, Diana Weynand starts with basic video editing techniques and takes you all the way through Final Cut Pro's powerful advanced features. Using world-class documentary footage, you'll learn to mark and edit clips, color correct sequences, create transitions, apply filters and effects, add titles, work with audio, and more.

Apple Pro Training Series: Advanced Editing Techniques in Final Cut Pro 5
0-321-33549-X

Director and editor Michael Wohl shares must-know professional techniques for cutting dialogue scenes, action scenes, fight and chase scenes, documentaries, comedy, music videos, multi-camera projects, and more. Also covers Soundtrack Pro, audio finishing, managing clips and media, and working with film.

Apple Pro Training Series: Advanced Color Correction and Effects in Final Cut Pro 5
0-321-33548-1

This Apple-authorized guide delivers hard-to-find training in real-world color correction and effects techniques, including motion effects, keying and compositing, titling, scene-to-scene color matching, and correcting for broadcast specifications.

Apple Pro Training Series: Optimizing Your Final Cut Pro System
0-321-26871-7

Written and field-tested by industry pros Sean Cullen, Matthew Geller, Charles Roberts, and Adam Wilt, this is the ultimate guide for installing, configuring, optimizing, and trouble-shooting Final Cut Pro in real-world post-production environments.

Apple Pro Training Series: Final Cut Pro for Avid Editors
0-321-24577-6

Master trainer Diana Weynand takes you through a comprehensive "translation course" designed for professional video and film editors who already know their way around Avid nonlinear systems.

The Apple Training Series:

Apple Training Series: iLife '05
0-321-33020-X

Apple Training Series: GarageBand 2
0-321-33019-6

Apple Training Series: Mac OS X Support Essentials
0-321-33547-3

Apple Training Series: Desktop and Portable Systems, Second Edition
0-321-33546-5

Apple Training Series: Mac OS X Server Essentials
0-321-35758-2

Apple Training Series: Security Best Practices for Mac OS X v 10.4
0-321-36988-2

Apple Training Series: Mac OS X System Administration Reference
0-321-36984-X

To order books or find out about the Apple Pro Training Series, visit: **www.peachpit.com/appleprotraining**

Apple Pro Training Series: Soundtrack Pro
0-321-35757-4

Apple Pro Training Series: Shake 4
0-321-25609-3

Apple Pro Training Series: Shake 4 Quick Reference Guide
0-321-38246-3

Apple Pro Training Series: Getting Started with Motion
0-321-30533-7

Apple Pro Training Series: Motion
0-321-27826-7

Encyclopedia of Visual Effects
0-321-30334-2

Apple Pro Training Series: Logic Pro 7 and Logic Express 7
0-321-25614-X

Apple Pro Training Series: Advanced Logic Pro 7
0-321-25607-7

Apple Pro Training Series: DVD Studio Pro 4
0-321-33482-5

Apple Pro Training Series: Getting Started with Aperture
0-321-42275-9

Apple Pro Training Series: Aperture
0-321-42276-7

Apple Pro Training Series: Color Management with Mac OS X
0-321-24576-8

Apple Pro Training Series: Final Cut Express 2
0-321-25615-8

Apple Pro Training Series: Xsan Quick Reference Guide
0-321-36900-9

To order books or find out about the Apple Pro Training Series, visit:
www.peachpit.com/appleprotrainir